T5-ART-411

DEVOTIONS®

Commit to the
LORD **whatever
you do, and
your plans will
succeed.**

—Proverbs 16:3

JANUARY

Photo © Liquid Library

Gary Allen, Editor

DEVOTIONS® is published quarterly by Standard Publishing, Cincinnati, Ohio, www.standardpub.com. © 2008 by Standard Publishing. All rights reserved. Topics based on the Home Daily Bible Readings, International Sunday School Lessons. © 2004 by the Committee on the Uniform Series. Printed in the U.S.A. All Scripture quotations, unless otherwise indicated, are taken from the HOLY BIBLE, NEW INTERNATIONAL VERSION®. NIV®. Copyright © 1973, 1978, 1984 by International Bible Society. Used by permission of Zondervan. All rights reserved. Where noted, Scripture quotations are from the following, used with permission of the copyright holders, all rights reserved: *King James Version (KJV),* public domain. *New Century Version*® *(NCV)* © 1986, 1988, 1999 by Thomas Nelson, Nashville, Tennessee. *The Revised Standard Version of the Bible (RSV),* copyrighted 1946, 1952, © 1971, 1973. *Holy Bible, New Living Translation (NLT),* © 1996. Tyndale House Publishers.

Tasting God's Word

O taste and see that the Lord is good: blessed is the man that trusteth in him (Psalm 34:8, *King James Version*).

Scripture: **Psalm 34:4-14**
Song: **"Come and Dine"**

"I don't like that." Many times I heard this when I placed new foods on our dinner table. I realized that children are reluctant to try new foods; mine were no exception. Because of this, we adopted a rule in our home. Each person was to taste *at least one spoonful* of everything on the table. It was amazing how foods they supposedly "didn't like" became favorites after the first taste.

Sometimes folks are quick to say, "I can't read that." They believe that reading the Bible is difficult, even though they have never given it a good try. But after that first taste, so many begin to love partaking of the Word as a regular mode of living.

My husband told the children, "If your mother went to all the trouble to fix this for you, then you can go to all the trouble to taste it." It's difficult to imagine all the goodness of God unless we first taste it ourselves. And, for further encouragement, the psalmist tells us the words of Scripture are sweet to the taste, even sweeter than honey.

Heavenly Father, You have given me words to live by, words that will comfort and encourage me. I pray that You would guide me as I read and study them this day. I pray in the name of Your Son, Jesus. Amen.

January 1–4. **Carol Russell**, of Fort Scott, Kansas, has written articles and stories in Christian magazines, as well as take-home papers for children and adults.

The Way He Chooses

What man is he that feareth the LORD? Him shall he teach in the way that he shall choose (Psalm 25:12, *King James Version*).

Scripture: **Psalm 25:12-22**
Song: "Follow On"

Me? You want me to have a speaking ministry? These were the thoughts rolling around in my head. I never before considered a speaking ministry, but the more I prayed and listened for God's answer, the more I knew He was leading me into another avenue for service. I'd taught Sunday school and Bible studies for many years. Now it appeared that God was revealing a new direction for me.

The Scriptures inform us that God will lead us in the way He has chosen. And, thankfully, He will never ask us to do anything He has not equipped us to do. He will give us the tools—the spiritual gifts, strength, and wisdom—for the task, no matter what the ministry may be.

The Bible offers countless examples of the ways He prepares people for His work: David had a sling, Dorcas had a needle, Samson had a jawbone. Similarly, God called Moses for a special mission. This great shepherd of God's people initially had great doubts, but he followed the way that God chose for him. With doubts, I began a speaking ministry, but the doubts soon faded. What way has God chosen for you?

Dear Lord, I thank You for showing me the pathways to tread. In your strength, may I be an effective servant for you. In Jesus' name, amen.

Standing in Awe

Let all the earth fear the LORD: let all the inhabitants of the world stand in awe of him (Psalm 33:8, *King James Version*).

Scripture: **Psalm 33:8-18**
Song: **"America the Beautiful"**

"Wow, there really are stars!" At the age of 10, after I received my new glasses, I saw the stars for the first time. What an awesome sight. Such beauty and majesty to behold!

Because of my poor eyesight, I had been unable to see the multitude of those twinkling lights in the night sky. I thought people were making up stories about stars and airplanes. I would usually respond with something like "Sure" or "Yes, of course" whenever someone mentioned something I could not see.

A kind of spiritual blindness sometimes hinders us from seeing the beauty of God. Other times, we fail to notice the wonders of creation because we're just too wrapped up in our own lives. We fail to see and stand in awe of His beauty and goodness toward us.

Mother cried when she realized I'd never seen the stars. How it must hurt God when His children gloss over the beauty of His world, along with the care and love He has for each of us. Why not stop for a moment today to really see the beauty of God's creation—and savor the wonders of His gracious blessings in Your life?

Heavenly Father, help me to see not only the beauty of this world, but also the glory of Your plan of salvation for me. Through Christ I pray. Amen.

Obeying God

The midwives feared God, and did not as the king of Egypt commanded them, but saved the men children alive (Exodus 1:17, *King James Version*).

Scripture: **Exodus 1:8-21**
Song: **"I Will Pilot Thee"**

The manager put the report back on my desk and gave me this instruction: "Just change the inventory a little. Show we sold more of the promotional suits and drop some of the other sales."

I knew he wanted to look good in the company supervisor's eyes, but this was wrong. "I'm sorry, Mr. Smith. My ethics just won't let me do as you ask." Although he was displeased with me, he did allow me to give an accurate report to the supervisor.

When Pharaoh told the midwives in Egypt to kill all the baby boys, they had a problem. They knew they were responsible to God and that His was a higher authority. However, what would Pharaoh do if they disobeyed?

While our superiors may condone certain behaviors, it is God's law we are to obey. Today, employment relationships can bring us many problems, especially when supervisors ask us to do something we know is wrong.

Just as the midwives must choose Pharaoh or God, we frequently face similar choices. Whom do we obey?

Lord, *thank You for Your laws and guidance. Help me always remember that I am accountable for my actions, that I must sometimes say "No," even at great personal cost. I pray through my deliverer, Jesus. Amen.*

Somebody Has to Follow

Just as we fully obeyed Moses, so we will obey you. Only may the LORD your God be with you as he was with Moses (Joshua 1:17).

Scripture: **Joshua 1:10-18**
Song: **"Follow Me, the Master Said"**

The Israelites didn't exactly obey Moses in all things . . . but they should have. Somebody has to follow. After all, there can't be leaders without followers. The Bible everywhere tells us that. Take, for example, those who followed David, both in exile and on the throne. Or consider the men and women who went where Jesus went, all over Galilee and then up to Jerusalem. In our Scripture passage today, we read of those who pledged Joshua obedience upon entering the land of promise. Somebody has to follow.

A dean at a woman's college sent a questionnaire to parents of prospective students. "Is your daughter a good leader?" one of the questions asked. After the responses came in, the dean wrote to the parents of a particular applicant: "Thanks for sending your daughter to be a member of our first-year class. Inasmuch as the class numbers 325, and we've already been assured of 324 leaders, we are delighted your daughter is coming along to be a follower."

Dear God, as a disciple of Jesus, may I follow Him where He goes in that part of the world where I live. In His name I pray. Amen.

January 5–11. **Phillip H. Barnhart** ministered in eight churches in three states for over 45 years. He has written 14 books and lives on Perdido Bay, Florida.

Faith Gets the Job Done

It was by faith that the people of Israel marched around Jericho seven days, and the walls came crashing down (Hebrews 11:30, *New Living Translation*).

Scripture: **Hebrews 11:23-31**
Song: **"My Faith Looks Up to Thee"**

Read the 11th chapter of Hebrews and you come away feeling you can do just about anything—if you have faith. "By faith . . . by faith . . . by faith . . ." the cadence goes on and on. Sacrifice offered, blessing given, deliverance managed, exodus accomplished, victory achieved—all by faith.

By faith mountains are moved, Jesus said. Faith is best understood as *response*, our response to God's faithfulness. Who God is, what God does, comes first. Faith responds to the character and action of God, both of which are revealed and, ultimately, experienced as trustworthy.

We are led to faith by the evidence of God's grace and power. We lift the sails because we've seen God send the wind. As someone has put it: "Sorrow looks back, worry looks around, faith looks up." And the uplook of faith produces the outlook of confidence.

Faith as response is why Jeremiah could buy a field in Anathoth, Elijah could see rain in a cloud the size of a man's hand, and two midwives could refuse to obey the wicked command of a powerful pharaoh.

Dear God, by faith I go forward each day. Faith takes fear out of my challenges, puts love in my relationships, brings hope to my plans, and gives power to my walk. Thanks be to You, through Christ my Lord! Amen.

Word Gets Around

We have heard how the Lord dried up the Red Sea when you came out of Egypt (Joshua 2:10, *New Century Version*).

Scripture: **Joshua 2:8-11**
Song: **"Tell Me the Story of Jesus"**

Rahab became Israel's ally because she had heard what God had done. God's reputation preceded Him. Drying up a sea, eliminating a couple of formidable kings, ruling Heaven and earth—all this God had done. All this Rahab had heard. And hearing stories about God's greatness made Rahab a believer.

Dr. Peter Joshua, renowned minister and evangelist, was won to Christ by the witness of one girl. An unemployed actor, he slept in alleys at night and accepted handouts by day. One evening, in London's Hyde Park, he saw a Salvation Army girl standing up to speak. Wanting to give her support, he found himself her only audience. Instead of speaking, she began singing a hymn about the worthlessness of the world compared to the glories and goodness of Christ.

Looking Joshua in the eye, she quoted several Bible verses, turned, and went her way. Peter Joshua received Christ. Word got around to him. Word gets around to us.

Dear God, thank You for those who told me the story of Jesus. I stand on the shoulders of their witness, looking into the face of Your glory. Their testimony is my creed, their words my life. What they told to me, I tell to others. In the holy name of Jesus, my Lord and Savior, amen.

Helping People on Their Way

So she let them down by a rope through the window, for the house she lived in was part of the city wall (Joshua 2:15).

Scripture: **Joshua 2:15-21**
Song: **"Help Somebody Today"**

Rahab believed, then she acted. Rahab was a helper. Acknowledging what God had done, she made a deal with the two spies and helped them on their way.

Long-stemmed flax, like what had hidden the spies on Rahab's roof, had been spun and braided into a strong rope. Down that rope the spies shinnied to safety and returned to tell Joshua that it was time to enter the land of promise.

There's a story of an old man who carried a little can of oil with him everywhere he went. If he passed through a door that squeaked, he poured a little oil on the hinges. If a gate was hard to open, he oiled the latch. Basically, he passed through life making it easier for those who came after him.

Some misunderstood the old man and called him odd. But he went steadily on, refilling his can when it went empty, oiling all the hard places he found.

For me, his example means simply this: I should be an equal opportunity Christian, helping everyone I can.

Dear Father, may I see each day the people You give me to help. May I love them as You love them and give myself to them as You give yourself to me. May I put them on the strength of my heart and carry them into Your presence. In the name of Your Son, my Savior, I pray. Amen.

Saved . . . to Do Good

Likewise also was not Rahab the harlot justified by works, when she had received the messengers, and had sent them out another way? (James 2:25, *King James Verson*).

Scripture: **James 2:21-26**
Song: **"A Charge to Keep I Have"**

We are not saved *by* works, but we are saved *for* works. The conflict some see between Paul and James on this subject misunderstands both of these great biblical writers. Paul argues against a false doctrine that keeping the law, apart from faith, will accomplish salvation. James does not see faith alone as deficient, but argues that a genuine faith will always result in good deeds.

They both agree that if saved people produce no works, they probably aren't saved in the first place. Similarly, Jesus said we will know people are saved when they bear fruit in the kingdom.

In the courtyard of a quaint little church in a French village stood a beautiful marble statue of Jesus with His hands outstretched. During World War II, a bomb struck and dismembered the statue. Later, the villagers gathered up the statue's fragments to reconstruct it . . . but could not find the hands. They planned to have a new statue built until one of them came up with an alternate idea. They attached a plaque at the base of the statue that read, "I have no hands but your hands."

God, lead me from belief to behavior, from doctrine to duty, from creeds to deeds. And may it all be done in Your strength. Through Christ, amen.

How Did They Get There?

. . . and Salmon the father of Boaz by Rahab . . . (Matthew 1:5, *Revised Standard Version*).

Scripture: **Matthew 1:1-6**
Song: **"Amazing Grace"**

Rahab ran a successful little establishment in the red-light district of Jericho. Yet there she is in the genealogy of Jesus Christ. Tamar duped her father-in-law into having sex with her, got pregnant, and gave birth to twins. Yet there she is in the genealogy of Jesus Christ. Bathsheba committed adultery with David, became pregnant, and allowed her husband's murder to confuse paternity. Yet there she is in the genealogy of Jesus Christ.

How did they get there? They got there by the grace of God. The list of names in Matthew's first chapter is a genealogy of God's grace, the undeserved favor that always has room for the unlikely, the unlovely, the uncredentialed. God's grace exists for those who don't have a very good record, and it is lightning fast on its feet of forgiveness.

Did Rahab deserve God's grace? Did Tamar deserve God's grace? Did Bathsheba deserve God's grace? To deserve grace nullifies its definition. Grace is what we *don't* deserve but get anyway. Grace happens.

Lord, *thank You for the grace I need when I've done something I shouldn't have and can't get over it. Thank you for the grace I need when my mind is confused, when my heart is confounded, when there is conflict in my soul. Thank You so much, in the name of Jesus. Amen.*

Promises: Made for Keeping

Joshua said to the two men who had spied out the land, "Go into the prostitute's house and bring her out and all who belong to her, in accordance with your oath to her" (Joshua 6:22).

Scripture: **Joshua 2:1-4, 11-14; 6:22-25**
Song: **"Standing on the Promises"**

Joshua insisted the promise made to Rahab would be kept. She and her family would be rescued from Jericho, just as she was told they would be.

Promises are made for keeping. Hudson Taylor, pioneer missionary in China, firmly believed God knew his needs and would meet them. On one occasion, when Taylor's assets were down to 87 cents, he wrote a friend, "We have this amount—and all the promises of God."

A promise is a pledge that proclaims a reality not yet present. There are thousands of promises in the Bible about what we can expect from God. Those promises are not subject to review. He keeps them.

With every call of God comes the promise to provide what is necessary to carry out that call. When God puts us on the road, He shows up to walk with us, just as He promised He would. As Dwight L. Moody once said, "God never made a promise that was too good to be true."

No matter how dark things get, **Dear God,** *I hold on to the promise of light. No matter how lost I am, dear God, I hold on to the promise of rescue. No matter how rough the passage is, I hold on to the promise of a safe landing. In Jesus' precious name, amen.*

Stay Strong

Aaron and Hur held his hands up—one on one side, one on the other . . . Moses built an altar and called it The LORD is my Banner (Exodus 17:12, 15).

Scripture: **Exodus 17:8-16**
Song: **"There Is a Fountain"**

There are times when my grandchildren, ages 13 through 25, come to me and tell me their woes. Listening closely makes them know they are very important to me and their granddad. We assure them as we pray for them—and they know that Jesus cares as well.

Encouragement is just what they hope to receive. A tender touch, a warm smile, and agreement with their good choices keeps them headed in the right direction.

Have you noticed how encouragement seems to strengthen the ones we love? And what encouragement Aaron and Hur offered Moses! They stood strong by his side as they held up his arms to ensure victory.

When Moses said, "The Lord is my Banner," these men knew where their strength came from. Through all of our battles, the Lord God is with us. He is our ever-present strength, and we can proclaim that strength to all we meet, as a blessed word of encouragement.

Father, I come to You, knowing You are my all and all, the strength I need for each day. Your mercy and grace bring me through each decision I make. Thank You, in Jesus' name. Amen.

January 12–18. **Maxine E. Holder** founded a Christian writer organization in Texas that has now grown to seven chapters.

He Renews Our Strength

If the Lord is pleased with us, he will lead us into that land. . . . Only do not rebel against the Lord . . . Their protection is gone, but the Lord is with us (Numbers 14:8, 9).

Scripture: **Numbers 14:6-10**
Song: **"The Love of God"**

Since committing my life to the Lord, I've prayed for eyes to see what He expects of me. And I trust Him to unfold His will for me, even though sometimes the answer is "no" or "wait."

After I suffered a long, nine-year bout with painful injuries following an automobile accident, my doctors found a way to ease my pain. And, thankfully, I was able to avoid living in a wheelchair. Through that time I came to the end of myself and learned to trust God deeply.

The Lord was with me through every difficult day, hour, and moment. Some believers thought I should be instantly healed, but I knew from studying His Word that He would heal me when, and if, He chose to do so. In any case, I simply determined to enjoy His constant presence.

In biblical days, those two wise men, Joshua and Caleb, lived with deep sorrow—until Joshua realized that the people had finally rejected their advice. Still, these men continued to depend on God. And, as He promises to do for us, He renewed their strength.

Heavenly Father, *how I praise You for Your indwelling Spirit! Help me to depend on Your strength every day as You lead me into paths of kingdom service. In the name of Jesus, my Savior, I pray. Amen.*

Finish the Job

May the LORD, the God of the spirits of all mankind, appoint a man over this community . . . one who will lead them out and bring them in, so the LORD's people will not be like sheep without a shepherd (Numbers 27:16, 17).

Scripture: **Numbers 27:12-23**
Song: **"Savior, Like a Shepherd Lead Us"**

Moses didn't want to leave his leadership position without making sure someone was fully trained to lead in his place. He first asked God to help him find that certain person, and that person was Joshua. Eventually, Moses guaranteed his people that Joshua was qualified. Confidence in this new leader helped make the transition.

Years ago I founded a Christian writer's organization that has now grown to seven chapters throughout Texas. Part of my job was to make sure our leaders realized our purpose: *ministry*. This requires leadership that is trained and accountable.

I'm so encouraged when I see Moses laying his hands on Joshua as the Lord instructed. Like Moses, we writers set up a formula for raising up leaders among us: pray, select, develop, and commission. It's a process we can apply in almost any form of ministry. After all, the Great Commission is always before us; let us continue to finish the job.

Dear Heavenly Father, I know that You hold me accountable to use my spiritual gifts in service to You and Your people. Give me the grace and strength to do so, day by day. I pray in Jesus' name. Amen.

Strong in Him

Be strong and courageous. Do not be afraid or terrified because of them, for the LORD your God goes with you; he will never leave you nor forsake you" (Deuteronomy 31:6).

Scripture: **Deuteronomy 31:1-8**
Song: **"Fear Not, O Little Flock"**

There was a war going on, and Joshua was to inherit the leadership position from Moses. For Moses realized he was about to die.

Moses also knew that the people must learn to depend on God for their future. Therefore, he showed them how to shake off their fears and forge ahead. God himself would go before them. In His strength, they could face any challenge.

There were times when I dreaded taking a test in school or facing someone who laughed at me for my faith. Do you know what helped the most? Repeating God's Word in my heart. That simple act seemed to renew my strength and keep me strong.

Life is often a giant challenge for us human beings. But my attitude is: Better to go to my knees and draw on God's mighty resources than to wallow in fear or despair. Then I do not face my fears alone; I can "be strong and courageous," depending solely on the Almighty Lord of all. He created and controls all things. And He lives within my heart.

Lord, how good to know You are ever near! You lift me up when I am down and bring renewed faith when I ask. Thank You, in Jesus' name. Amen.

He Redeems the Situation

The LORD said to him, "This is the land I promised on oath to Abraham, Isaac and Jacob when I said, 'I will give it to your descendants.' I have let you see it with your eyes, but you will not cross over into it" (Deuteronomy 34:4).

Scripture: **Deuteronomy 34:1-19**
Song: **"Near to the Heart of God"**

Because of his disobedience, Moses wasn't allowed to cross over into the promised land. But God took the great leader to Mount Nebo and allowed him to see that land before he died. Though he had his faults, what an impressive man was Moses! He was the only person who ever spoke with God, face to face. Yet, with Moses—as it is with us—disobedience brings discipline.

Years ago, as I ran from God, I had a terrible automobile accident that caused crippling and pain. I needed a lot of help, both physical and spiritual. And somehow, through the gentle invitation of God himself, I was able to turn to Him with an open heart. In spite of all my anger and pain, I faced Almighty God in openness and received a deep desire to follow Him.

Yes, He disciplines us, but He does it in love. He grieves to see us entangle ourselves in self-destructive actions that limit our potential. Yet He redeems every situation that we offer to Him with an open heart. That is how it was with Moses, and that is how it is with me.

Dear Lord, *like Moses, help me constantly turn to You, to open my heart and life to Your indwelling Spirit. I ask in Jesus' name. Amen.*

Wherever We Go

Do not let this Book of the Law depart from your mouth; meditate on it day and night, so that you may be careful to do everything written in it. Then you will be prosperous and successful. Have I not commanded you? Be strong and courageous. Do not be terrified; do not be discouraged, for the LORD your God will be with you wherever you go (Joshua 1:8, 9).

Scripture: **Joshua 1:1-9**
Song: **"My Jesus, I Love Thee"**

Joshua didn't promise the future would be easy. But he knew that obeying God's law would ultimately bring success to God's people.

Years ago, after attending a Christian marriage retreat, my husband, Marshall, and I longed to grow deeper in our relationship to God. Together, we prayed regularly and spent much time reading His Word—and we were soon put to the test! When Marshall's company was bought out, our future was on the line. Things got downright scary. But our prayers for the new company's leaders were answered; they sent a good man to protect Marshall's job.

Yes, after many months of praying and waiting, we were able to rejoice in a negotiator who saved the day for us. Yet it was our God in control. And like Joshua, we grew in our faith that He is with us wherever we go.

Lord, I praise You for granting me strength and courage as You did Joshua. You are with me and continue to lead the way. You are my All in All. For it is in Your holy name I pray. Amen.

Draw Close

Joshua told the people, "Consecrate yourselves, for tomorrow the LORD will do amazing things among you" (Joshua 3:5).

Scripture: **Joshua 3:1-13**
Song: **"Have Thine Own Way Lord"**

Most of us know about the ark of the covenant, carried only by the Levites. Worshipers had to stay back from the Ark a thousand yards because of its holiness. It contained the tablets of the Ten Commandments, a jar of manna, and Aaron's staff. What holy and sacred treasures!

The consecration ceremony in this Scripture passage shows us the importance of approaching God with a pure heart. How can we do it?

For one thing, we can simply stop for awhile during our days to enjoy God's intimate presence. In the days of Joshua, the presence of the Lord was, in a sense, "contained" in an external object. But the promise was always underneath: Someday God would actually dwell within His people and lead them from the heart.

We know how that promise unfolded: on the day of Pentecost, the Holy Spirit came to live within every believer. Just as Jesus promised, we worship Him in spirit and truth as He works to purify our lives. Yes, in every age, the call to consecration rings out. For Joshua and his people, it meant staying back. For us—thanks to the cross of Christ—it means drawing ever closer.

Heavenly Father, *thank You for the cross of Your Son that brings me access into Your presence. Through Him I pray. Amen.*

The Original Hippies

Throughout the period of his separation he is consecrated to the LORD (Numbers 6:8).

Scripture: **Numbers 6:1-8**
Song: **"Servant of God, Well Done!"**

During the 1960s, teenagers began wearing their hair longer as a symbol of rebellion. In ancient Israel, long hair conveyed the opposite attitude. The Nazirite was to use no razor on his head for the entire length of his vow. A man with long hair attracted attention, but in a positive way. He was a Nazirite, a man dedicated to God's service.

The well-known story of Samson begins with the angelic announcement that he is to be a Nazirite. The secret of Samson's strength was not his hair but his vow. Cutting his hair severed the vow, and the Spirit of God (along with Samson's strength) departed.

Cut off from God we are weak. Dedicated to his service, we remain strong.

I have worked with a number of dedicated Christians. I have studied under teachers who were models of Christian humility and wisdom. There was little in their outward appearance that highlighted their dedication to the Lord. But the inner spirit would shine through in such a way that it was as noticeable as shoulder-length hair.

Lord, use me in Your service. Help me fulfill my vows of dedication and service in each situation I meet this day. In Jesus' name, amen.

January 19–25. **Dan Nicksich** is now entering his 10th year of ministry with First Christian Church in Somerset, Pennsylvania.

Choose Him Who Chose

When the angel of the Lord had spoken these things to all the Israelites, the people wept aloud (Judges 2:4).

Scripture: **Judges 2:1-5**
Song: **"I'd Rather Have Jesus"**

John the Baptist stood up to a king and denounced his sinful behavior. He was imprisoned and later beheaded for his words. The prophet Jeremiah proclaimed the truth, even when he knew a king would be enraged. And Daniel risked the lion's den in defiance of a king's edict.

It makes me wonder: Is pleasing God more important to me than pleasing people? Would I proclaim God's truth, even to a king?

The Bible abounds with examples of those who stood against the ungodly in the face of imprisonment or death. Sadly, we also see those times when the nation of Israel failed to put God ahead of its own self-interest. Yet God's commands were clear: Do not make a covenant with these people, do not follow their gods, do not bow down at their altars.

We all face times when pleasing those around us may seem more important than pleasing God. Sometimes, of course, we can do both! But more often, it's a question of commitment and loyalty to one or the other. May God help us to choose the one who has already chosen us.

O heavenly Father, may it be that nothing would ever become so important in my eyes that my dedication to You would suffer. In the name of my Lord and Savior, Jesus Christ. Amen.

Awesome Responsibility

After that whole generation had been gathered to their fathers, another generation grew up, who knew neither the LORD nor what he had done for Israel (Judges 2:10).

Scripture: **Judges 2:6-10**
Song: **"Tell It Again"**

"The church is one generation away from extinction." It's a rather bleak forecast, isn't it? But let's face it: The church is *always* one generation away from extinction. That is, if one generation of parents fails to teach its children about the Lord, we would soon see a repeat of the sad state of affairs depicted in Judges 2:10.

Joshua inspired the people throughout his lifetime. No doubt many had heard of his faithfulness on that day when he and Caleb stood alone among the 12 spies sent to assess the possibilities for conquest in the promised land. They spoke boldly then, saying that with God's help, Israel could surely achieve victory.

But somehow the generation that followed failed to teach its children that kind of vibrant faith in God. The Israelites reached the point where they "knew neither the Lord nor what he had done for Israel."

Let us always remember that each of us has a part in training the next generation. What an awesome responsibility, and what a humbling task!

Lord, bring me to those young people who could benefit from my Christian example. And give me wise words to say, too, at just the right times. In Jesus precious name I pray. Amen.

Returning His Slingshot

Unlike their fathers, they quickly turned from the way in which their fathers had walked, the way of obedience to the Lord's commands (Judges 2:17).

Scripture: **Judges 2:11-17**
Song: **"Falter Not"**

A 12-year-old boy and a slingshot. Sounds like a recipe for trouble, right? And trouble it was. So Mom took away my slingshot.

I can still recall the day she finally gave it back to me, saying, "Here, I think you're old enough to handle this now." I was 40!

At times, Israel's history reads like the continuing failures of a 12-year-old boy heading in and out of trouble. Judges depicts a particularly distressful time, with Israel failing time and again. God had promised protection, fruitful abundance, and blessings in return for faithfulness. If unfaithful, the people would land in their enemies' hands. Either way, it was their choice, and thus we read that their defeat was "just as he had sworn to them."

A good parent lays out the choices: Obey, and you will be blessed; disobey and face the consequences. God, the most faithful of parents, does the same. Thankfully, He gives us all the grace and strength we need to keep following Him. And when we stumble, He lifts us up that we may start again—even if it's 28 years down the road!

Lord, open my eyes to the dangers of disobedience today. May I learn from those who are faithful and from those who are not. In Jesus' name, amen.

Follow the Leader

When the judge died, the people returned to ways even more corrupt than those of their fathers, following other gods and serving and worshiping them (Judges 2:19).

Scripture: **Judges 2:18-23**
Song: **"Where He Leads Me"**

President Roosevelt encouraged his people not to fear "fear itself." John F. Kennedy challenged us to put a man on the moon before the end of a decade. And Martin Luther King, Jr., inspired us with a single, dramatic statement, "I have a dream." Good leaders challenge and inspire like that. They point the way, sometimes into uncharted territory, hopefully onto paths of righteousness.

Israel was good at following the leader. As long as a godly leader pointed the way, the people remained faithful to God. Whenever the good leader died, though, his or her example was quickly forgotten. Israel's history is a series of such failures.

We tend to crave tangible, visible leaders. If they de-emphasize character and morality, many seem to follow suit. We've even heard of those who insist, "Character doesn't count." How sad when those in authority will take such a stance!

God calls His leaders to be examples worthy of following. Are you a leader? Set the right example. A follower? Set your sights on a godly leader.

__Lord,__ please raise up leaders who are worthy of respect, in Your church and in our nation. May they look to You for guidance. In Jesus' name, amen.

By Luck or By Plan?

"We are doomed to die!" he said to his wife. "We have seen God!" But his wife answered, "If the LORD had meant to kill us, he would not have . . . shown us all these things" (Judges 13:22, 23).

Scripture: **Judges 13:15-23**
Song: **"Count Your Blessings"**

An old song complains: "If it weren't for bad luck, I'd have no luck at all." But the serious question is: Do you tend to assume something painful is always lurking just around the corner? And is God the one you blame whenever bad things occur?

It's strange how quickly we forget God's abundant blessings when tough times tumble down into our lives. Manoah's wife correctly reasoned that God's blessings are more than adequate proof of His love and acceptance.

One of the best-known verses of Scripture (John 3:16) assures us: God loved us so much that He came to us in person, willingly leaving all the glories of Heaven. If God's intention were to harm us, would He have suffered on our behalf as He did?

In the person of Jesus, we have seen God himself. But in that beautiful vision, we will not die. In fact, because of what we see and believe in His words and deeds, we shall surely live forever. Not by luck, but by plan (from before the foundation of the world), His motive was never anything other than our eternal good.

Father, help me see the unmistakable signs of Your love in my life. Reassure me whenever I tend to fear the worst. Thank You, in Jesus' name. Amen.

Come—He Blesses!

The woman gave birth to a boy and named him Samson. He grew and the LORD blessed him (Judges 13:24).

Scripture: **Judges 13:1-13, 24**
Song: **"Growing Dearer Each Day"**

Israel may have fallen, but God was already planning its deliverance. To a country in oppression and to a woman who was barren came the good news: a son would be born who would one day deliver the nation.

It reminds me of a friend who once sat in a prison cell after being arrested for drunk driving. It was a long night of self-evaluation and introspection. Her life had hit rock bottom, but the good news was that she knew exactly where to look for help. She confessed her failings and renewed her faith in Christ. She would later say that during one very dark night she came to appreciate God's grace.

Even in the midst of our most extreme failures, God extends His good news. No matter the sin, no matter the depths of our self-destruction, God offers His blessings to us as we open our hearts to Him.

How we know our failures! But we often fail to appreciate God's long-standing offer of grace at just the point of our most desperate needfulness. In other words, we don't have to "clean up" to come to Him. We just come; He just blesses.

*There are times, **Dear God,** when I need to spend some serious time in reflection and introspection. Help me examine my life in the light of Your Word, and lead me to repentance. Through Christ I pray. Amen.*

The Silent Call

[Elisha] took his yoke of oxen and slaughtered them. He burned the plowing equipment to cook the meat and gave it to the people. . . . Then he set out to follow Elijah (1 Kings 19:21).

Scripture: **1 Kings 19:15-21**
Song: **"Great God, A Blessing from Your Throne"**

One chilly evening, hundreds of tiny sparrows landed in the trees and berry bushes outside my window. The flock had found a safe place to rest amidst plentiful food.

But suddenly they departed as a whole. Led by an unnamed leader within, they gave up all they had. And off they flew in a beautiful formation. Each bird knew its place and was totally submitted to it.

I marveled at the complexity of the organization among such simple creatures. It called to mind Psalm 19:1—"The heavens declare the glory of God; the skies proclaim the work of his hands."

Elisha proclaimed God's glory too. He was a family man of means. Yet when God called, Elisha gave up all he had—fortune, family, and freedom. He left it all behind to serve God's servant, Elijah. You see, Elisha knew his place and was totally submitted to it, because he knew the one who called him and promised to lead him.

Lord, as I submit to Your will, teach me to recognize Your call and follow in Your footsteps. Help me to rest in the knowledge that just as You care for the tiny sparrow, You will care for me. In Christ's name, amen.

January 26–February 1. Author **Barbara E. Haley** has worked as an elementary school teacher and piano instructor. She lives in San Antonio, Texas.

The Best I Can Do

Elijah said to Elisha, "Tell me, what can I do for you before I am taken from you?" (2 Kings 2:9).

Scripture: **2 Kings 2:9-15**
Song: **"What a Friend We Have in Jesus"**

Herman Wilkerson believed in prayer. One day, he attended a church service led by a missionary. Afterward, the missionary confessed he was hungry and had no money to buy food. Herman invited the man to his home for dinner, knowing full well there was no food in his house for a proper meal. But Herman prayed, and when he got home, a stranger knocked at his door.

"I accidentally hit this turkey with my car," the stranger said. "I'm just passing through, so I can't use it. But I thought maybe you could." As the two men "gamely" figured out how to prepare and cook that bird, they enjoyed lively fellowship and developed a lasting friendship.

The Bible tells of Elijah being taken into Heaven. Just before he goes, he asks Elisha, "What can I do for you?"

May I suggest that prayer is the most powerful thing we can do for others? What a blessing it would be if every time we prepared to leave someone, we asked, "How can I pray for you before I go?" We would be communicating three important things: we care; we are listening; we know who holds the answer.

*Thank You, **Father,** for caring and for listening to my prayers. Please remind me daily to bless others as I lift up their concerns to You in an attitude of faith and love. In Christ's name, amen.*

Persistence Pays Off

Elisha turned away and walked back and forth in the room and then got on the bed and stretched out upon him once more. The boy sneezed seven times and opened his eyes (2 Kings 4:35).

Scripture: **2 Kings 4:27-37**
Song: **"God Will Make a Way"**

A stone cutter pounded a rock a hundred times—to no avail. But he didn't give up, and with one more strike, the rock split in two.

Did that single blow do the job? No, the break simply required 101 blows. Perhaps the cutter's personal experience, or trust in someone's word, motivated him to keep going.

The prophet Elisha demonstrated this same persistence. He made three attempts to revive a dead child before the boy recovered completely. At one point, the boy's body grew warm. But Elisha didn't accept a partial miracle—he believed God for more. Elisha prayed again, and the boy fully awoke.

How many times do we settle for second best instead of waiting on God's perfect way? We might even give up on praying. But as we read of God's great power, our faith—the power behind our prayers—blossoms and grows. Let us persist, then, in clinging to His almighty presence.

O God, as I come to You in prayer, remind me to persist and not give up or settle for second best. Thank You for Your promise to supply all of my needs according to Your glorious riches in Christ Jesus. In His name, amen.

Even When We Hurt

Elisha was suffering from the illness from which he died. Jehoash king of Israel went down to see him and wept over him. "My father! My father!" he cried. "The chariots and horsemen of Israel!" (2 Kings 13:14).

Scripture: **2 Kings 13:14-20**
Song: **"Sanctuary"**

Elisha was suffering when Jehoash came to see him. Yet even in his discomfort, Elisha agreed to counsel the king. Even illness couldn't keep Elisha from effective ministry.

A wise person once compared the effect of suffering to that of boiling an egg and a potato. While the egg becomes hard-boiled, the potato emerges soft and pliable. Likewise, suffering may cause us to become calloused and unresponsive or resilient and adaptable.

Suffering is a universal experience, yet we all react differently. Often, pain and hardship limit us or even cause our ministry to grind to a halt. But it doesn't have to. As Billy Graham once said, "The Christian life is not a constant high. I have my moments of deep discouragement. I have to go to God in prayer with tears in my eyes, and say, 'God, forgive me,' or 'Help me.' "

Graham knew this great truth: As we ask God to comfort, strengthen, and use us, He will do it, even amidst our most painful days.

***Dear Lord,** thank You that I am not alone in my suffering. Soften my spirit as I remember that You will use this experience to help me fulfill the plans You have for my day. In the name of Jesus I pray. Amen.*

Level Ground

"I tell you the truth," he continued, **"no prophet is accepted in his hometown"** (Luke 4:24).

Scripture: **Luke 4:23-30**
Song: **"Blessed Be the Tie That Binds"**

The Civil War had ended when General Robert E. Lee visited a church in the north and knelt beside a black man during the Lord's Supper. Later, an observer asked him how he could do that. He replied, "My friend, all ground is level beneath the cross."

Jesus experienced a kind of prejudice when He returned to His hometown. At first the people gloried in His eloquent words and were filled with hope. They focused on what Jesus could do for them, God's chosen people, and they enjoyed the blessings this prophet offered. But they became furious when Jesus spoke approvingly of the healing of Namaan, a Syrian, in Israel's ancient days. That foreigner had been a hated enemy!

Today, we still find it hard to reach out to our so-called enemies as God commands us to do. In fact, we often prefer to stick with our close circle of friends, those from whom we receive so much love and support. But as Charles Swindoll once said, "You can tell a lot about a person by the way they treat those who can do nothing for them."

Dear Lord, *thank You for providing for my salvation, though I deserve it not. Help me follow Your example as I extend Your hand of love and grace to all who come into my life. Through Christ I pray. Amen.*

Mercy Walk

Be merciful, just as your Father is merciful (Luke 6:36).

Scripture: **Matthew 10:40-43**
Song: **"I Want to Be More Like You"**

One day, a responsible student forgot her homework and came to me in tears. "That's OK," I said, wrapping the child in my arms. "I ate my mercy-flakes this morning. Just bring your work in tomorrow. I'll accept it without penalty."

One of my dictionaries defines mercy as the compassionate treatment of one in distress. It certainly helps the one in need, and I've found that providing relief and comfort makes *me* feel good too. But what about showing compassion to an offender or abuser who seems so clearly undeserving? That's a lot tougher! It's true that such people often don't *deserve* our mercy. But, of course, that's the point: the very definition of mercy makes it an *undeserved* extension of care and favor.

So how can we show mercy, when we don't feel it in our hearts? Like love, forgiveness, or any other Christlike virtue, to offer mercy is a choice of our will.

Today's Scripture passage puts feet to the choice. We are to love, do good to, bless, pray for, and give to those who may never do the same for us. For, as Martin Luther once said, "It is the duty of every Christian to be Christ to his neighbor."

Father, teach me to be more like You in loving even the most unlovable. For that is exactly how You have treated me! In Christ's name, Amen.

DEVOTIONS®

***B*e merciful, just as your Father is merciful.**

—Luke 6:36

FEBRUARY

Photo © istockphoto

Gary Allen, Editor

DEVOTIONS® is published quarterly by Standard Publishing, Cincinnati, Ohio, www.standardpub.com. © 2008 by Standard Publishing. All rights reserved. Topics based on the Home Daily Bible Readings, International Sunday School Lessons. © 2004 by the Committee on the Uniform Series. Printed in the U.S.A. All Scripture quotations, unless otherwise indicated, are taken from the HOLY BIBLE, NEW INTERNATIONAL VERSION®. NIV®. Copyright © 1973, 1978, 1984 by International Bible Society. Used by permission of Zondervan. All rights reserved. Where noted, Scripture quotations are from the following, used with permission of the copyright holders, all rights reserved: The *Revised Standard Version of the Bible (RSV),* copyrighted 1946, 1952, © 1971, 1973.

Impossible Dream?

The woman became pregnant, and the next year about that same time she gave birth to a son, just as Elisha had told her (2 Kings 4:17).

Scripture: **2 Kings 4:8-17**
Song: **"Awesome God"**

Years ago, when the research head of General Motors called a meeting in order to solve a problem, he placed a table outside the meeting room displaying this sign: "Leave slide rules here." This kept his employees from reaching for their slide rules and jumping up to say, "Boss, you can't do that!"

In our Scripture passage today, the Shunammite woman had no son and was married to an old man. From her perspective, having a child was absolutely impossible. So she had simply given up on her dream. But God saw beyond the impossible and blessed her with a son. Even when she couldn't believe the promise, God kept His word. And, of course, that is how He works with us too.

What a wonderful Bible passage to remember when we are praying for a seemingly impossible situation. For as the apostle Paul put it, God is "able to do immeasurably more than all we ask or imagine, according to his power that is at work within us" (Ephesians 3:20).

Dear Father, it's such a relief to know that my prayers are not limited by what I can imagine or understand. Thank You, in Jesus' name. Amen.

February 1. Author **Barbara E. Haley** has worked as an elementary school teacher and piano instructor. She lives in San Antonio, Texas.

Pray Over Your Schedule

In the spring, at the time when kings go off to war, David sent Joab out with the king's men and the whole Israelite army. They destroyed the Ammonites and besieged Rabbah. But David remained in Jerusalem (2 Samuel 11:1).

Scripture: **2 Samuel 11:1-5**
Song: **"Take Time to Be Holy"**

Time management is one of the most important skills I use in life. I constantly check my calendar and evaluate my priorities to keep myself on schedule and on task.

On those rare occasions when I fail to show up where I have responsibilities, I pay a huge price. I damage my reputation and lose valuable ministry opportunities.

I doubt King David had a Day-Timer™, but however he kept up with his schedule, one spring he decided *not* to go to war with his men, even though that was his custom. As it turned out, the army didn't need David to win their battles.

But because David wasn't where he should have been, he lost his own battle. While the army was away, David succumbed to sexual temptation, and it nearly destroyed him. It did destroy others.

The bottom line for us: As we schedule our days, may we ask God to help us make the best possible choices.

Lord, as I form my schedule today, help me make choices that will give me the best chance of success in Your kingdom. In Jesus' name, amen.

February 2–8. **Michael Helms** is a minister, author, and amateur photographer. He lives with his wife, Tina, in Moultrie, Georgia.

Doing the Right Thing

Uriah said to David, ". . . My lord's men are camped in the open fields. How could I go to my house to eat and drink and lie with my wife? . . . I will not do such a thing!" (2 Samuel 11:11).

Scripture: **2 Samuel 11:6-13**
Song: **"Find Us Faithful"**

An accountant once told me she was asked to enter some false numbers into the company's records. She refused, and the owner of the business fired her.

It's not uncommon. In fact, history abounds with stories of people who have set aside their personal well-being to do the right thing. Sometimes what we lose is greater than a job, though. Sometimes our choices put our very lives on the line.

Such was the fate of Uriah, Bathsheba's husband. David brought him back from the war and encouraged him to go home and enjoy his wife. David hoped this would cover his sinful act—and Uriah would think the baby Bathsheba had conceived was his own. But Uriah wouldn't relax while his comrades suffered on the battlefield.

Uriah, countless people in history, and my accountant friend remind us: It takes courage to do the right thing. Sometimes we do it at great cost, but always to the pleasure of God.

Lord, give me the courage I need to stand firm when tempted to make choices contrary to Your will. Help me be a person of integrity, unwilling to sacrifice morality for pleasure or ethics for gain. May I remember that in all situations I am Your earthly ambassador. Through Christ I pray. Amen.

Can Others Count on Me?

Put Uriah in the front line where the fighting is fiercest. Then withdraw from him so he will be struck down and die (2 Samuel 11:15).

Scripture: **2 Samuel 11:14-21**
Song: **"There's No Disappointment in Heaven"**

I met Mrs. Washington on a dirt road in Virginia, Liberia, on the campus of Ricks Institute. She's a refugee of the civil war that ravaged the country for 13 years. Abandoned by all of her children after her husband died, she lives alone in a stick hut on the 1000-acre campus. In a country where there is no Social Security, no welfare, no food stamps, and no government assistance of any kind, children are the life-source for aging parents. When they leave, parents suffer.

How hard it is to be abandoned by those who should support us! I wonder what went through Uriah's mind in those last moments as he noticed his comrades pulling back. Alone, he could hardly defend himself against an overpowering enemy. The pain of abandonment surely pierced his soul before an arrow pierced his heart.

If the Golden Rule serves as our guide, we will not abandon friends in their time of need. If fact, why should we abandon them ever, no matter the situation?

Lord, thank You for never leaving or forsaking me. As You are faithful to me, help me remain faithful to others. I want my friends and family to be able to count on me through good days and bad, just as I count on You. In the name of the Father, the Son, and the Holy Spirit, I pray. Amen.

Grief: Evidence of Love

When Uriah's wife heard that her husband was dead, she mourned for him (2 Samuel 11:26).

Scripture: **2 Samuel 11:22-27**
Song: **"Be Still, My Soul"**

I was 16 years old when I first experienced the death of someone I loved. I was hauling hay with my father. As we passed my grandmother's house, we noticed she had fallen over in the swing on the front porch. I watched as Dad gave her CPR. The color left her skin as she drew her last breath.

Over the next several months I observed the different stages of grief in Mom as she adjusted to life without her mother. I grieved, too, along with our entire family.

At that time I didn't know I'd be a minister, frequently walking with people through their own griefs. Most of the time, someone in my church faces loss and mourning. It's so painful, so difficult.

After Uriah died on the battlefield, Bathsheba, his wife, mourned his death. It was only natural, for grief is the price we pay for loving others. Have you ever thought of it that way? The only way to escape grief is never to have loved. But if we never love, then we never truly live.

Dear Father in Heaven, if I had my way I'd never deal with grief. It hurts too much. When I have significant loss in my life, remind me that grief is normal and that it's healthy. After a significant period of mourning, bring healing to me and the desire to love again. I pray this prayer in the name of Jesus, my merciful Savior and Lord. Amen.

Only God Can Do It

Have mercy on me, O God, according to your unfailing love; according to your great compassion blot out my transgressions. Wash away all my iniquity and cleanse me from my sin (Psalm 51:1, 2).

Scripture: **Psalm 51:1-9**
Song: **"Create in Me a Clean Heart"**

The *Boston Globe* reported in 2006 that scientists are investigating a possible way a way to cool down the overheated earth and reverse global warming. Could they shoot tons of particles into the atmosphere that would block the sun's rays? One model experiment indicated that if 20 percent of the sunlight over the Arctic Ocean were blocked, it would be enough to restore sea ice there.

We can come up with creative solutions to many of our problems. But the Bible offers no man-made solution to our sin problem. The transgressions we commit against God can be blotted out only by God himself.

David, overcome by his sin with Bathsheba, knew he couldn't fix his problem. Only God, in His great mercy, could rescue David from sin.

What great advances in technology since the days of David! However, nothing has changed when it comes to a soul's salvation. Only God can accomplish it, through the precious blood of His Son.

Father, I am not looking for justice, for I would not survive it. Like David, I need Your mercy. I am not hoping to get what I deserve; I am depending on Your great compassion to forgive me of my sins. In Jesus' name, amen.

February 7

In the Restoration Business

Restore to me the joy of your salvation and grant me a willing spirit, to sustain me (Psalm 51:12).

Scripture: **Psalm 51:10-19**
Song: **"He Keeps Me Singing"**

For almost a decade, the 1965 Ford Comet deteriorated. Only partially garaged, the back half of the white car was mostly black with stains from the pecan trees above it. That Comet, which belonged to my aging grandmother, was the only car I ever saw her drive.

Before Grandma died, I bought it and had it completely restored, inside and out. What joy on the day when I brought her outside to see that "brand new" work of art!

Life can pile its share of stain on us, can't it? David, marred by his own sin, longed for his joy to be restored to its original condition. So he called out to God for help.

Praise God, He's still in the restoration business. As someone once put it, "There is only one requirement for salvation: we must first be lost." Coming to God, admitting our deep need—the stains of our sinful choices—we ask for what God does best. He extends His loving arms of compassion and opens up the floodgates of grace. He restores us to a new reality: "Therefore, if anyone is in Christ, he is a new creation; the old has gone, the new has come!" (2 Corinthians 5:17).

Lord, in the rhythm of life, sometimes the cadence becomes erratic. Instead of dancing, I feel agitated by the beat. In such times, bring my heart back into rhythm with Your will. Then will I know joy. Through Christ, amen.

Being God's Messenger

Then David said to Nathan, "I have sinned against the LORD" (2 Samuel 12:13).

Scripture: **2 Samuel 12:1-7, 13-15**
Song: **"Redeemed, Restored, Forgiven"**

"Don't shoot the messenger." It's a common phrase meaning, Why be angry with the one who simply tells us the truth?

It's rare for someone to tell us what we *need* to hear rather than just what we *want* to hear. But mere "yes men" won't help us grow. And such relationships remain superficial at best.

It's risky to speak the unvarnished truth, though. Friendships can become strained. Yet the risks come laced with the rewards of personal growth. We begin seeing personal liabilities that once evaded our vision.

Nathan took a huge risk in going to King David as God's truthful messenger. He didn't accuse directly; he simply told a story that hooked David's heart and held a mirror to his soul. The story of a rich man's thievery became the story of David's own dark deeds with Bathsheba and Uriah.

Thankfully, David was able to respond to the painful revelation: "I have sinned against the Lord." I wonder, though, how I might have responded in a similar situation. Can I look in the mirror and see what's *really* there?

Lord, I'm not very comfortable pointing out the sin of others. But on occasion, I may need to be a Nathan to someone. Help! In Jesus' name, amen.

Transforming Training

The girl pleased him. . . . Immediately he provided her with her beauty treatments and special food (Esther 2:9).

Scripture: **Esther 2:1-11**
Song: **"More Like the Master"**

A full year of special treatments and training prepared Esther and the other girls for presentation to the king. They'd be the potential candidates for his next queen. No contender could just rush into the king's presence. First, 12 months of beauty prep!

In *Pygmalion*, by George Bernard Shaw, Professor Henry Higgins had his hands full when he took on the challenge of transforming lowly Eliza Doolittle into a high society lady. Her lower-class upbringing—including her speech, manners, and clothes—had to change so he could pass her off as a well-bred duchess.

I, too, am being transformed so I'll be ready to stand in the presence of God for eternity. My sin stood in the way of my being presentable, but His Son paid the price for my sins. Now His Holy Spirit is busy in my life (and in yours, if Christ is your Savior). He is transforming me, working into me the wonderful fruit of the Spirit: "love, joy, peace, patience, kindness, goodness, faithfulness, gentleness and self-control" (Galatians 5:22, 23).

*Thank You, **my Father,** for providing salvation for me through Your Son. May I allow Your Holy Spirit to transform me! In Jesus' name, amen.*

February 9–15. **Sue Miholer** is a newly-retired busy grandmother in Salem, Oregon, where she runs Picky, Picky Ink, her own freelance writing business.

Special Gifts

So he set a royal crown on her head and made her queen (Esther 2:17).

Scripture: **Esther 2:15-18**
Song: **"Love Divine"**

When we want to show our appreciation to someone, we go out of our way to find the perfect gift. Chocolates? Flowers? A special meal? A fancy card? It has to be something we know the person will value.

I doubt any of us will be able to top what King Xerxes gave Esther—a crown, a banquet in her honor, and a holiday to mark the occasion. He also distributed gifts with "royal liberality."

My king made me His own when I accepted His offer of salvation. Although the day wasn't marked by a crown or calendar change in my honor, He has showered me liberally with His gifts. Even Queen Esther's brilliance fades in light of what God will do for me when I am eternally in His presence.

No matter how you interpret the book of Revelation, for those who are baptized into Christ, the future is full of beautiful things. Heaven will be perfection—beyond anything we can imagine. Just being in His presence will be enough to keep us worshiping Him forever.

*I thank You, **Father,** that You have chosen me to be Your own. What You have given me is beyond imagining, and I can hardly fathom what it will be like to enjoy Your presence throughout eternity. May I live in gratitude for Your immense favor this day! Through my Lord Jesus I pray. Amen.*

Right Place, Right Time

Mordecai was sitting at the king's gate (Esther 2:21).

Scripture: **Esther 2:19-23**
Song: **"I'll Go Where You Want Me to Go"**

Heads of state and other powerful individuals have people whose job it is to protect them. In the USA, one of the duties of the Secret Service is to guard the president and vice president.

The Secret Service employs approximately 3,200 special agents, 1,300 uniformed division officers, and more than 2,000 other technical, professional, and administrative support personnel. A Secret Service applicant undergoes a thorough background investigation, including employment history, police records, credit history, school transcripts, neighborhood references, and military records. Then another six or more months of training follows.

But all King Xerxes needed was Mordecai. He uncovered a plot to kill the king and quickly reported it. The perpetrators were executed, a note was entered in the king's records, and that was that. Mordecai had no special training, but God had put him in the place where he'd hear what he needed to hear.

Where has God placed you today? What particular situation has He called you to enter, to make a difference there in God's strength?

Dear Lord, *I know You have placed me where I am today. Keep me alert to what You want me to know and do, that I might bring glory to Your name. All praise to You, in Christ's name. Amen.*

Let Go of the Banana

If it pleases the king, let a decree be issued to destroy them (Esther 3:9).

Scripture: **Esther 3:7-13**
Song: **"Is Your All on the Altar?"**

I've heard about a creative way that hunters use to capture a particular kind of monkey in South America. They put a banana in a narrow-mouthed jar and bury the jar in the ground, leaving the top open and exposed. The monkey smells the banana and grabs it. But because the jar is too narrow for him to remove his paw—which now clings tenaciously to the prize—he's caught. He will shriek about his dilemma, but he will not let go.

In our Scripture today, I suppose only one person out of hundreds refused to bow to the king. But it was that one person, Mordecai, who so infuriated Haman. He was in such a rage over the slight that he determined to kill Mordecai—and hatched an even grander scheme when he learned about Mordecai's ethnic heritage.

Like the monkey who won't let go of a banana, Haman was captured by his insistence on getting what he demanded.

Most of us have some monkey-like attitudes, right? We want to hang on to the "banana" of a less-than-God-pleasing attitude or habit. It too can enslave us with anger, bitterness, or just a sad longing for what truly satisfies.

Lord, *I want to hold on to wrongs that have been done to me. It's so hard to let go, and I need Your power to do it. Thank You, in Jesus' name. Amen.*

What's Eating You?

A gallows seventy-five feet high . . . He had it made for Mordecai (Esther 7:9).

Scripture: **Esther 7:1-10**
Song: **"I Surrender All"**

What we eat can cause chronic indigestion, migraines, and countless other maladies. But often it's not so much what we eat as "what's eating us" that makes us ill.

Unresolved stressful situations can trigger physical symptoms. For example, raging at other drivers raises our blood pressure. If we don't deal with and let go of such stressors, we can actually put our lives in danger.

Haman, consumed by his rage at Mordecai, got the king's permission to do away with all the Jewish people in the kingdom. His fury spelled trouble for him.

The dramatic intensity of today's passage would make a great movie scene. Haman relishes the honor of dining with the king and queen—until Esther reveals her heritage. Haman immediately realizes his life is in danger. He grovels before a Jew for his life, which has been consumed by rage because a Jew would not bow to him. What irony.

What's "eating you" today? Whatever it is, would you like to commit the situation to God? In a simple prayer, just open Your heart to Him. Let Him take away the sting of the hurt.

Lord, I release to You whatever stands in the way of my growth in Christ. Heal the hurts that come from living here on earth. In Jesus' name, amen.

A New Decree

Now write another decree in the king's name in behalf of the Jews as seems best to you, and seal it with the king's signet ring—for no document written in the king's name and sealed with his ring can be revoked (Esther 8:8).

Scripture: **Esther 8:3-8**
Song: **"I Call the World's Redeemer Mine"**

To counter the decree fashioned by Haman, Esther and Mordecai were to craft a new decree on behalf of the Jews. Jesus, by His death and resurrection, also crafted a decree—a new testament "by His blood"—on our behalf. The law of grace now dictates His dealings with us and our dealings with Him.

When I drove a school bus, I had to follow precise steps upon approaching a railroad crossing. I had to stop a specified distance from the tracks in the farthest right lane, turn on my warning lights, open the door, open the window, and listen for a train. Then I could cross the tracks. (That always reminded me of the rituals the ancient Hebrews had to follow in order to approach God.)

However, when I'm in my car, unless there is a stop sign, I am free to drive across those tracks without stopping. That's a good picture of the easy access we have, because of grace, to the throne of God the Father. Because of the death and resurrection of His Son, the Father bids us draw near.

*Thank You, **Jesus,** that the blood You shed on my behalf gives me instant access to the Lord of All. I pray to the Father in Your name. Amen.*

"For Such a Time as This"

Who knows but that you have come to royal position for such a time as this? (Esther 4:14).

Scripture: **Esther 4:1-3, 9-17**
Song: **"For the Deep Love That Kept Us"**

My brother-in-law was raised in the Philippines as the son of missionaries. He also spent the majority of his 25-year career with the State Department attached to the embassy in Manila. Even after he retired to teach at a university in the United States, he kept his security clearance so he could fill in overseas when needed.

In the summer of 2001, he was assigned to Manila for six weeks. During that time, rebel forces captured American missionaries Martin and Gracia Burnham. The mission agencies were glad they had someone at the embassy who understood the rebels' mind-set.

Fast forward to summer, 2002. Frank was assigned to Manila for just three weeks that year, but in that exact window of time, Martin and Gracia were shot and released—Martin to God's presence and Gracia to U.S. authorities. Frank was there to assist Gracia with her press conferences (very familiar territory for him). He also worked out many of the details for her return home.

God had uniquely prepared and placed Frank, in His place and at His time, "for such a time as this."

*Oh, **Lord,** I thank You that You uniquely prepare each of us so You can use us to accomplish Your will. Keep me walking close to You so I'm ready for Your plans to unfold. In the name of my Savior, Jesus Christ, amen.*

Treasure This!

After this I looked, and there before me was a door standing open in heaven. And the voice I had first heard speaking to me like a trumpet said, "Come up here, and I will show you what must take place after this" (Revelation 4:1).

Scripture: **Revelation 4:1-6a**
Song: **"I Stand in Awe"**

A rock? I'd invested hours typing this graduate student's geology thesis . . . and this ugly chalky gray mineral was my compensation? "I'm sorry I can't pay you monetarily, but I hope you'll treasure this. I found two others in the field also." I rolled the knobby hunk between my palms and muttered, "Umm . . . thank you."

He then retrieved it and whacked it in half. Wow! Inside was a cavity populated with purple crystals of indescribable beauty. We were the first to witness their magnificence inside this geode.

When John was given a glimpse into Heaven, he observed splendors so dazzling that he could hardly speak. Lamps blazed. Lightning flashed. Thunder crashed.

While we may not be the first to view a particular wondrously beauty here on earth, it is possible to daily experience, firsthand, the dazzling freshness of God's grace. Whenever we do, let us deeply treasure it.

My Father, let me always be open to Your matchless beauty amidst the ordinary routines of my days. I love You! In Jesus' name, amen.

February 16–22. **Vicki Hodges** lives in the lap of the Colorado Rockies and works as a Spanish teacher at her local public high school.

Perpetual Praise

You are worthy, our Lord and God, to receive glory and honor and power, for you created all things, and by your will they were created and have their being (Revelation 4:11).

Scripture: **Revelation 4:6b-11**
Song: **"Holy, Holy, Holy"**

The school's doors and windows vibrated as each note blasted from the speakers, every beat assaulting the glass and metal frames. This was my first experience chaperoning a hip-hop and rap concert at our local high school. I literally checked my watch every three minutes, wondering how much longer I'd have to endure the psychic battering. When the evening ended, my head's throbbing rivaled that of the school building.

By contrast, John ushers us into the throne room of Heaven to witness a most pleasant, eternal concert. The four creatures, and all those in attendance, worship the Lord continuously in a chain reaction of praise. Time constraints will never limit this concert.

When I consider that God created everything from the substance of His Word and that He sustains everything by His wisdom and power, I am in awe. Worship is the natural overflow of this knowledge, and my entire being throbs with praise.

Heavenly Father, when I exhaust the words to praise You, it's exciting to think all eternity will be sufficient time to learn to glorify You continuously. Glory to the Father, and to the Son, and to the Holy Spirit; as it was in the beginning, is now, and will be forever! Amen.

We're Moving!

The LORD had said to Abram, "Leave your country, your people and your father's household and go to the land I will show you" (Genesis 12:1).

Scripture: **Genesis 12:1-5**
Song: **"Move Forward"**

Every spring the nerves in my stomach knotted and eventually strangled my emotions. Springtime was our family's D-Day: Dad decided whether or not to sign his newly offered teaching contract for the upcoming school year. Once he accomplished his professional goals in one location, he would accept new challenges . . . and we would have to move. It was wonderful for him, but torment for us kids. I admit that I envied children who could claim a hometown.

God directed Abraham to move, a command that held both promise and hope. God's agenda targeted big objectives. *"Leave"* packed and delivered a powerful punch: God prepared to revolutionize Abraham's life, and to manipulate the course of history. His goals were deliberate and purposeful.

Ours may not be a drastic calling to move, geographically. Perhaps God is orchestrating a shift in our thought processes or redirecting our areas of service. Possibly, God desires us to pursue a new dream! Whatever the journey, He longs to guide and join us.

Father, the joy of journeying with You outweighs the tyranny of venturing into the unknown. Thank You for Your good plans. In Jesus' name, amen.

Among the Stars

I will make your descendants as numerous as the stars in the sky and will give them all these lands, and through your offspring all nations on earth will be blessed (Genesis 26:4).

Scripture: **Genesis 26:1-5**
Song: **"All Heaven Declares"**

The best estimates indicate that the Milky Way Galaxy contains at least 100 billion stars. And the universe holds approximately 100 billion galaxies, all populated with stars. There are more stars in space than there are grains of sand on the Earth.

Try this: Hold a dime at arm's length and aim at a night sky. That dime would hide about 15 million stars from your view, if it were even possible to see with such power.

Obviously, it was huge when God promised Abraham that his descendants would be as the stars of the universe. Abraham believed God's promise, even though he and Sarah had been unable to have children. The promise referred not only to Abraham's physical offspring, but also to his spiritual children, including all who belong to Jesus, Abraham's divine descendent. As the apostle Paul would write, centuries later: "If you belong to Christ, then you are Abraham's seed, and heirs according to the promise" (Galatians 3:29).

Lord, give me Your heart and eyes for the lost of all nations. Help me love and serve people, never losing sight of the worth of the individual. For Your love knows no cultural or geographical boundaries. In Jesus' name, amen.

The Hard Way

The angel of the Lord came and sat down under the oak in Ophrah that belonged to Joash the Abiezrite, where his son Gideon was threshing wheat in a winepress to keep it from the Midianites (Judges 6:11).

Scripture: **Judges 6:11-23**
Song: **"Faith Is the Victory"**

What is she doing? When I peeked in the kitchen, Aimee's little hands were plunged into the mixing bowl and plastered with eggs, flour, and chocolate chip goo. "I'm just following directions, Mom. It says to mix by hand." Apparently, I hadn't taught her that "mixing by hand" simply meant using a spoon, instead of an electric mixer. Our literalist was doing it the hard way, accidentally.

As the enemy Midianites were so near, Gideon threshed wheat the hard way. He beat the grain in a winepress, since that was quieter and less likely to attract enemy attention. Gideon, a man of valor, rejected the easy way—and even took on additional work from God. Not only would Gideon thresh grain, but he'd also thresh the Midianites!

In our technological age, we expend great energy trying to discover simple, painless means of accomplishing our work. The way is generally hard for a follower of Jesus, but He sufficiently enables and strengthens us to accomplish His will.

Lord, thanks for equipping me. Help me to serve with a willing mind and daring heart—the right way, easy or hard. Through Christ, amen.

S-O-C-K-S!

That night God did so. Only the fleece was dry; all the ground was covered with dew (Judges 6:40).

Scripture: **Judges 6:36-40**
Song: **"There Is Joy in the Lord"**

That's the way it is: *Eso sí que es.* My high school students delighted in the simple technique for remembering this idiomatic expression, "that's the way it is," in Spanish. By rapidly spelling socks, one produces an acceptable pronunciation for these four Spanish words.

My students frequently shout it to their friends outside of school. And in the classroom, if they groan about an assignment, I simply say, S-O-C-K-S to remind them the task is purposeful, nonnegotiable, and I will help them accomplish it.

God revealed His mission to Gideon, a mighty warrior. The assignment seemed impossible; after all, Gideon's clan was the weakest in Manasseh, and he was the least in his family. Gideon wanted verification of the assignment, so he tested God a couple of times. Each time, God patiently reinforced His S-O-C-K-S message to Gideon.

God faithfully demonstrates His power and wisdom, always equipping us to do His will, no matter how mind-boggling the goal might seem. Every time the impossible is accomplished, He is glorified, and that's the way it is.

Lord, I realize You don't need my help for anything. You set the universe in motion and are capable of doing everything by yourself. But thank You for the privilege of being part of the action. In Jesus' name, amen.

Pick Me!

Then I heard the voice of the Lord saying, "Whom shall I send? And who will go for us?" And I said, "Here am I. Send me!" (Isaiah 6:8).

Scripture: **Isaiah 6:1-8**
Song: **"Here I Am, Lord"**

"Staff, this year Anaheim, California, will host the curriculum convention. Three teachers will represent our school. During your convention free time, you might even want to visit Disneyland and the Pacific Ocean. Who wants to go to the convention?" The room exploded with willing volunteers. It's rarely my experience to win something, even if the odds tip in my favor. However, I volunteered and wrote a proposal, listing the reasons I'd make a good attendee. And . . . my principal selected me!

Isaiah, perhaps caught up in the awesomeness of God's presence, volunteered to be God's man. He knew neither the assignment nor what would be required of him. (It's possible the fervor of the nearby seraphim kindled a flame within him.)

Isaiah's passion for serving God, in the capacity of a forgiven sinner, allowed him to welcome any commission from on high. He witnessed God's holiness. What would it take for followers of Jesus to sense His holiness and mission? What would cause us to jump up and down, wave our arms, and yell, "Send me!"?

Lord, *I want a fiery zeal for serving You. Help me love and enlighten others with the truths of Your salvation. Through Christ, I pray. Amen.*

Shining with God's Favor

The LORD saw how great man's wickedness on the earth had become . . . But Noah found favor in the eyes of the LORD (Genesis 6:5, 8)

Scripture: **Genesis 6:1-8**
Song: **"Father, Whose Everlasting Love"**

Maribeth Parsons' family was gathered in celebration of her 80th birthday. While toddlers bounced in mothers' laps, adults caught up on the latest family happenings. Excited grandchildren crowded about the woman, each wanting to be first with the cards in their outstretched hands. A stack of wrapped presents awaited the arrival of the birthday cake. Around the room, other occupants of Sunny Acres smiled at the charming scene.

Maribeth was a favorite of both staff and residents. She always had a smile or cheerful word for whomever she met. When asked the source of her happy state, she just said, "God's been good to me."

Just as Noah's obedience found favor in God's eyes, Maribeth's life also reflected God's pleasure. In a world gone berserk with mayhem and bedlam, someone whose life reflects the favor of God shines like a diamond. That is the kind of person I want to be, today, tomorrow, and at the end of my days.

Lord, help me remember that I am Your representative here on earth. Show me ways to share Your love with others. I pray in Jesus' name. Amen.

February 23–28. **Gay Ingram** enjoys writing from her home in East Texas. Besides devotionals, she has published two novels and a book on her hometown's history.

A Willing Offering

The LORD said to Moses, "Speak to the people of Israel, that they take for me an offering; from every man whose heart makes him willing you shall receive the offering for me" (Exodus 25:1, *Revised Standard Version*).

Scripture: **Exodus 25:1-9**
Song: **"Lord of My Life!"**

"Not that shirt, Mom. It's my favorite."

"But Douglas, you haven't worn this in ages." She held up a blue T-shirt.

"It's the only Superman shirt I have, Mom. And I love it even if I can't wear it anymore."

Douglas thought of that shirt in Sunday school class, as he listened to Mr. Brown speak about the people he served as a missionary. "They are very poor. Most live in houses, made of scrap pieces of wood, that have dirt floors." Mr. Brown paused and looked around the room at the attentive, uplifted faces. "But even if all they have to eat is a crusty piece of bread, they will share it with someone who has none."

Douglas thought about Mr. Brown's words all the way home. After lunch he disappeared to his room and stayed for a long time. When he came out, he carried a cardboard box, clothes, and toys spilling over the top. "Here, Mom. Add this shirt to the things you're taking to the homeless shelter."

Father, help me remember that all I have is on loan from You. Open my eyes to how I can share my blessings with others. I pray in Jesus' name. Amen.

Don't Be Distracted

Let me pass through your land; I will go only by the road, I will turn aside neither to the right nor to the left (Deuteronomy 2:27, *Revised Standard Version*).

Scripture: **Deuteronomy 2:26-30**
Song: **"The King's Highway"**

Mrs. Bolton decided to bake a dessert for supper. When she found herself without enough eggs, she called to her son, Jimmy. "You'll need to go to the store, Jimmy. I can't make my chocolate cake without more eggs."

"Yum, chocolate cake. OK, Mom." As he stepped out the door, his friend Steve called. "Want to shoot some hoops?" Jimmy decided it was early and he had time. An hour later, Jimmy set off for the store. Leaving the store, he met up with Roger and Blake. He stopped to talk and, before he knew it, their conversation turned to the next big game. By the time their conversation ended, it had grown dark.

As Jimmy stepped into the kitchen, his mother asked, "Where have you been?" Without waiting for an answer, she said it was so late she hadn't time to bake a cake now. "Your Dad will be home soon, and I need to fix supper."

Sadly, it's so easy to turn aside, even from a once cherished destination. What will it take for you and me to keep our feet on the straight and narrow path Christ has set before us today?

Lord, I'm tempted to forsake the path you have set before me. Keep me faithful, in spite of the multitude of distractions. In Jesus' name, amen.

Quick Obedience?

Oh that they had such a mind as this always, to fear me and to keep all my commandments, that it might go well with them and with their children for ever (Deuteronomy 5:29, *Revised Standard Version*).

Scripture: **Deuteronomy 5:28-33**
Song: **"O Blessed Souls Are They"**

"Danny, you still need to sweep the driveway before you go to practice."

"I won't forget, Mom," he replied, his attention focused on the baseball magazine he was reading. His mother left, and the house grew quiet.

Fully engrossed, Danny didn't notice the time going by until he happened to look at the bedside clock. "Ooops!"

With only five minutes to get to the practice field, Danny changed into his uniform. Grabbing his mitt, he flew out the door, hopped on his bike, and pedaled down the street.

That evening, Danny's mother informed him: "Before you're allowed to go to practice again, the driveway must get swept."

Even we adults have our problems responding to God's call in a timely fashion. Why? Perhaps we hope things will "just work out on their own," with little effort on our part. However, the call of God usually involves hard work on behalf of His people. When others need us, we need to respond. Driveways don't clean themselves!

Father, I want to be quick to obey your commandments. Give me a willing heart and a loving motive, for Your glory. In Jesus' name, amen.

Attitude of Gratitude

Take heed lest you forget the LORD your God, by not keeping his commandments and his ordinances and his statutes, which I command you this day: . . . then your heart be lifted up, and you forget the LORD your God, who brought you out of the land of Egypt (Deuteronomy 8:11, 14, *Revised Standard Version*).

Scripture: **Deuteronomy 8:11-20**
Song: **"Hail, Thou Source of Every Blessing"**

He was born December 4, 1905, in Houston, Texas. At the young age of 19, he inherited the Hughes Tool Company, a million-dollar business. A lifetime aircraft enthusiast, he set many world records, and through his company, pioneered many innovations in aerospace technology.

Cowboy aviator, Hollywood playboy, military contractor, maverick financier—young Howard Hughes captivated the American imagination with his flamboyant lifestyle. But in later life, his eccentricities and excesses degenerated into madness. At his death, Hughes was a stringy-haired old man whose obsessive fear of germs made him a virtual hermit.

Some people live their lives as if every blessing comes from their own efforts. But God calls us to a continuous attitude of gratitude.

Every blessing comes from His gracious hand. Take heed!

Father, I acknowledge that everything I have comes from your loving heart. Let me live my days in thankfulness, pointing to Your unconditional favor. In the name of Your Son, my Savior, I pray. Amen.

Protective Love

What does the LORD your God require of you, but to fear the Lord your God, to walk in all his ways, to love him, to serve the LORD your God . . . to keep the commandments and statutes of the LORD, which I command you this day for your good? (Deuteronomy 10:12, *Revised Standard Version*).

Scripture: **Deuteronomy 10:12-21**
Song: **"Ye Righteous in the Lord Rejoice"**

"Judy, will you go collect the books for Library Hour from Mrs. Johnston?" The Johnstons lived only two streets away in their neighborhood, and Lacy Johnston was Judy's best friend.

Sack in hand, Judy turned the corner beside a yard enclosed in a white picket fence. A yellow sign reading "Beware of Dog" hung on its gate. As she passed, a rottweiler rushed toward her, barking furiously. Judy picked up a stick and began poking through a gap, laughing at the dog's aggressive reaction. Suddenly, the dog took a flying leap over the fence and pushed Judy to the ground

Arms covering her face, Judy crouched in fear of the dog's attack. But the dog's owner quickly came to the little girl's rescue, and Judy ran home. The phone rang as Judy's mother comforted her. "Yes, I understand," Judy's mother said as she hung up. "Didn't you see the sign, Judy? It was there for your good, to protect you from harm."

Father, help me see that Your commandments are not harsh. Through them You protect me from my own self-destructive attitudes and behaviors. I love You because You first loved me! Thank You, in Jesus' name. Amen.

My Prayer Notes

My Prayer Notes

My Prayer Notes

DEVOTIONS®

"You show that you are a letter from Christ . . . ."

—2 Corinthians 3:3

MARCH

Photo © Getty Images

Gary Allen, Editor

DEVOTIONS® is published quarterly by Standard Publishing, Cincinnati, Ohio, www.standardpub.com. © 2008 by Standard Publishing. All rights reserved. Topics based on the Home Daily Bible Readings, International Sunday School Lessons. © 2005 by the Committee on the Uniform Series. Printed in the U.S.A. All Scripture quotations, unless otherwise indicated, are taken from the HOLY BIBLE, NEW INTERNATIONAL VERSION®. NIV®. Copyright © 1973, 1978, 1984 by International Bible Society. Used by permission of Zondervan. All rights reserved. Where noted, Scripture quotations are from the following, used with permission of the copyright holders, all rights reserved: *Holy Bible, New Living Translation (NLT)*, © 1996. Tyndale House Publishers. *The New King James Version.* Copyright © 1982 by Thomas Nelson, Inc. *New American Standard Bible (NASB)*, © The Lockman Foundation, 1960, 1962, 1963, 1968, 1971, 1972, 1973, 1975, 1977, 1995.

Come Home to Peace

I will gather you from the nations and bring you back from the countries where you have been scattered, and I will give you back the land of Israel again (Ezekiel 11:17).

Scripture: **Ezekiel 11:14-21**
Song: **"Return, O Wanderer, to Thy Home"**

Ezekiel announced that the scattered Israelites would return to their homeland some day. It happened most recently in 1948, when the "new" Jewish state was re-constituted once again. Was this the final return of God's people before the day of the Lord? We don't know for sure, but we can watch with faith as history unfolds before us.

There's an application here for us too. We often feel scattered, don't we? But what does it take to bring us "back home" to God's peace (see Philippians 4:7)? For me, it requires carving out times for quietness and prayer.

Of course, my initial impulse is to seek some form of escape or entertainment. Yet when I've stayed quiet for a while, I've found the need for escape lessening. Soon the desire to get away from my hurts gives way to a deeper desire for the one who can heal them. As the great 17th-century preacher John Bunyan once put it: "If we have not quiet in our minds, outward comfort will do no more for us than a golden slipper on a gouty foot."

Dear God, keep bringing Your people home—including me, this very day. I pray in the name of Jesus, my Savior and Lord. Amen.

March 1. **Gary Allen** is editor of *Devotions*. He lives in southwest Georgia with his wife and Yorkshire Terrier, Robbie Burns. Tim and Dan are his two adult sons.

Who's in Charge Here?

I have installed my King on Zion, my holy hill (Psalm 2:6).

Scripture: **Psalm 2:4-11**
Song: **"King of Kings"**

"Who are the authorities at school?"
"My teachers, the principal, the bus driver."
"What about at home? Who's in charge there?"
"Mom!"
I had to laugh at this definitive answer, straight from the lips of a 9-year-old. She knew exactly who was in charge of her life.

Who is the authority in your life? It's a valid question, no matter who you are or what position you hold. Even those enjoying positions of power in this world will one day stand before the King of kings. The wise ruler recognizes this and governs accordingly.

Who is the authority in your life? You may never rise to such a grandiose position as those who rule over nations. Yet it's vitally important that you live as one who recognizes His authority.

We live in an age where it seems more common to question, resist, or defy authority. Some would even stand in defiance of God's divinely installed king. What about you—who is the authority in your life?

Lord, help me submit to Your authority in the most practical ways today. May I follow the King of kings in all things. In Jesus' name, amen.

March 2–8. **Dan Nicksich** serves as senior minister of First Christian Church in Somerset, Pennsylvania. He and wife Donna have two sons, Andrew and Derek.

Share the Gift

I have other sheep that are not of this sheep pen. I must bring them also. They too will listen to my voice, and there shall be one flock and one shepherd (John 10:16).

Scripture: **John 10:11-18**
Song: **"Bring Them In"**

One of the best-known pictures of Jesus is that of the shepherd who leaves the 99 sheep behind to go and search for the one missing lamb. But I like John's picture of Jesus as well—that of a shepherd who brings *other* sheep in and makes them part of the flock as well.

I doubt the apostles understood the worldwide implications of these words of Jesus. How could they possibly know He was referring to a harvest among Gentiles when He referred to "other sheep that are not of this sheep pen"? How could they ever envision the world we live in today—and the penetration of the gospel to virtually every corner of the earth?

I was once challenged by a preacher who said, "We have received the greatest gift in the world. Why are we so selfish with it?" In other words, there are other sheep not yet part of the flock. What can we do to bring them in? Why hold so tight to the greatest gift mankind could ever receive?

Dear Father in Heaven, I confess my complacency in taking Your Word to others. I acknowledge my fear and ask that You renew my heart and open my eyes to openhearted people. I pray this prayer in the name of Jesus, my merciful Savior and Lord. Amen.

His Dream Job

You have granted him the desire of his heart and have not withheld the request of his lips (Psalm 21:2).

Scripture: **Psalm 21:1-7**
Song: **"Be Glorified"**

It was the job he'd been dreaming about for a long time. He was called in for a second interview, this one with a vice president of the firm.

"How do you feel about traveling for the company?"

"Well, I don't mind traveling, but I have to tell you that I'm a Christian. If it ever got to the point where traveling interfered with my family and my time of worshiping with them, I'd have to do something about it."

Zack could hardly believe what he had just said. He realized this bold statement could cost him his dream job. The silence was deafening. After a moment that stretched to an eternity, the other man smiled and said, "I like that."

No matter what we stand to lose (even a dream job), why not proclaim our dedication and thanks to the Lord? Even with his dream job on the line, Zack proclaimed his devotion to God and his family. Since we trust in Him, let us not be shaken. Zack was hired—and God was glorified.

Lord, remind me that in putting You first I stand to reap the greatest of blessings. Indeed, it is You who grant the desires of my heart. Help me to glorify You with my life. In Jesus' name I pray. Amen.

When You Need to Talk

You love righteousness and hate wickedness; therefore God, your God, has set you above your companions by anointing you with the oil of joy (Psalm 45:7).

Scripture: **Psalm 45:1-7**
Song: **"What a Friend We Have in Jesus"**

Paul McCartney, best known as one of the Beatles, revealed in December 2006 that he had been seeing a psychiatrist for help following the breakup of his marriage. His explanation was unapologetic and to the point: "It's not a bad idea to have someone to talk to."

We all need someone to talk to. Even the best-known fictional heroes are firmly linked to their sidekicks. Who thinks of Batman without quickly connecting him with Robin? Robin Hood had Little John, and the "Lone" Ranger was something of a misnomer—since he was rarely without his friend Tonto.

The psalm-writer sings the praises of his king. His praise speaks of a relationship of shared joy and mutual respect. Yet he firmly understands that God is the source of the king's strength and blessings. Men may triumph over their enemies, but it is God who grants the victory. It is God who raises humans to positions of power and might. For no king, no matter how mighty he may be, will endure forever. Wise are those who serve the king whose throne endures forever.

*Thank You, **God**, for my close friends. They bring comfort in times of sorrow, encouragement amidst despair. Through Christ my Lord, amen.*

Whatever You Want

Endow the king with your justice, O God, the royal son with your righteousness (Psalm 72:1).

Scripture: **Psalm 72:1-7**
Song: **"Happy the Home When God Is There"**

After Solomon offered a thousand burnt offerings, God responded: "Ask for whatever you want me to give you" (2 Chronicles 1:7).

Rather than riches or long life, Solomon asked for wisdom. Faced with the daunting task of ruling Israel after David's death, Solomon sought God's assistance. God not only granted his request, he also blessed him with what he did not ask: riches *and* long life.

Many know Solomon as the wisest man ever to walk the earth. Few know that David, his father, had also prayed that Solomon would receive God's guidance in order to govern wisely.

What do you wish for your children? While Psalm 72:20 reveals this to be a prayer of David, it reads much like a prophecy of Solomon's reign. David understood the relationship between God's wisdom and success in Solomon's divinely appointed task.

Do you see your children (or children you know) filling a role in God's kingdom? Do you pray accordingly?

Lord, guide children and teens that they might seek You always. Help me to be a good example, and, if possible, a good mentor too. Instill within all of our youth the desire to seek Your will, especially when they face tough ethical choices and temptations. Through Christ I pray. Amen.

When God Takes an Oath

The LORD has sworn and will not change his mind: "You are a priest forever, in the order of Melchizedek" (Psalm 110:4).

Scripture: **Psalm 110**
Song: **"'Tis So Sweet to Trust in Jesus"**

Did you ever cross your heart and hope to die? Did you ever swear on a stack of Bibles? Do you remember any childhood pacts to be best friends forever?

Jesus says any such oaths are unnecessary. Our yes should be yes and our no should be no. In other words, we should be people known so much for honesty and integrity that anything beyond our word wouldn't be required.

The writer of the book of Hebrews quotes Psalm 110:4 to show that Jesus is the indestructible, eternal high priest. He also makes the point that God cannot lie; therefore, any oath He has taken can be trusted throughout eternity. In the same way, any promise He has given stands forever.

The Lord will not change His mind. He has redeemed you and empowered you to serve Him as a minister of the new covenant. The Lord has given His word that He will be with you no matter what difficulty comes your way. It is His oath, His promise to you. Are God's promises sufficient for you?

*What great assurance we have, **O Lord,** since all the wonderful promises You have given are sure to be fulfilled! I give You praise, in the name of the Father, the Son, and the Holy Spirit, amen.*

Appreciate Him!

I will bless them and the places surrounding my hill. I will send down showers in season; there will be showers of blessing (Ezekiel 34:26).

Scripture: **Ezekiel 34:23-31**
Song: **"There Shall Be Showers of Blessing"**

Christine couldn't stop praising God. "Eva will be 2-years-old in another month, and I don't think there's been a day we haven't thanked God for her. And now we have a healthy baby boy too. We are so blessed. What have we done to deserve all this?"

The day of delivery often brings a mixture of thanksgiving, exhaustion, and relief. But Christine was obviously expressing what, for her and her husband, Dan, has become a daily habit of praise and thanksgiving. Most of us have received showers of blessings from God. Sadly, we often fail to appreciate those blessings on a day-in, day-out basis. Christine reminded me to give thanks again for an often unappreciated blessing—my family.

God is the shepherd who guides, supplies, and protects His people from all that could possibly harm them. Yet the ancient Israelites needed frequent reminders to *appreciate* their shepherd. Let it never be said of us that we failed to see how blessed we are!

Dear Father in Heaven, how inspiring to hear Your name lifted in praise! Thank You for allowing me to share in the joy of birth and new life. Help me to live each day in remembrance of Your great goodness. I pray this prayer in the name of Christ my Lord. Amen.

Serenity Prayer

Give us aid against the enemy, for the help of man is worthless (Psalm 60:11).

Scripture: **Psalm 60:1-5, 11, 12**
Song: **"Peace, Troubled Soul"**

My favorite written prayer is "the Serenity Prayer," in which we ask God for ability to face the things we can't change, the courage to change the things we can, and the wisdom to know the difference. Many people, like me, have prayed those words when they've felt challenged, overwhelmed, or powerless. The prayer often appears on walls at the meeting places for addiction-recovery groups, as well as in hospitals and churches.

I don't pray the Serenity Prayer because of an addiction to alcohol or drugs. No, my particular compulsion is far more subtle but just as powerful. I don't know of any meetings for people like me, but if there were one, I'd have to stand up and announce: "Hello, my name is Lisa, and I'm a control freak."

But the events of the past year have shown me that trying to control my life is like trying to hold back the tide with my hands. All my efforts to be strong fell apart, and I was left with this truth: God's abiding love restores me. With God, I am serene, despite the storms.

Lord, *thank You for Your strong, gentle arms that wrap around me, encouraging me to put all my trust in You. In the name of Jesus, amen.*

March 9–15. **Lisa Konzen** is an administrative assistant and freelance writer. She enjoys reading, cooking, and taking lazy afternoon naps with her cat, Simone.

Under the Light?

Restore us, O God Almighty; make your face shine upon us, that we may be saved (Psalm 80:7).

Scripture: **Psalm 80:1-7**
Song: **"The Light of the World Is Jesus"**

When my mother was in the hospital last year, I visited her almost every night after work. She enjoyed the visits, but she always worried about my safety at night. So, after kissing me good night, she'd ask me the same question, night after night, until it got to be our little joke: "Are you parked under the light?"

However, no night I visited her was ever darker than the one in which she passed away. Suddenly, it seemed that even if I'd parked under a search light, I would still be engulfed in darkness.

But when I was too sad to find my own way to the light, Christ reached down to me through the members of my church family. They rallied around me. They helped me in so many ways, never drawing attention to themselves, but always reflecting God's glory. Some made meals, others helped me clean up and organize Mom's house to sell it. Still others just sat with me as I cried. Through them, God's light warmed me, saved me from despair, and renewed my spirit.

*Sometimes the dark is so deep that I can almost feel it. But then I lift my head, **Savior,** and I see You. Your love shines through Your servants, piercing the blackness and filling me with light. Help me to be a reflection of Your light to others this day. In Your name I pray. Amen.*

Mondaymorningitis

I will listen to what God the LORD will say; he promises peace to his people, . . . but let them not return to folly (Psalm 85:8).

Scripture: **Psalm 85:1-9**
Song: **"Father, Speak Your Word Again"**

A disease runs rampant throughout churches in America, afflicting people of all ages, races, and genders. Its name: Mondaymorningitis. This tragic condition is marked by enthusiastic worship and attention to the sermon on Sunday, followed by spiritual amnesia the next day. Sufferers are usually well-meaning, regular churchgoers. But they find the cares and demands of the workaday world crowding out the message of the gospel they've heard only 24 hours earlier.

Some complications of this disease include irritable mood, loss of satisfaction in one's prayer life, and weakness of spirit. Researchers believe some of the causes may be mental distractions (such as children running late for school) bosses breathing down one's neck, and a spouse who once again forgot to take out the trash. (Yes, I did the research myself.)

There is only one cure. It is drastic, but 100% guaranteed: Daily doses of time spent quietly with the Savior have proven quite effective. (A common side effect is peace; take as directed by your divine physician.)

Healer of my soul, I too soon forget the message of Your love. The closeness I feel to You on Sunday evaporates with the jarring alarm clock on Monday morning. Forgive me, Lord! In Jesus' name, amen.

Restored to God—and Renewed

Restore us to yourself, O Lord, that we may return; renew our days as of old (Lamentations 5:21).

Scripture: **Lamentations 5:15-21**
Song: **"Let the Beauty of Jesus"**

It was an old, broken-down wooden chair that my father, recently deceased, had made for me many years before. Dad had taken great pride in crafting the child-sized chair. But what once had been my favorite perch was now busted in the middle, with the paint chipped and peeling. I was ready to toss it in the trash pile, until a friend from church stopped me.

"Would you mind if I take a stab at it?" Denny asked. He explained that his hobby was restoring furniture. I knew he'd worked on a piece for a mutual friend, so I decided to let him try.

About ten days later, he returned with a chair I didn't recognize at first. He hadn't just *restored* the chair to its former charm. He *renewed* it, making it better than it had ever been before.

God does that with us. When we repent, He doesn't just return us to the way we were before. He restores us to himself, to a new and better way that only He can give. That's spiritual renewal, from the inside out.

Master Craftsman, who created the universe, I'm astounded that You love me so much. Your love transforms me, a lump of clay that You breathe the breath of life into, day by day. Because of Your mercy, I am a new creation. Help me to live for You every day of my life. In Jesus' name, amen.

The Unruly Calf

I have surely heard Ephraim's moaning: "You disciplined me like an unruly calf, and I have been disciplined. Restore me, and I will return, because you are the LORD my God" (Jeremiah 31:18).

Scripture: **Jeremiah 31:7-9, 16-20**
Song: **"O Gift of Gifts!"**

The artist Winslow Homer painted a picture called "The Unruly Calf." In it, a young boy tugs on a rope attached to a calf. The boy is obviously struggling, but the stubborn calf refuses to be led.

Today's verse brought that painting to mind. While God is certainly stronger than any young boy, man, or mountain, He still calls us an unruly calf. But this makes no sense. Surely, if our God is that strong, we couldn't refuse to be led by Him, right?

But that is the mystery and wonder of His loving gift of free will to us. God graciously allows us to make our own choices. He will not overpower us into submission. Rather, He desires our willing acceptance of His leading so we may respond in heartfelt love.

Along with that loving gift of free will comes a great risk. If we remain in disobedience, and like an unruly calf refuse to be led by Christ, we may find ourselves outside the pasture.

Good Shepherd of sheep (and unruly calves), Your yoke is easy and Your burden is light. Help me to follow You freely—with joy and peace in my heart—without stumbling. Through Christ I pray. Amen.

Restored for Service

Therefore this is what the LORD says: "If you repent, I will restore you that you may serve me" (Jeremiah 15:19).

Scripture: **Jeremiah 15:15-21**
Song: **"All for Jesus"**

Many of my friends are retired from regular employment, but they don't sit back in rocking chairs with nothing to do. Most of them seem busier now than when they drew a paycheck. They stay active for the glory of God, and they say they enjoy volunteering because they "love feeling useful."

We all need direction and purpose in life, don't we? Maybe that's why books like *The Purpose-Driven Life*, by Rick Warren, are so successful. Warren speaks to the fact that we human beings are on a constant quest, a seemingly endless search for meaning in our lives.

But as noble as that search may be, it can be dangerous if it leads us to focus purely on our own self-fulfillment. In fact, turning inward in pure self-interest is what sin is all about. Christ calls us to repent—literally, to turn around—so that the focus of our search moves us toward Him. Then we can find the true fulfillment Warren describes. It's something my retired friends already know: Serving God restores us as nothing else can.

Dear Lord, You have redeemed me for a purpose. I am called to be Your servant, Your hands and feet in this world, and a voice of eternal praise in the next. Thank You for saving me and giving me the most wonderful reason to live. In the name of Jesus, Lord and Savior of all, I pray. Amen.

Hearts of Flesh

I will give you a new heart and put a new spirit in you; I will remove from you your heart of stone and give you a heart of flesh (Ezekiel 36:26).

Scripture: **Ezekiel 36:22-32**
Song: **"Give Me Thy Heart"**

Stones can be quite handy. They can prop a door open or line a pathway. The big ones can even be climbed on for exciting recreation. But there's one thing about stones that makes them difficult: They're awfully hard to move.

Imagine having a heart of stone, literally. On average, you'd be carrying around a 10.5-ounce lump in your chest (9 ounces if you're a woman). Of course, you wouldn't be carrying it anywhere, because, as noted, stone is awfully hard to move. And a heart of stone couldn't contract to pump blood through your body. You'd be a corpse— "stone-cold" dead.

I know this is just a silly analogy. But think of it in spiritual terms. Sin creates a heart of stone in us, making us incapable of really living. Christ died and rolled away the stone, though, not just the one at His grave, but also the stony places in our hearts. We did nothing to earn this gift. Yet, because of His mercy, He gives us hearts of flesh, hearts that live in and for Him. What a blessing!

My Lord God, You've chiseled away the stone of my heart, giving me new life. I know I don't deserve such love, and I also know I could never have removed that stone myself. But now that You've redeemed me, help me to serve You with every beat of my heart. In Christ's name, amen.

God Will Do Something New

Forget the former things; do not dwell on the past. See, I am doing a new thing! (Isaiah 43:18, 19).

Scripture: **Isaiah 43:14-21**
Song: **"The Guiding Hand"**

Twelve years ago the company I worked for relocated. I had invested 20 years and loved my job; it was a difficult time of transition. But God led me to a special promise that helped me look to the future.

I'm going through another change in my career right now. After managing a team for five years, I've chosen, for reasons too numerous to mention, to step down into more of a service role. I wonder: Will it work out? Will I love it as much as I've loved my old job?

And once again I'm reminded of today's Scripture—the same passage that encouraged me 12 years ago; the same passage that I shared with a friend at work this week; the same passage that began my week of assigned devotional writing.

Obviously, God wanted to get my attention! He has reminded me of His power and faithfulness with Israel and of His power and faithfulness today for my own future. He wants me to remind you of the same things.

Lord, forgive me for not trusting You after You've proven Yourself over and over again. Help me look to the future, to the new thing You will do, and not dwell in the supposed security of the past. Through Christ, amen.

March 16–19, 22. **Maralee Parker,** a new grandma in Elgin, Illinois, invests her days working on publications at Judson University in the adult education division.

Soar Like an Eagle

Those who hope in the LORD will renew their strength. They will soar on wings like eagles; they will run and not grow weary, they will walk and not be faint (Isaiah 40:31).

Scripture: **Isaiah 40:25-31**
Song: **"It Is Well with My Soul"**

Do you know that an eagle can soar above storms? The eagle can tell when a storm is coming and will fly to a high spot, ready to catch the winds that will lift it above the storm.

I love that image! I have a lot of storms in my life, many related to our 18-year-old autistic/bipolar daughter. Life is stressful most of the time, so I often remind myself of the promises found in these verses. It's wonderfully encouraging, and incomprehensible, to know that the almighty creator of the universe—the one who hung the stars in place and calls each one by name—gives me strength and power each day.

Yes, the soaring eagle gives me a visual to cling to as I'm going through yet another stormy day. I remind myself that because of the grace and strength God gives, I can choose to rise above my circumstances and soar, just as eagles do. It all depends upon waiting on the Lord. We can rise above it all, as we wait patiently on Him for our needed strength, guidance, and peace.

Almighty God and Heavenly Father, help me trust You through the storms of life. Remind me that You hold all power and that You're able to help me with anything that comes my way. In Jesus' name. Amen.

A New Covenant

In the same way, after the supper he took the cup, saying, "This cup is the new covenant in my blood, which is poured out for you" (Luke 22:20).

Scripture: **Luke 22:14-23**
Song: **"The Old Rugged Cross"**

How's your memory?

I'm not too proud to confess that I struggle these days with remembering. So I make use of practical reminders on a regular basis. I need them in order to accomplish everything I must get done in a day. When I'm out in the car, I'll call myself on my work phone and leave a message to remind me about something. Or I'll send an e-mail from work to my home computer. I also use computer pop-up windows to help me remember.

I tell my family that I have too many details to be responsible for, and that's why I have these problems. Nevertheless, reminders are essential to my success in life these days.

So I'm thankful that Jesus, in all of His omniscience, knew that I would need a reminder. May I never forget the great sacrifice He made for me on the cross of Calvary. He told His disciples to take the bread, and the cup, that they might remember Him often. We need to do the same. Don't forget.

O Lord, how can I give enough thanks to You, the one who willingly poured out Your life for me? May I never forget your amazing, merciful sacrifice on my behalf. Because of Jesus, I pray. Amen.

Be Reconciled

We are therefore Christ's ambassadors, as though God were making his appeal through us. We implore you on Christ's behalf: Be reconciled to God (2 Corinthians 5:20).

Scripture: **2 Corinthians 5:16-21**
Song: **"I Come to the Cross"**

It's my observation that some teen girls seem to enjoy living in a constant state of drama. I've seen this over and over in my daughter's life. She and her friend can get "bent out of shape" over the most trivial things—sometimes evoking tears, hurt feelings, and angry words. Often phone calls are ignored—thanks to caller I.D.—or the phones themselves are slammed down without even a decent good-bye.

More than once I've had to serve as mediator between my daughter and her girlfriend. It happens regularly when they're together (and we parents are far away from home), and a rift develops between the girls. Those times are stressful for everyone. We talk it out, and they eventually reconcile. Then everyone heaves a sigh of relief when they come back together, ready to forgive and move on.

Thus it is with God and us. He wants us to be reconciled to Him, and it can only happen through Christ. Isn't it wonderful that God provided the mediator? He sent Christ for us so we can be reconciled to Him forever.

Merciful Father, thank You for loving me so much that You sent the answer before I knew there was a problem. Thank You for reconciling me to You, through Your Son, Christ Jesus. In His name I pray, Amen.

The Pathway to Hope

The LORD is good to those whose hope is in him, to the one who seeks him (Lamentations 3:25).

Scripture: **Lamentations 3:19-31**
Song: **"Whispering Hope"**

Directing our thoughts into dark memories of mistakes made, sins committed, and sufferings endured can lead us to despair. What starts as a simple pity-party can quickly degenerate into a major depression. Once in such gloomy depths, it's hard to pull oneself out into the sunshine again.

Jeremiah knew all about sorrow that comes from sad thoughts, as he remembered what the Israelites had lost because of their sins. But he also knew exactly what he needed to do whenever his inner turmoil became overwhelming: He turned his thoughts to the Lord. He remembered God's great love for him; he took comfort in knowing that he could always count on the Lord to be there for him, no matter what he was going through. Each morning brought a brand new start and another opportunity to experience God's great faithfulness. Such thoughts put him back on the right path.

Which path are you on today? If your thoughts are gloomy, spend some time remembering how much God loves you and how He has provided for you in the past. Put yourself on the pathway to hope.

Gracious Father, help me remember the ways you have blessed my life. Fill my heart with joy and hope, as I walk today's path in your presence. Amen.

March 21, 22. **Cheryl J. Frey** runs an editorial services out of her home in Rochester, New York. She spends her spare time with family—especially her grandchildren.

How to Escape Quicksand

[The Lord] lifted me out of the slimy pit, out of the mud and mire; he set my feet on a rock (Psalm 40:2).

Scripture: **Psalm 40:1-5**
Song: **"My Hope Is Built"**

Would you like to know how to escape from quicksand? Today's psalm has good advice on that subject. Contrary to the scary images from the movies where people are sucked under quicksand never to reappear, scientists now know that a person can float out if they stay calm. Rather than flailing around in a panic trying to pull yourself out, just relax, stretch out on your back to increase the surface area, and wait for your legs to pop free. Moving your legs in a circular motion will stir in water and help you float out eventually.

Although David might not have been in quicksand, he was stuck in a slimy mudpit. And he knew what to do: he cried out to the Lord and waited patiently for God to pull him out and set his feet on the rock.

When the trials of life are grabbing us and pulling us under, our first impulse is to panic and try to fight our way out. But the best escape from a terrible mess that has us trapped is to cry out a hearty "Help!" to the Father, relax, and wait patiently for Him to rescue us.

Heavenly Father, how I long for the faith to stop trying so hard to save myself. Remind me when I am the most desperate to relax into your arms of love and trust You to rescue me. In the name of Jesus, my Savior, I pray. Amen.

Do You Hear What I Hear?

I will attach tendons to you and make flesh come upon you and cover you with skin; I will put breath in you, and you will come to life. Then you will know that I am the LORD (Ezekiel 37:6).

Scripture: **Ezekiel 37:1-14**
Song: **"This Is My Father's World"**

It's cicada time in the Midwest. Cicadas are shrimp-size creatures with transparent wings and red eyes that come alive every 17 years. If you live in an area with old trees, you may be "blessed" with hoards of them, several million per acre. When they sing their cicada song, it can sound like a 747 airplane overhead.

They crawl out of the ground, fight to get out of their outer shell, and then look for a mate. After they're successful, the male dies and the female lays eggs in trees. Later, the eggs hatch into nymphs, which fall from the trees and burrow into the ground, where they snack on tree-root sap. At the appropriate time—exactly 17 years later—they claw their way up and out into the world, and the whole cycle is repeated. God has truly created an amazing world!

In Ezekiel's passage, we see another illustration of His awesome power with raising the dry bones. He can do anything. Nothing is too hard for the Lord!

Creator of all, I am in awe of the ways You reveal Yourself in our world. Help me to realize that my amazement should turn toward You, in glorifying You. You are worthy of admiration and praise! I love You, and I pray this prayer in the name of Jesus, my Savior and Lord. Amen.

That First Bath

Wash yourselves and be clean! (Isaiah 1:16, *New Living Translation*).

Scripture: **Isaiah 1:12-17**
Song: **"Are You Washed in the Blood?"**

When my second child was born, I was offered the "privilege" of cutting the umbilical cord and watching baby's first bath. I accepted, of course! When it came time for the bath, my 8-pound, 3-ounce boy began screaming at the top of his little lungs. He didn't like the bath at all. It was all I could do to keep from crying in sympathy.

In retrospect, I can understand my son's problem. He was used to a nice, warm environment inside Mommy. But change begins with new life. Besides, he really needed that bath.

As Christians, when we're baptized we are washed clean of our unrighteousness by the Holy Spirit. We are made new, a new creation. Our sin is separated from us "as far as the east is from the west." While we sometimes "get dirty" with poor decisions, we remain in a position of acceptance before the Father, all because of Christ and His cross. Certainly, there are consequences for our decisions. But we can boldly enter the throne room of God because we have been cleaned.

Dear Father, thank You for washing away my sin. Help me remember that You now have a plan for my life. In Jesus' name, amen.

March 23–29. **Pete Anderson** is a fourth-grade teacher who lives in Ocala, Florida, with his wife of almost 25 years and the younger of his two boys.

The Waters of Rebirth

He saved us, not because of righteous things we had done, but because of his mercy. He saved us through the washing of rebirth and renewal by the Holy Spirit (Titus 3:5).

Scripture: **Titus 3:1-7**
Song: **"Nothing But the Blood"**

"What can wash away my sin? Nothing but the blood of Jesus!" That is what the old hymn says, and it is so true. Jesus redeemed us through the washing of rebirth, and we are renewed by the Holy Spirit.

Clearly, we cannot earn salvation. No amount of money I give, nor amount of service I do, can earn me rebirth. I can only accept God's gift of salvation by faith. I accept what He did on the cross for me—His death and His resurrection—by faith. And I enter into the waters of baptism, what Paul calls the washing of rebirth. To God be the glory!

Just as we take a shower to wash away any dirt from our physical bodies, so Christ washes us to cleanse us completely. Nothing is overlooked, nothing is left uncleaned.

Don't you enjoy the waters as you bathe? Likewise, the washing of rebirth is just as glorious—even more so. In it Christ gives us himself—the living water.

Dear Heavenly Father, thank You for saving me through the life and death of Your precious Son, Jesus. Thank You for the waters of rebirth, and thank You for Your Holy Spirit who renews me daily. In the name of the Father, the Son, and the Holy Spirit, I pray. Amen.

Like Spring Rains

As surely as the sun rises, he will appear; he will come to us like the winter rains, like the spring rains that water the earth (Hosea 6:3).

Scripture: **Hosea 6:1-6**
Song: **"The Water of Life"**

"April showers bring May flowers." I said that many times while growing up to demonstrate my superior knowledge of Spring weather patterns. I also said, "Rain, rain, go away; come again another day. Little Phillip (my younger brother) wants to play!" When I was young, I wanted to be outside playing, but the rain would prohibit my fun.

I'm older now, and I know we need the spring rains to water our earth. If anything is going to grow—from grass to crops, from weeds to trees—we need the rain. (Thankfully, we have had the beginning of the end to the drought here in Florida this month.)

And just like the rain that our earth needs, we humans need Jesus. "As surely as the sun rises, he will appear," the prophet Hosea said. We don't know exactly when the rains will come, but we know they *will* come. Likewise, we may not know when Jesus will return, but we know He *will* indeed come to earth again, just as He promised (see John 14:3 and Acts 1:11).

Father, I am thankful for the rain that waters the earth. I know that just as it will rain, Your Son will return one day. Help me to live each day knowing that He may enter into my world at any moment. In Christ's name, amen.

Are You Prospering?

He is like a tree planted by streams of water, which yields its fruit in season and whose leaf does not wither. Whatever he does prospers (Psalm 1:3).

Scripture: **Psalm 1**
Song: **"Like a River Glorious"**

Ever been to a riverbank? It seems that most riverbanks abound with lush vegetation: green grass, leafy trees, thriving plants. Any plant blessed enough to be near a river gets all of the water it needs. The roots of the tree can even grow under or into the river to get needed moisture. Trees simply thrive when planted near a river.

Maybe we ought to live like trees planted near streams of water. I don't mean that we need leaves or a broad trunk! But I do mean that we should be solidly "planted" by our living water, Jesus. Then the "bad weather" that comes into our lives won't seem so devastating. As art critic John Ruskin once said: "Sunshine is delicious, rain is refreshing, wind braces up, snow is exhilarating; there is no such thing as bad weather, only different kinds of good weather."

When our faith, our trust, our lives are *in* Jesus, we thrive, no matter the weather. Then the fruit of our labor is full and sweet to our Savior. While we are "doing His good will, He abides with us still." So may our lives be firmly rooted in Christ.

Dear Lord, *help my fruit, my testimony, to be strong and sweet for Your sake. Help me thrive in my relationship with You. Through Christ, amen.*

Give Me Living Water

If you only knew the gift God has for you and who I am, you would ask me, and I would give you living water (John 4:10, *New Living Translation*).

Scripture: **John 4:7-15**
Song: **"Nearer, My God, to Thee"**

Legend says that as the "unsinkable" ship *Titanic* sank, music swelled above the chaos. The hymn, "Nearer, My God, to Thee" was being played on deck by a small ensemble. As hundreds of passengers without lifeboats jumped into the frigid waters of the North Atlantic, death was inevitable. The hymn was prophetic, for most of those hapless victims were only moments from encountering the living God. How many met Him as Savior . . . and how many met Him as judge?

In contrast to those deathly Atlantic waters, the water Jesus offers is living. Christ isn't offering water whereby we will be thirsty again. He is offering life-giving water for eternity. He is offering salvation. Anyone who partakes of this water will never thirst again.

This simple passage of Scripture reminds me that everyone needs the living water. And, as Christians, we are called to share this water with others . . . or the lost will find themselves in dark, uninviting waters indeed.

O great and merciful Father, thank You for Jesus, my Savior. Help me to be nearer to You, O Lord, and give me the words to say and the boldness to speak so others can know the life-giving waters of salvation. In the precious name of Jesus, I pray. Amen.

He's in the Cleaning Business

"Blessed are those who wash their robes, that they may have the right to the tree of life and may go through the gates into the city" (Revelation 22:14).

Scripture: **Revelation 22:12-17**
Song: **"For Those Tears I Died"**

Death. It's not a popular subject to write about, talk about, or dream about. Yet we will probably all experience it. Unless Jesus returns before our physical death, our lives on this earth will end in a grave. But death is *not* the end of the story for Christians; it's the next step. The Bible reminds us: "away from the body and at home with the Lord" (2 Corinthians 5:8).

Each believer can face death with courage and be sure of a future with Christ. Have you made some bad decisions or done some terribly wrong things in your past? You can come. The simple message of the Bible is that anyone can come and wash their robes and be made clean. In order for us to enter the heavenly city and enjoy eternal life, Jesus first makes us clean. I am so thankful on this Saturday in March 2009 that God is still in the "cleaning business"!

One last thing: We are the bride of Christ. The Spirit *and* the bride say, "Come!" You're invited!

Merciful Father, thank You for saving my soul and cleansing me. Thank You for offering the water of life freely to all who desire to come. Help me to extend that invitation to others too. In the name of Jesus, amen.

Water from the Sanctuary

Fruit trees of all kinds will grow on both banks of the river. Their leaves will not wither, nor will their fruit fail. Every month they will bear, because the water from the sanctuary flows to them (Ezekiel 47:12).

Scripture: **Ezekiel 47:1-12**
Song: **"I've Got a River of Life"**

I live in Florida. If you don't, you may have images of fruit trees in full bloom, lots of sunshine, and a certain "mouse" that is widely popular down here. And while these images are, for the most part, true, they are not absolutes. Our fruit trees aren't always in bloom. And while we certainly have a good deal of sunshine, we do have rain, hurricanes, and our share of bad weather. (Let's not talk about Mickey.)

Our Scripture today has Ezekiel at the entrance of the temple. He observes water coming out from under the threshold, and he receives this promise: The trees will bear fruit every month.

Imagine a place where fresh fruit is always available. A place with abundant fresh water. That is our destination. And while some people may believe that, if you live right, you will go to Florida when you die, we know that if you trust Jesus, you'll spend eternity with Him (probably not in Florida).

Father, thank You for the encouragement of knowing that You have me in the palm of Your hand. Help me appreciate the beauty in what You have created—especially the glory of Your plan of salvation. In Jesus' name, amen.

Greater Than Foolishness

The word of the cross is foolishness to those who are perishing, but to us who are being saved it is the power of God (1 Corinthians 1:18, *New American Standard Bible*).

Scripture: **1 Corinthians 1:18-25**
Song: **"The Cross of Jesus"**

I thought divorce was my way out of the constant pain in my heart. God surely couldn't want me to be so unhappy or desire our children to live with such angry, bickering parents. In my misery, I prayed, "God, please come into my life. I've made such a mess of things without You, and I desperately need Your wisdom. I don't know anything about the Bible, but help me follow Your directions."

I soon sensed God saying to me, "Ask your husband's forgiveness." I thought, *Will that really change anything?* The Holy Spirit continued to prompt me, "Pray for your husband, be submissive to him." It was all foolishness to my way of thinking. Yet, as I acted on God's leading, my husband began to respond in loving ways, and the Lord restored our marriage.

Yes, He revived a love that was dead. Thirty-four years later, I am still thankful: God's wisdom was greater than my foolishness.

Lord, *You rescued me from my foolishness by Your great wisdom. Thank You for bringing Your great power into my life. In Jesus' name, amen.*

March 30, 31. **Marty Prudhomme** is a great grandmother who teaches Bible studies and leads a friendship-evangelism ministry called *Adopt a Block*.

Jesus, the Prophesied

He was pierced through for our transgressions, He was crushed for our iniquities; The chastening for our well-being fell upon Him, and by His scourging we are healed (Isaiah 53:5, *New American Standard Bible*).

Scripture: Isaiah 53:1-9
Song: "Sweet Savior, in Thy Pitying Grace"

I stood in the hospital room watching Sam as he slept. (This was his third heart attack.) I prayed, "God, please let Sam wake up so I can tell him about Jesus. Don't let him leave this life unless he goes with You."

I gave him a little nudge. As Sam opened his eyes, I reassured him, "God must be keeping you alive for a purpose." Sam agreed with me. We talked for awhile, and then I asked him, "Have you considered the possibility you may not live through the next attack? Where would you spend eternity?"

Sam's answer amazed me. He said, "I have never thought about it." So that day I told Sam about Jesus, who suffered and died for his sins. Sam accepted God's forgiveness that day in his hospital room.

Isaiah predicted Messiah's sufferings thousands of years ago, but he never saw this prophecy's fulfillment. We now know the great truth: The chastening for our well-being fell on Jesus of Nazareth, the incarnate Lord. Because of His infinite sacrifice, we can live forever.

*Thank You, **Father,** for salvation through the atoning death of Jesus. Help me tell others the good news of Your Son. In His name I pray. Amen.*

DEVOTIONS®

Gary Allen, Editor

"Therefore my heart is glad and my tongue rejoices; my body also will live in hope."

—Acts 2:26

APRIL

Photo © iStockphoto

DEVOTIONS® is published quarterly by Standard Publishing, Cincinnati, Ohio, www.standardpub.com. © 2008 by Standard Publishing. All rights reserved. Topics based on the Home Daily Bible Readings, International Sunday School Lessons. © 2005 by the Committee on the Uniform Series. Printed in the U.S.A. All Scripture quotations, unless otherwise indicated, are taken from the HOLY BIBLE, NEW INTERNATIONAL VERSION®. NIV®. Copyright © 1973, 1978, 1984 by International Bible Society. Used by permission of Zondervan. All rights reserved. Where noted, Scripture quotations are from the following, used with permission of the copyright holders, all rights reserved: *New American Standard Bible (NASB)*, © The Lockman Foundation, 1960, 1962, 1963, 1968, 1971, 1972, 1973, 1975, 1977, 1995. *Holy Bible, New Living Translation (NLT)*, © 1996, 2004. Tyndale House Publishers.

Humble Enough?

"You don't know what you are asking," Jesus said. "Can you drink the cup I drink or be baptized with the baptism I am baptized with?" (Mark 10:38).

Scripture: **Mark 10:32-45**
Song: **"Behold My Servant, See Him Rise"**

My friend Regina serves her husband and children faithfully, without complaint, while living in a simple house trailer. She has allowed many hurting teens to live with her family from time to time. Regina serves in the church nursery, and occasionally she cooks for sick people in the community.

And more than once Regina has come to my rescue when I've been rushing to finish a church project. Regina doesn't have much by worldly standards, but she is a loyal, humble servant who lays down her life every day for her Lord Jesus. What a godly example to me!

Many people crave honor and desire power, but do not realize the price that comes with elevated positions. James and John wanted to be honored and raised above the rest of Jesus' disciples. Jesus knew they didn't understand the meaning of greatness in His kingdom. Honor there comes only to those humble enough to receive it.

Lord, I want to serve You without complaint. By Your grace, help me to lay down my life in Your service, starting today with the smallest acts of kindness and love. I pray in the name of Jesus, my Savior and Lord. Amen.

April 1, 2, 4, and 5. **Marty Prudhomme** is a great grandmother who teaches Bible studies and leads a friendship-evangelism ministry called *Adopt a Block*.

Appropriate Tears

God, with undeserved kindness, declares that we are righteous. He did this through Christ Jesus when He freed us from the penalty for our sins (Romans 3:24, *New Living Translation*).

Scripture: **Romans 3:21-26**
Song: **"Love Divine"**

Steve lives alone in a little yellow house and rides his bicycle to his job at a donut shop several miles away. I met Steve while working in his neighborhood with our church's "Adopt a Block" ministry. As I stood in his front yard talking to Steve, his eyes began to fill with tears. The smell of alcohol was evident on his breath (at only 10:30 in the morning.)

"I remember everything you said to me last week," Steve said. I had prayed with him then, "Lord, please give Steve favor at work and let him know Your love for Him."

The idea that I would come to tell him about God's gift of love amazed him. Steve knew he was a sinner; no one had to tell him that. But the reality that God sent His Son to redeem him brought Steve to tears.

It truly is a profound reality: When we trust God's loving kindness, we are declared righteous, placed in right standing with God, freed from the penalty of sin. Upon such a pronouncement of pardon, tears are thoroughly appropriate!

Father, You loved me when I was so unlovable. Now help me to love others with Your kind of love. In Christ's holy name I pray. Amen.

Spotless!

Their sins and lawless acts I will remember no more (Hebrews 10:17).

Scripture: **Hebrews 10:10-18**
Song: **"Nothing but the Blood of Jesus"**

I once lost a dryer load of my own clothes because of stains I couldn't get out. This unhappy event started innocently enough with my throwing a pair of my young daughter's jeans into the washer along with several of my best dresses. Unknown to me there were three crayons in one of her pockets. The clothes all made it safely through the wash cycle, since I used cold water. However, once the crayons encountered the heat of the dryer, they quickly melted and spread in interesting patters over my clothes. Stained beyond salvaging, they all had to be thrown away.

Realizing my shortcomings in the stain department, I'm happy to know that the job of removing the stain of sin from my soul is not up to me. Because of Jesus' one time sacrifice on the cross for my sins, I can wear a spotless robe of righteousness. Washed in His blood, I bear no trace of the former stains—they are both gone and forgotten. Hallelujah, what a Savior.

*Thank You, **Lord,** that we "have been made holy through the sacrifice of the body of Jesus Christ." You have provided the cleansing that we could never achieve on our own. Help us to keep our hearts pure and free from sin. In Jesus' name, amen.*

April 3. **Cheryl J. Frey** runs an editorial services out of her home in Rochester, New York. She spends her spare time with family—especially her grandchildren.

Flee from Sin

Flee immorality. Every other sin that a man commits is outside the body, but the immoral man sins against his own body (1 Corinthians 6:18, *New American Standard Bible*).

Scripture: **1 Corinthians 6:12-20**
Song: **"Yield Not to Temptation"**

Cindy was sexually abused by her mother's boyfriend when she was 8-years-old. She now lives with her grandparents in a tiny house, where she sleeps on the sofa.

Cindy has suffered tremendously during her young life. Her mom never really wanted to hurt her child, but that's exactly what happened as she kept making bad decisions. Mostly, her mom "just wanted to have fun;" she certainly didn't want God telling her what to do.

Like Cindy's mother, many people believe God is trying to spoil their fun. All those rules and commandments! But God warns us not to sin, simply because it will destroy us and our families. As Benjamin Franklin once said: "Sin is not harmful because it is forbidden, but it is forbidden because it is hurtful."

If only we would believe it: God wants us to be filled up, overflowing with abundant life, joyful and productive. But the self-destructiveness of sin leaves us hopeless and hurting. So . . . flee!

Dear Lord, I know my body is the temple, the dwelling place, of the Holy Spirit. You gave Your life so I could be washed clean. Please help me flee immorality and live a holy life. Help me remember that Your rules and commands indicate Your deep care for me. In Jesus' name, amen.

Life Out of Death

"Father, forgive them; they do not know what they are doing."
And they cast lots, dividing up His garments among them-
selves (Luke 23:34, *New American Standard Bible*).

Scripture: **Luke 23:32-47**
Song: **"It Is Not Death to Die"**

Each year I visit my friends Gail and Greg in Oregon—where the ocean is wild and dazzlingly beautiful and where the forests are vast, gigantic, and gorgeous. But last year I saw a forest that had burned during an extremely dry summer season. Black, charred trees stretched for miles.

Such devastation made me want to cry. But Gail said: "Fire cleanses the land, ridding it of dead and diseased trees. New growth comes out of these fires." In fact, certain seeds lay dormant until there's a forest fire. Only under great heat will these seeds open and take root, creating a healthy new tree. From destruction comes beauty.

Christ, too, gave us beauty for our ashes. Those who crucified Him didn't know that His violent death would give us the greatest victory of all time.

Christ still uses the "fire storms" in our lives to give us the greatest triumphs. Are we willing to endure, though, when the heat soars?

Dear Father in Heaven, I thank You for the salvation and peace that came from Your suffering on the cross. Help me to be convinced, daily, that all of my trials can be redeemed for the good by Your power. Help me even to be willing to suffer for Your sake that Your glory may become evident to all. In the name of Jesus, my merciful Savior and Lord. Amen.

God's Promises

We tell you the good news: What God promised our fathers he has fulfilled for us, their children, by raising up Jesus (Acts 13:32, 33).

Scripture: **Acts 13:26-33**
Song: **"Standing on the Promises"**

Life can be so sad. This afternoon, I've learned that two people who are dear to me have both been placed under hospice care. They were surrogate father and mother to me when I needed guidance early in my ministry. They live in a distant city. Not long ago, when I phoned them at the nursing home where they live, I identified myself, as I always do, "Hi, Drexel here."

There was a long pause at the other end of the line, and then he said: "I don't know who you are." This was the man who had helped to mold my life over many years. His response stunned me.

I don't like sad endings. But this week's reading reminds me that beyond all our earthly grief, discontent, and distress, there is a happier ending ahead. The power by which God the Father raised Jesus is the same power that will resurrect us to new life some day. Then we will know for sure that the words of the old gospel song are true: "It will be worth it all, when we see Jesus."

Help me to remember, **God,** *that Your promises are filled with hope and joy—and the sure prospect of Heaven. Through Christ, amen.*

April 6–12. **Drexel Rankin,** now retired, served the Christian Church (Disciples of Christ) as an ordained minister for more than 35 years.

Remembering in Prayer

Ever since I heard about your faith in the Lord Jesus and your love for all the saints, I have not stopped giving thanks for you, remembering you in my prayers (Ephesians 1:15, 16).

Scripture: **Ephesians 1:15-23**
Song: **"Help Us Accept Each Other"**

For a whole week I fished with my son and three of my friends. We experienced good fishing and bad during those days—times when smallmouth bass and walleyes were plentiful, and days when it was tough to find a fish anywhere in the lake.

What a special time for us! We were so active. We traveled, boated, fished, and ate together. I learned what had unfolded in the lives of my friends since we'd last been together. And I discovered in more depth what was happening in the life of my son and his family.

There were times, however, when I simply wanted stillness and quiet. I took several long walks up a dirt road, away from camp. During those unscheduled times of quiet, I reflected on the struggles of my son and friends—and the hopes they harbored for better days.

I prayed during those undisturbed walks, giving thanks—and also interceding for these beloved ones, that they continue growing in Christ. Isn't this how Paul recalled the believers in Ephesus? His heart was constantly pulled back to prayer and thanks for those he loved.

Lord, for family and friends who love me, advise me, help me, and lead me—may I always give thanks. In the name of Christ, amen.

Never Futile!

If the dead are not raised, then Christ has not been raised either. And if Christ has not been raised, your faith is futile (1 Corinthians 15:16, 17).

Scripture: **1 Corinthians 15:12-26**
Song: **"Because He Lives"**

I look into the sky and think I can see forever, billions of miles into the universe. Of course, it is nighttime. During the day, when all is sunlit and bright, I can see no farther than our sun. But when the darkness enfolds me, then and only then am I able to see thousands of suns, billions of miles away.

Only in the darkness can I see forever.

Have you noticed that, in the midst of crisis, we often sense more fully the presence of our resurrected Christ? When I feel lost, sick, tired, dejected, and dying the risen Christ propels himself into my life. He is always there, always in the midst of my life, even when impenetrable darkness seems to surround me. In fact, the darkness itself can help me perceive Him.

The resurrection reminds me that Christ is not bound by space or time. He is not bound by a tomb with a rock in front of it. He is present in my life, here and now. And my faith never was futile—nor shall it ever be!

O Lord, for Your ever-present love that overcomes the darkness of life, I thank You. May I experience the resurrected Christ in every moment of life that You grant me. And may I rejoice amidst every trial, for You are there with me in all circumstances. In Jesus' name, amen.

The Thursday Before

Having been buried with him in baptism and raised with him through your faith in the power of God, who raised him from the dead (Colossians 2:12).

Scripture: **Colossians 2:6-15**
Song: **"Lead Me to Calvary"**

On the Thursday before the first Easter, Jesus breaks the bread and pours the cup as He gathers His disciples around a table in an upper room. "This is my body, which is for you," He tells them. "This cup is the new covenant in my blood" (see 1 Corinthians 11:24, 25). It is a glorious meal, but betrayal looms in the darkness. And, even in His faithfulness, Jesus struggles in Gethsemane, sweating great drops of blood while contemplating the horror of Friday's cross.

Too often, we Christians arrive at the joy of Easter Sunday without experiencing the pain and agony of Thursday and Friday. Without these two days, the story is incomplete.

Today, as we prepare for the "Hallelujah" of Sunday, let us grapple with, and agonize through, the events of Thursday and Friday. After all, there is no resurrection if there has been no death. And, as Paul tells us, in baptism it is just as if we ourselves were put to death there with Christ. Only then are we free to love and serve Him by faith. What a Savior we have!

Father, help me to rejoice in Christ's life while recalling His sobering command: "Take up your cross and follow me." In His name, amen.

Good Friday—Today

Now if we died with Christ, we believe that we will also live with him (Romans 6:8).

Scripture: **Romans 6:3-11**
Song: **"Lift High the Cross"**

Good Friday recalls the day of Christ's death, and Easter Sunday is the day we celebrate His resurrection. Without these two days, we are left with an interesting teacher whose influence somehow outlived Him. That's the spiritual equivalent of very watered-down soup!

Otherwise, we end up seeing a God who is life-sized, manageable, marginally helpful, but not likely to ask much of us. These two days compel us to see that our reconciliation with God will not be accomplished on our own terms. We cannot write the script.

The bread, the wine, the thorns, the wood, the nails, the death, burial, and resurrection. Apart from those, we will not know God.

By Friday evening, evil appears to have the final word. Jesus has breathed His last. The tomb embraces Him. The entrance, sealed securely, seems to speak of what might have been.

It's important that we recall the whole story that climaxes in the glory of the resurrection.

*Transform my life, **Dear God,** into a close walk with You that takes me down pathways of both dying and rising. Give me the courage to "let die" everything in me that refuses to follow Your will each day. And raise up in me all the lovely fruits of Your Spirit. I pray in Jesus' name, amen.*

Waiting for the Dawn

Since, then, you have been raised with Christ, set your hearts on things above, where Christ is seated at the right hand of God (Colossians 3:1).

Scripture: **Colossians 3:1-11**
Song: **"Are Ye Able, Said the Master"**

The Saturday before the first Easter was a time of fearful anxiety. The disciples were ready to pack it in, call it quits. All they had hoped for was gone. Their dreams were shattered. For them, Jesus had summed it up perfectly: "It is finished."

Paul, however, knew that the outcome was hardly gloomy; instead, it was glorious. And, since Christ arose from the dead, we who are "in Him" through baptism are raised to new life as well. The apostle's writings constantly reflect this great truth of our identification with Christ and His work of salvation. For example:

"If we died with Christ . . ." (Romans 6:8).

"I have been crucified with Christ . . ." (Galatians 2:20).

"Since you died with Christ . . ." (Colossians 2:20).

On the surface, not much about the Christian life is unique. Christians look the same, suffer the same pains, and die the same deaths as others. Yet, Christians live on the basis of "the hope that is stored up" for them in Heaven (see Colossians 1:5). And that hope rests solely on the one who went there before them, direct from a cold grave.

God, help me recall my identification with Christ's death, burial, and resurrection. May I walk in newness of life this day! In Jesus' name, amen.

Resurrection Day!

He is not here; he has risen! (Luke 24:6).

Scripture: **Luke 24:1-12**
Song: **"Thine Is the Glory"**

I remember how much I enjoyed going to the Saturday morning movie matinees as a boy. It wasn't just the idea of going to the movie; it was also the feeling of *urgency* that gnawed inside of me.

You see, the reason I just couldn't miss a Saturday morning kids' show was because they came as unending serials that linked together from week to week. And each week always ended in some dreadful event that put the hero's life in danger—concluding with the words: "To Be Continued". The same design shows through in our cliff-hanger TV shows today.

The women who went to visit the tomb on that first Easter morning were startled by the question of the two men inside. And the disciples treated the tale of the returning women as an idle story.

What resulted, however, quickly showed that this saga of Jesus Christ would be labeled: "To Be Continued." There was more to come.

Because Christ lives, we too are resurrected from the darkness of sin. In Christ, we are made alive, born anew. And because of Easter, our story, also, is "To Be Continued" eternally.

Almighty Father, help me always to rejoice in Your mighty work of salvation on my behalf. I pray through my deliverer, Jesus. Amen.

Listen!

He is not here; he has risen, just as he said (Matthew 28:6).

Scripture: **Matthew 28:6-10**
Song: **"Christ Has Arisen, Alleluia"**

I didn't listen when experienced gardeners told me, "Take it slowly. Buy only one or two rose bushes until you know how to take care of them." Instead, I bought over a dozen. I lost half of them during the first winter. Now, even the remaining bushes need more maintenance than I had imagined. How I wish I had started out small. How I wish I had listened!

The women who came to Jesus' tomb to anoint a dead body had trouble listening too. Repeatedly, Jesus had told them He would rise on the third day. But they thought they knew better. After all, didn't they see Him crucified only days before? Didn't they watch as His disciples placed His lifeless body in a tomb? What Jesus had said didn't make sense in light of what they had seen and how they felt. So they went to the tomb expecting to find a corpse.

He is risen! What Jesus said would happen, happened. No doubt the women were much better listeners after their experience. And so am I.

*Thank You, **Lord Jesus,** for being my risen and living Savior. Teach me to open my ears to the sound of Your voice. Instruct me in Your ways, O Lord, for Your servant is listening. In Your name I pray. Amen.*

April 13–19. **Patricia Mitchell,** former Editorial Director at Hallmark Cards, writes from the home she shares with two people and four cats in Kansas City, Missouri.

What's in a Name?

Jesus said to her, "Mary" (John 20:16).

Scripture: **John 20:11-18**
Song: **"The Name of Jesus"**

I've become better at remembering names. When I'm introduced to someone, a few little "tricks" have been helping—like quickly repeating the person's name aloud, or associating the name with something I notice about the person's appearance. I'm more successful, however, when I simply focus my full attention on the one standing before me. Then, the next time we meet, I can usually extend one of the grandest human compliments: using his or her own name.

I know how good it feels when someone I've met remembers my name. It tells me I'm not just another face in the crowd. I'm not anonymous, not invisible; someone thought enough of me to remember my name. Those people remind me that even the Lord knows me by name—just as he knew Mary. No one is too "small" for His notice. No name is too difficult or too foreign for Him to pronounce.

Census figures tell us that the world's population tops 6.5 billion. Even so, Augustine's words still hold true: "God loves each of us as if there were only one of us." He calls me—and He calls you—by name.

*Thank You, **Heavenly Father,** that You have chosen to honor me by adopting me into Your family. Thank You for desiring such a close, personal relationship with me! All praise to You, through Christ my Lord! Amen.*

Along the Road

He asked them, "What are you discussing so intently as you walk along?" They stopped short, sadness written across their faces (Luke 24:17, *New Living Translation*).

Scripture: **Luke 24:13-23, 28-31**
Song: **"Lord, Take My Hand and Lead Me"**

Someone once said, "I didn't know I'd have to be torn down before I could be built up." Certainly the disciples on the road to Emmaus had been torn down. They had heard Jesus teach and had watched Him perform miracles. They had followed Him and placed their hope in Him, only to see Him crucified and buried. Granted, a rumor floated around about an empty tomb, but who knew? No wonder the disciples walked along with "sadness written across their faces."

When life tears us down, sadness seems the only logical response. Missed opportunities. Financial setbacks. A broken marriage. Sickness and disability. The loss of a loved one. But while things crumble, Jesus builds. On the road to Emmaus, He walked along with the despondent disciples, teaching them, strengthening their faith, and opening their eyes to their risen Lord and Savior. In the same way, He walks along with His "torn down" disciples of today. He comforts, encourages, and strengthens.

*Thank You, **Lord**, for walking with me in those times when I feel most alone. Build in me compassion, understanding, and wisdom so that I too may walk along with others and build them up in love. In the name of the Father, the Son, and the Holy Spirit, I pray. Amen.*

Show Me

Then Jesus told him, "Because you have seen me, you have believed; blessed are those who have not seen and yet have believed" (John 20:29).

Scripture: **John 20:24-29**
Song: **"I Am Content, My Jesus Ever Lives"**

I live in Missouri, the Show-Me state. One story attributes that motto to Willard Duncan Vandiver, Missouri's state representative in Congress early in the 20th century. He once said that "frothy eloquence neither convinces nor satisfies me. I am from Missouri. You have got to show me."

The disciple Thomas made a similar statement. Sure, he had heard talk of Jesus' resurrection. Talk, however, didn't convince him and didn't satisfy him. "You've got to show me," he told the other disciples. So Jesus showed him His hands and His side. And what Thomas saw convinced him. He bowed down and worshiped His Lord and Savior.

After His resurrection, Jesus physically appeared to many. Most people, though, from the beginning of time until today, have never seen His nail-wounded hands and His spear-pierced side. But that doesn't mean He has nothing to show us. He shows us His truth in Scripture, His love among believers, and His blessing on faith that has not seen yet still believes.

Dear God, keep me faithful to Your Word, and show me the way that leads to You, even when I find it hard to believe. In Christ's name I pray. Amen.

Comfort Zone

Simon Peter said, "I'm going fishing" (John 21:3, *New Living Translation*).

Scripture: **John 21:1-14**
Song: **"In Thee Is Gladness"**

"When things get tough, the tough get going." The rest of us run to our comfort zones, right? Some people watch TV or listen to music. Others cook, garden, or go for a walk. Some eat; I sew. After the astonishing events of Jesus' trial, crucifixion, and resurrection, Peter . . . went fishing.

In upsetting or traumatic times, we're eager to get back to normal. We fly to familiar surroundings. We regain control by doing something we know we can do—an activity (or non-activity) that brings us peace. But deep down inside, we know our lives have changed, as the lives of Jesus' disciples certainly had. Because of His glorious resurrection, they were no longer just fishermen. Now they were preachers of the good news to all the world.

When the Holy Spirit works faith in the heart, lives change. We're no longer satisfied by the temporary "comforts" this world offers. No matter what's going on in our lives, our comfort comes from Christ, who calls each one of us to rest at ease in His peace and love.

Lord, thank You for understanding my worries and fears. Thank You for being there for me through all the times of my life. Though the world may change around me, in You I have comfort, security, and peace. In the precious name of Jesus I pray. Amen.

Tell the Story

What I received I passed on to you as of first importance: that Christ died for our sins according to the Scriptures, that he was buried, that he was raised on the third day according to the Scriptures (1 Corinthians 15:3, 4).

Scripture: **1 Corinthians 15:1-8**
Song: **"I Love to Tell the Story"**

"We desperately need a teacher for fourth grade. Will you do it?" Not being a trained teacher, I couldn't picture myself taking on a weekly after-school religion class. Besides, it would mean leaving early from work every Wednesday, which would mean reporting to work earlier on Thursday morning. Ouch! Since the commitment was for only one semester, however, I decided to go ahead. That was ten years ago, and counting.

I've picked up a few teaching techniques along the way. I can name no better role model, however, than the apostle Paul. Paul simply taught the gospel message that was passed on to Him from the apostles and other eyewitnesses of the risen Lord. He stuck to the facts and let the Holy Spirit take care of the rest.

Children receive the gospel only if we pass it on to them. Is there a little one in your life who has not heard about Jesus and His love?

*Thank You, **Lord,** for everyone in my life who has gladly and willingly passed on to me the message of salvation by grace. Bless them, Lord, for all they have done to enlighten, encourage, and inspire me in my faith-walk. In the name of Jesus, Lord and Savior of all, I pray. Amen.*

Well Dressed

I am going to send you what my Father has promised; but stay in the city until you have been clothed with power from on high (Luke 24:49).

Scripture: **Luke 24:44-53**
Song: **"Holy Spirit, Light Divine"**

I was pleased with myself for having landed an elegant designer dress on sale. The first time I wore it, a colleague, who had formerly worked as a buyer at an upscale department store, spotted it right away. At first glance, she could name the designer, and she knew exactly where I had bought it!

The spiritual clothing we wear every day is just as noticeable. Our loved ones, friends, associates, and even strangers hear our words and observe our actions. They recognize love, joy, gentleness, and kindness when they see it. They can readily spot peace, patience, goodness, faithfulness, and self-control. These things stand out, especially in a world accustomed to much the opposite.

As the Holy Spirit continues to work in you, your "spiritual clothing" becomes even more elegant, more attractive, more remarkable to others. Christians who see it won't need to ask, "Where did you get that?" They know! But someone else might not know. What will you tell them about the power-clothing you're wearing?

Lord, clothe me with Your power so that my words and actions, my thoughts and attitudes, reflect the riches of Your spiritual graces. In all I do, let others see evidence of Your work in my heart. In Jesus' name, amen.

My Mother's Likeness

Don't you know me, Philip, even after I have been among you such a long time? Anyone who has seen me has seen the Father. How can you say, "Show us the Father?" (John 14:9).

Scripture: **John 14:8-14**
Song: **"O to Be Like Thee!"**

One day I said, "Whenever I look in the mirror, I see my mother." This puzzled my small grandson, for he knew my mother had died several years ago. He stared at me and asked, "How can that be?"

My grandson never knew my mother and didn't realize how much I look like her. But it isn't only my physical appearance that so resembles Mom. She influenced the way I think and act, and she instilled many of her character traits in me. Mother is the one who taught me to sew and cook, to be a good wife and mother, and to care for my home. I even teach a Sunday school class of preschoolers in the same room where she taught little ones for many years.

My mother was a godly woman, and I am pleased to follow in her footsteps. It is a good reminder to look in the mirror each day and see Mother looking back at me. I hope I will leave a good image to reflect in the lives of my children and grandchildren.

Dear Father, thank You for sending Jesus into the world to reveal Your character and Your love. I come to You in His name. Amen.

April 20–26. **LeAnn Campbell** is a retired special education teacher. She and her husband have six children, eleven grandchildren, and two great-grandsons.

A Sorry Sight

I will not accuse forever, nor will I always be angry, for then the spirit of man would grow faint before me—the breath of man that I have created (Isaiah 57:16).

Scripture: **Isaiah 57:14-21**
Song: **"Afflicted Saint, to Christ Draw Near"**

One morning after breakfast, I tossed a leftover waffle outside for our little dog, Muffin. My husband and I went for our daily walk, and Muffin trotted alongside with the waffle in her mouth. Later in the day the waffle was gone, but the next morning it reappeared—dirty and tasteless (in our opinion), because Muffin had buried it for a while. But she dug it up to carry around again. This went on for several days, and the waffle looked more unappetizing every time she dug it up.

Muffin's waffle was a lot like we are when someone makes us angry. Perhaps we bury our feelings for a while—but not too deep. We want to keep them close enough to the surface so we can dig them up to drag around again. But as today's Scripture tells us, it is not good always to be angry, for that makes a person's spirit grow faint. Just as that waffle looked worse every day, anger and accusations drag us down to a pretty sorry sight.

Dear Lord, I don't want to carry anger around, nor do I want to direct it toward others. When I'm angry, help me to forgive the one who has hurt me, even though I may need to hold him accountable. Also, help me direct all that energy toward the problem—and a solution. In Jesus' name, amen.

Mercy in Little Things

The LORD has heard my cry for mercy; the LORD accepts my prayer (Psalm 6:9).

Scripture: **Psalm 6**
Song: **"He Leadeth Me"**

Five months after Mom's death from Alzheimer's disease, the doctor gave us the diagnosis for my mother-in-law: "Alzheimer's," he said. How could we face this memory-robbing disease a second time? We cried to God for mercy. He didn't cure the Alzheimer's—it lasted 25 years from my mother's first symptoms in the 1960s until my mother-in-law's death in 1999. Even though we lived with the disease all those years, we know God heard and answered our cries. His mercy came to us in small, every-day ways.

Friends let us know they cared. One asked, "Is your mother having problems?" Just five words, but they were enough to show her concern. In the later years, a support group formed where we could share with other families our struggles and victories. Monthly suppers with my husband's siblings turned out to be an invaluable support system when we had to make tough decisions about my mother-in-law's care.

We have wonderful memories of both mothers. There are funny and touching stories to share when our families get together. Each rings with the mercy of God.

God, thank You for the mercy of others that conveys Your own goodness. May the good memories be the ones we remember. In Jesus' name, amen.

Sustain Me

The LORD will sustain him on his sickbed and restore him from his bed of illness (Psalm 41:3).

Scripture: **Psalm 41**
Song: **"Precious Lord, Take My Hand"**

The college instructor asked questions on the history test that she had not covered in class, and I knew my grade would be bad, maybe even failing. That was 30 years ago, and now I've forgotten whether my score was good or bad on that test. What I do remember is how I worried over that grade. Although I should have turned my concerns over to God and asked Him to sustain me, I came home and fretted. I stretched out on the couch, covered up with an afghan, and gave in to my misery.

The test was already over, and all my anxiety couldn't change a thing. But like so many problems that plague us, my worries about the test grew worse during the night-time. And as morning dawned, the stress had made me physically ill.

What anxiety I could have saved myself if I had only done as David did when he was ill! He asked God for mercy and acknowledged that God would sustain him. Then he moved on to heartfelt worship: "Praise be to the Lord, the God of Israel, from everlasting to everlasting. Amen and Amen" (Psalm 41:13).

Heavenly Father, may I never forget that You are faithful to sustain me. I pray that I will come to You for mercy every day, rather than wasting energy with unnecessary worrying. Through Christ I pray. Amen.

"I'm Sorry"

"Return, faithless people; I will cure you of backsliding."
"Yes, we will come to you, for you are the LORD our God"
(Jeremiah 3:22).

Scripture: **Jeremiah 3:19-23**
Song: **"Lord, I'm Coming Home"**

"I'm sorry, Mom."

"I didn't mean to do it, Dad."

What parent hasn't heard these words at least once? The broken dish, wrecked car, stolen goods—children face many temptations and often backslide.

When one of our daughters was small, she eyed the clear plastic cane-shaped tube of candy near the cash register. After we left the store, I realized she had the colorful cane in her hand. We went back inside, and I stood beside her while she gave the candy to the clerk and apologized for taking it. The clerk accepted the candy, but she felt sorry for my little girl because I made her return it.

My daughter probably wasn't sorry that day, for she wanted the candy and didn't get it. But she learned that it's wrong to walk out of a store with something unless you've paid for it.

We don't always learn our lessons that quickly. Many of us, children and adults, are guilty of backsliding before we honestly admit that we're sorry and ready to change our ways.

Father, thanks for Your forgiveness when I confess that I'm wrong. And thank You for restoring our fellowship so quickly. In Jesus' name, amen.

When I Need Help

O Lord my God, I called to you for help and you healed me (Psalm 30:2).

Scripture: **Psalm 30:1-5**
Song: **"God Will Take Care of You"**

Throughout the week, as we camped in a wooded park, a flock of geese wandered through the campsites. One afternoon as we finished our lunch of hotdogs and chips, two of the geese came close to investigate. My sister-in-law tossed them a piece of bread, and the largest goose grabbed it. The piece was too large for him, so he pulled off a hunk and left the remainder on the ground.

He swallowed the bread—but it stuck on the way down! His neck began to convulse, and we knew he was in trouble, unable to finish swallowing. He'd take a tentative step toward the piece of bread still on the ground, but then backed away as he continued his struggle to swallow. None of us knew how to help him, for we knew the goose would either run away or attack if we tried to catch him. After several minutes, he managed to swallow the first bite and then grabbed the other piece.

I didn't know how to help the struggling goose, but when I have trouble I can call on God for help. He knows me through and through. And since most every problem I have is some form of "heart trouble," He is the perfect Physician to come to my aid.

*Thank You, **God,** for all the times You've been there, ready to help when I've called. Praise You for Your goodness and grace! In Jesus' name, amen.*

Use Those Abilities!

Peter went with them, and when he arrived he was taken upstairs to the room. All the widows stood around him, crying and showing him the robes and other clothing that Dorcas had made while she was still with them (Acts 9:39).

Scripture: **Acts 9:32-43**
Song: **"Give of Your Best to the Master"**

When our four daughters were small, their grandma crocheted each of them a red coat. The girls proudly wore those coats all winter. Grandma made them because she loved her granddaughters and wanted them to have beautiful clothes. The next year she crocheted extra lengths so they could wear their coats for another year.

When the pretty coats were finally outgrown, we had to put them away. But the girls still remember what Grandma did for them. She knew how to use a crochet hook, and it was a wonderful way to express her love.

Our Scripture reading today is about another woman who made clothing for her friends and neighbors. Dorcas must have been a fine seamstress, and she used her skill to make robes and clothes. When she died, the widows she'd befriended cried as they showed their garments to Peter.

Some of us can sew or crochet; others wield a hammer, a paintbrush, or concoct great recipes. What a privilege it is to use our talent and experience to help others.

Dear God, *guide me in using the spiritual gifts and abilities You've given me. Should I read to a shut-in, visit a grieving person, or provide transportation for someone with no car? Thank You, in the name of Jesus. Amen.*

April 27

Soaring Above the Canyon

You yourselves have seen what I did to Egypt, and how I carried you on eagles' wings and brought you to myself (Exodus 19:4).

Scripture: **Exodus 19:1-8**
Song: **"I Must Tell Jesus"**

The eagle stretched out its powerful wings and soared high above the canyon floor. It seemed to float effortlessly on the wind. I had come to the Grand Canyon to remember my maker. The majestic depths and vibrant colors of the canyon were awe-inspiring. Its vast beauty gave glory to the creator.

A week earlier, I had been diagnosed with cancer. The full extent of its invasive attacks was not yet known. I cried to the Lord and asked Him to keep the cancer from also attacking my soul with fear, doubt, and distrust.

As the eagles soared gracefully over the seemingly endless canyon, God reminded me: He promised to carry me on wings like eagles. If I rested on Him as the eagle rested on the wind currents, He would carry me over the canyons of seemingly insurmountable circumstances. He would save me from the depths of despair. From there, I would begin to see things from His perspective.

Creator of All, You are my maker, and You know everything about me. You promise to carry me through every circumstance that You allow into my life. Help me to trust You completely. In Jesus' name, amen.

April 27–30. **Julie Kloster** is a teacher, speaker, and freelance writer. She also enjoys singing with her church worship team. She lives in Sycamore, Illinois.

Depending on a Promise

If the inheritance depends on the law, then it no longer depends on a promise; but God in his grace gave it to Abraham through a promise (Galatians 3:18).

Scripture: **Galatians 3:15-18**
Song: **"All I Need"**

My 7-year-old daughter, Sarah, put her hand over her eyes to shade the stage lights. She scanned the audience. I smiled and waved. Sarah's little sisters bobbed up and down in excitement on their grandparents' laps. Sarah bit her lip and blinked hard when she saw that the seat next to me was still empty.

Sarah's daddy had promised to try to make it home from a business trip to attend her Christmas pageant, but an unexpected snowstorm was delaying flights. Suddenly, the back door to the auditorium opened. Her snow-covered daddy arrived just in time.

Sometimes it's quite difficult for people to keep their word; sometimes they fail. God, however, always keeps His promises. Abraham believed God and His promise to provide him an eternal inheritance. This promise was fulfilled in Jesus. Abraham did not receive eternal life by keeping the law—it hadn't even been given yet! No, Abraham was saved by faith, through Christ's work on the cross, just as we are. We can trust our ever faithful God to keep every promise He makes.

Faithful God and keeper of promises, I look with expectant hope to the promise of eternity with You. In the name of Your Son, Jesus, amen.

Pardon Me!

So the law was put in charge to lead us to Christ that we might be justified by faith (Galatians 3:24).

Scripture: **Galatians 3:23-29**
Song: **"This Is How It Feels to Be Free"**

"The law, whether human or divine, is no respecter of persons," said President Ford. It was September 8, 1974, and Ford was about to pardon former President Nixon for his role in the Watergate scandal. Ford continued, "I, Gerald R. Ford, President of the United States . . . do grant a full, free, and absolute pardon unto Richard Nixon for all offenses against the United States." At that moment, regardless of any guilt that might be proven by the law, Richard Nixon was free from punishment for any wrongdoing.

We humans, too, stand in need of a pardon. We have broken God's law. Yet God's law helps us to recognize that we are sinners in need of the Savior.

By God's wonderful grace, He offers all-sufficient pardon and eternal salvation. Through repentance and faith in Jesus Christ, we can become children of God, being baptized into His body. We thus receive a "full, free, and absolute pardon" in Christ. Released from the curse of sin, we can sing and shout God's praise with exuberant joy.

Father, thank You for the cross of Your Son, Jesus. He took the punishment that I deserved. How wonderful and glorious Your love for me must be! Now I am forgiven and free. May I give You glory and praise all the days of my life. In the holy name of Jesus, my Lord and Savior, I pray. Amen.

Fully Adopted, Fully Loved

When the time had fully come, God sent his Son, born of a woman, born under law, to redeem those under law, that we might receive the full rights of sons (Galatians 4:4, 5).

Scripture: **Galatians 4:1-7**
Song: **"Redeemed, How I Love to Proclaim It!"**

A splotch of "Molokai Blue" paint adorned Caitlyn's hair. She grinned. "I'm almost done painting her room," she said. "Carpeting comes tomorrow."

Caitlyn's 10-year-old daughter, Bridget, danced around her. "We want her room to be ready when we get the call to come and get her," Bridget explained. "Her name is Holly."

Bridget's family was adopting a baby girl from China. "We already love her, and we don't even know her yet," Bridget explained. "I have always wanted a baby sister. I can hardly wait!"

Under Roman law, an adopted child had all the legal rights of a biological child, even if the adopted child had formerly been a slave. The child wasn't second-class, but equal to other children in the family in every way.

The apostle Paul wanted the Galatians to understand that this is how God adopts us. We become His children, and He becomes our "Abba, Father" or "Daddy, God." As adopted children, we are first-class heirs to His kingdom.

Daddy God, *thank You for adopting me fully and completely as Your own dearly loved child. Thank You for the promise of eternity with You, as an heir to Your kingdom. In Christ's precious name, amen.*

My Prayer Notes

DEVOTIONS®

*T*he people all responded together, "We will do everything the Lord has said."

—Exodus 19:8

MAY

Photo © Getty Images

Gary Allen, Editor

DEVOTIONS® is published quarterly by Standard Publishing, Cincinnati, Ohio, www.standardpub.com. © 2008 by Standard Publishing. All rights reserved. Topics based on the Home Daily Bible Readings, International Sunday School Lessons. © 2005 by the Committee on the Uniform Series. Printed in the U.S.A. All Scripture quotations, unless otherwise indicated, are taken from the HOLY BIBLE, NEW INTERNATIONAL VERSION®. NIV®. Copyright © 1973, 1978, 1984 by International Bible Society. Used by permission of Zondervan. All rights reserved. Where noted, Scripture quotations are from the following, used with permission of the copyright holders, all rights reserved: *The New King James Version.* Copyright © 1982 by Thomas Nelson, Inc. *The Revised Standard Version of the Bible (RSV),* copyrighted 1946, 1952, © 1971, 1973.

What List Am I On?

Everyone who has left houses or brothers or sisters or father or mother or children or fields for my sake will receive a hundred times as much and will inherit eternal life (Matthew 19:29).

Scripture: **Matthew 19:23-30**
Song: **"All As God Wills"**

"A nine-figure fortune won't get you much mention these days, at least not on these pages," said Forbes.com on September 21, 2006. For the first time in history, the nation's wealthiest Forbes 400 each had at least $1 billion dollars! Forbes also noted that eight members on the list the year before had died. One couple had dropped off the list because they had given $1 billion dollars to charity.

Wealth in this world is highly acclaimed, but what is the *eternal value* of financial gain? We may not be on the Forbes 400 list, but if our name is written in the Lamb's Book of Life, we have eternal treasure. The tempting but temporal trappings of this world will never compare to the unending blessings of those Christ has redeemed.

Jesus made it clear that financial wealth can stand in the way of our understanding of the need for a Savior. God is the God of the impossible, however, and He can change the heart of any person. Are we willing to use all that we have for God's kingdom?

O Lord, all good things come from You. Use all the gifts that You have given to me for Your honor and glory. In Jesus' name, amen.

May 1–3. **Julie Kloster** is a teacher, speaker, and freelance writer. She also enjoys singing with her church worship team. She lives in Sycamore, Illinois.

More Christlike

The fruit of the Spirit is love, joy, peace, patience, kindness, goodness, faithfulness, gentleness and self-control. Against such things there is no law (Galatians 5:22, 23).

Scripture: **Galatians 5:16-25**
Song: **"Spirit of the Living God"**

"If you plant an apple seed, will you grow an orange tree?" I asked a group of preschoolers.

They laughed. "No! An apple tree!"

"You are silly," a curly-headed 4-year-old told me.

"You are right!" I answered. "The type of plant that grows depends on the seed that we plant."

This basic principle is true for our spiritual lives, as well. If the Holy Spirit is planted in our hearts and we listen to His voice, we will bear the fruits of the Spirit. If we do not keep in step with the Spirit, though, we will produce the acts of our own sinful nature. Without the Holy Spirit being planted in our hearts, we will be unable to consistently grow His fruit, the evidence that He is there.

God alone can plant the Holy Spirit in our hearts. He does this when we repent of our sins and are baptized into Christ. Once the seed is planted, we can listen to the Spirit's voice and grow to the heights of spiritual maturity. As we grow in the Spirit of Christ—amazingly—we become more and more like Christ himself.

Spirit of God, fill me with Your presence that I may bear Your fruit. I want to hear Your voice and follow You. Teach me through Your Word how to be more like Jesus. For in His name, I pray. Amen.

Guaranteed!

Having believed, you were marked in him with a seal, the promised Holy Spirit, who is a deposit guaranteeing our inheritance until the redemption of those who are God's possession—to the praise of his glory (Ephesians 1:13, 14).

Scripture: **Ephesians 1:3-14**
Song: **"He the Pearly Gates Will Open"**

I painted the white wicker chair, replaced the worn cushion with a new one in modern colors, and tucked it into a corner of the sun room. It was a treasure to our family—a piece of inheritance to add to our collection of items left behind by those we loved.

In the corner of one bedroom is a small, marble-topped dresser. Its edges are rough with use. The latch hangs crooked. Still, it is a treasure to us, having once belonged to my grandmother.

We have a few beautiful pieces of old china, several tarnished pieces of silver, an embroidered tablecloth on a small round table in our dining room, and an old German knife. They are all relics of the past that are now marked with age and use. Yet they are precious to us because we've inherited them from precious people.

Christians have an inheritance in Heaven that will never perish, spoil, or fade. At baptism, the Holy Spirit takes up residence in our hearts. His presence is a seal, a divine promise, guaranteeing our eternal inheritance.

Holy Spirit, thanks for living in me as a promise that I belong to God. I am so grateful for Your ever-present sustaining grace. Through Christ, amen.

Grace Has Come

Grace and truth came through Jesus Christ (John 1:17).

Scripture: **John 1:14-18**
Song: **"Here Is Love"**

Most of the time, Christians press on in their daily lives with God by faith, not experiencing visions or special revelations. But I believe God does sometimes break through in a special way. It happened to me once.

A group of us was praying in a friend's house, and the Lord Jesus stood in our midst. I seemed to see His feet as He stood there. He was very real to me, and He said, "You are acceptable to Me." His presence was like a beautiful perfume, which lingered with me for some days, then faded. Faith had to take over once again.

I was so overcome by the sweetness of His presence that I forgot to pass on the message! I knew it was for someone else at that meeting who truly needed encouragement in Christian growth—a person struggling with doubt and truth, with law and grace.

The apostle John wrote about the Jesus He knew well; he had experienced the Lord's grace and truth firsthand. We can experience it too. We may not see Him with physical sight until we stand before Him. But we can receive His goodness any time we open our hearts.

Lord, by Your grace, You forgive me and accept me. Now my heart is free to proclaim Your goodness to all in my world. In Jesus' name, amen.

May 4–10. **Marion Turnbull** and her husband, now retired in Manchester, UK, raised a family in England, then served together as missionaries in Africa.

Powerful Enough to Wait

The L<small>ORD</small> **will wait, that He may be gracious to you** (Isaiah 30:18, *New King James Version*).

Scripture: **Isaiah 30:15-21**
Song: **"We Rest on Thee"**

We hear a lot today about terrorists, young men ready to sacrifice everything, even their own lives, for their cause. They kill and maim in their zeal for their religion.

To many people, Paul was a terrorist. Extremely zealous for his religion, he dragged Christians into prison and death, thinking he was doing the will of God. When Jesus met him—and he saw that the whole time he had been fighting *against* God—he reeled into a state of collapse for days. He said that everything he had considered his best assets—pride in his national and religious heritage and all his own efforts to be righteous before God—he now counted these things as rubbish compared with knowing the Lord Jesus.

In that context, I find today's verse amazing. The Lord is waiting to be gracious to me? He waits until I come to the end of my own zealous efforts to earn His favor, until I give up the fight, until I simply allow Him to show me compassion. Some gods need to be supported and defended so they may go forth in power—not ours. He is powerful enough to wait; He leads His people with grace.

Thank You, **Lord,** *for being so patient with me. I will wait for You and receive all that You want to pour out upon me. Through Christ, amen.*

Hospitality or Fame?

I would rather be a doorkeeper in the house of my God than dwell in the tents of the wicked (Psalm 84:10).

Scripture: **Psalm 84:8-12**
Song: **"Close to Thee"**

I knew a gentle Welshman (now with his Lord) who was once a champion boxer. His name was Gerault James, and he came from a humble home. But a famous fight promoter spotted his talent. There is big money in boxing, and Gerault was on the way up from the beginning.

Gerault was a Christian. One day during a training session in the boxing ring, Gerault's small New Testament fell out of his dressing robe onto the floor. The fight promoter was watching and saw what it was. He climbed up and kicked the New Testament right out of the ring. "You can forget all *that*!" he said. "No place in your life for that now, my boy!"

Gerault knew he had to make a choice. Go on in his boxing career and make the kind of money he had dreamed about . . . or follow Jesus.

He chose Jesus. He and his wife ran a small hotel in Aberystwyth, Wales, and served God's people for many years. Such a choice is not too difficult for most Christians, those who have tasted that the Lord is good. In Gerault's case it meant preferring a life of kind hospitality to one of fame and affluence.

*Not just to the door, **Father,** You call me to enter right in to Your blessed presence. What can tempt me away from You? In Jesus' name, amen.*

He Knows My Pain

Although He was a son, He learned obedience by what He suffered (Hebrews 5:8).

Scripture: **Hebrews 4:14–5:10**
Song: **"God with Us"**

My sister lost her 19-year-old son in an accident. She had been looking for God for many years, and neither of us could understand this terrible tragedy. How can we? However, she went on to find Jesus, and I was able to direct her to a church near to where she lived.

One day she phoned me and said, with tears, "Isn't God good? He's given me a Christian friend who also lost a child—and she knows how it feels."

The friend, Norah, had a beautiful married daughter who died while giving birth. She took my sister into her arms and comforted her as I, who never lost a child, could not. Significant loss and pain had developed that extra dimension in Norah's life.

Not that God *wants* us to suffer; Jesus has suffered enough for all of us. But without experiencing a little pain, how can we know what it feels like?

My Jesus, Eternal Son of God, King of kings, needed this dimension too. He is so much more glorious because of it.

I cannot help but worship You, **Lord,** *so perfect in every way. You are not a high priest untouched by my sufferings. Thus You are able to comfort me in my worst times, knowing my pain. Please help me to rely on You amidst all circumstance, rejoicing in Your goodness. Through Christ, amen.*

Behave Like the Father

Just as he who called you is holy, so be holy in all you do (1 Peter 1:15).

Scripture: **1 Peter 1:10-16**
Song: **"Trust and Obey"**

Many people come to the UK from other countries with different cultures, customs, and laws. They want to stay here and be considered British. However, if they do, some things will have to change. They are not now under the laws of their own country, tribe, or family. If they are accepted into our society, they must behave themselves as British citizens. If not, they will be sent back home (in theory, anyway). The same is true of any country.

I am so glad I have been accepted into the family of God by a new birth. Now I have a wonderful Father who is holy. He calls me to be like Him, letting go of all that clings to me from my old life.

Yes, He calls His children to behave as He behaves, to forget the old ways. It's an impossibly high standard, of course. That's why He promises His indwelling Spirit to transform us by His grace in ways that we could never accomplish on our own. Ultimately, then, our goal is not so much to be *like* Him as to *grow close* to Him. Then, paradoxically, we do become more and more like Him as our lives in Him unfold. Thanks be to God!

Dear Heavenly Father, may I never look to the ways of this world to govern my behavior. I want to walk close to You daily, that You may work Your own character deep into my life. Thank You, in Jesus' name. Amen.

His Shining Face

The LORD make his face shine upon you and be gracious to you (Numbers 6:25).

Scripture: **Numbers 6:22-27**
Song: **"That I Should Gain"**

Someone very close to me came to our house one day. "I want God," she said. "Tell me how I can get Him." What a joy to lead her to Jesus! "Now," she said, "I must do something for God."

Because I knew Jean so well, I knew she had a great guilt, and she was feeling she must sacrifice something for God, to somehow atone for her past. So, looking her straight in the eye, I said, "When Jesus died on the cross, He wiped your slate clean. There is nothing left to pay, you know." The relief and joy showed in her eyes.

It's true. Consider the ancient Israelites, for example, who had so often been grumblers and idolaters in their relationship with God. Yet God pronounced His blessing on these constantly rebelling people and put His name on them. The Lord intended only good for them. Therefore, ever so patiently, by His infinite mercy, He redeemed and blessed them.

The enemies of God run before His angry face. But when He looks upon His people, we see only His shining countenance, the face of love and grace.

Gracious Father in Heaven, I come to You, not fearing any condemnation for my past failings. I come in the name of Your beloved Son, who always sees Your face; in Him I am blessed. Thank You, in His name. Amen.

The Results: Up to Him

We are God's workmanship, created in Christ Jesus to do good works, which God prepared in advance for us to do (Ephesians 2:10).

Scripture: **Ephesians 2:1-10**
Song: **"I Want to Serve the Purpose of God"**

Patricia St. John looked back on her life. "With so little to show for it, what had the years really achieved?" she wondered. Let's look . . .

She trained as a nurse and cared for the many wounded and shattered people of London during wartime bombings. Later, she went to Africa with her brother, helping him at a Christian hospital in a Muslim land. Seeing the need, she went to live alone in a hill town to care for the sick and preach Jesus in word and deed to the poor. After some years she was forced to move, but not before some found the Savior and willingly suffered for their faith.

She wrote favorite children's books, which still bless many children (including mine). She researched and wrote a book about revival in Rwanda; helped care for her brother's children and the little persecuted Christian community; nursed her mother in old age; helped her sister in war-torn Lebanon; blessed children everywhere.

Achieved? She had only taken up what came to hand. That is all we can do—take the steps prepared in advance for us. God will assess the results.

*I thank You, **Father,** that You have work prepared for me to do. I take up what comes to my hand—and I do it with joy. In Christ I pray. Amen.*

Shadow Creatures

He reveals the deep things of darkness and brings deep shadows into the light (Job 12:22).

Scripture: **Job 12:13-25**
Song: **"The Light of the World Is Jesus"**

An almost cartoonish image presents itself in this verse. We can imagine a hideous, snaggletoothed shadow creature—long operating under the happy delusion that it wields an unbeatable power—suddenly yanked from the shadows and forced into the blinding light of God. The creature, assumed to be an unstoppable power, has no choice but to kneel beneath the far mightier authority.

The believer looks around at this world and observes with sadness many wicked people flaunting their immoralities. Like the soldiers who crucified Jesus, they spit in the face of God. And it wounds those of us who love Him. However, it might help us to have compassion if we remember that these shadow creatures lurk behind every sinning person. They perform their awful ministry from the secrecy of deep shadow.

We can chase away some of the shadows of our world with our small lights. But we know that one day the great light will come; it will permanently disable every creature of shadow.

Light of the world, living in this shadowy place is difficult! I long for the day when Your beauty illuminates the universe. In Jesus' name, amen.

May 11–17. **Rhonda Brunea** lives in a tiny town in New York state with her kids and her Lord. She is encouraged by recalling that she has family everywhere.

Secret Society

Blessed are your eyes because they see, and your ears because they hear (Matthew 13:16).

Scripture: **Matthew 13:10-17**
Song: **"Open My Eyes, Lord"**

Christians are members of the ultimate secret society. Nothing sinister, just secret. Some of us are blessed to live in countries where we may openly profess our belief in Christ. Even with this freedom, our unbelieving neighbors often won't have a clue what we're talking about. We simply see things with different eyes than those who see only with their natural eyes. We are perceived as simple-minded and odd, at best. Being misunderstood can grow burdensome.

From time to time, we recognize one of our own as we pass through the ordinary hours of our days. We clasp hands and smile. We confess, "I'm a believer too." And for a moment we recall with relief that there are others like us, those who see what we see and hear what we hear.

Actually, there are brothers and sisters everywhere, in every imaginable guise. They too are listening for God's voice, peering intently into the things of the Spirit and then carrying them out into a largely blind and deaf society to give away. How blessed to be a member of this secret society!

Dear Lord, help me to remember that I'm part of a beautiful family of believers who love You as I do. Many more would love You if they only knew You. Give me courage to speak up! In the name of Christ, amen.

Behind the Veil

No wise man, enchanter, magician or diviner can explain to the king the mystery he has asked about, but there is a God in heaven who reveals mysteries (Daniel 2:27, 28).

Scripture: **Daniel 2:25-30**
Song: **"Be Thou My Vision"**

Maria wants nothing more in the world than to train her children in godliness. She wants to protect them from the deceit of the world. But cruel circumstances constantly intervene to make her good intentions impossible. So she watches helplessly as her beloved children slip farther and farther from God. Her agonized prayer comes through in one word: *"Why?"*

Why? So much we don't know! God has veiled His universe in mystery. When it serves His purposes, He lifts the edge of the veil ever so slightly, revealing a bit of the secret. As when a magician reveals a trick, the child of God experiences a moment of delighted "Aha." Then comes the relief of understanding—and finally the question, "Why didn't I see that before?"

We aren't allowed to observe much that transpires behind the veil separating us from Heaven. Thus our ignorance gives rise to painful questions. But perhaps there is a more helpful response than questioning God: trust. For her part, Maria has determined to wait with a patient heart . . . until she is given a peek behind the veil.

O God, so often I'm confused, and sometimes I just have to weep. Yet I will trust in the one who holds the key to all mysteries. In Jesus' name, amen.

Teamwork

Surely the Sovereign LORD **does nothing without revealing his plan to his servants the prophets** (Amos 3:7).

Scripture: **Amos 3:1-8**
Song: **"It Is No Secret"**

The owner of the store gathers her employees for a meeting. "This," she says, "is what I plan to do." She gives her workers an overview of what she intends to accomplish. Then she assigns specific tasks to each person. Her team waits, listening, ready to do all that their employer requires.

They want to please their superior, and so they listen carefully, fully intending to follow her plan. She, in turn, realizes that her workers need certain information in order to function best in their positions. While she may not reveal every detail of her grand plan, she will let them in on all they need to know.

Similarly, God honors His "team" by trusting us to help Him carry out His work in the world. As someone has said, "We are the only hands and feet that Jesus has on earth until He comes again. " Our part is to listen carefully for His plan to be revealed, since to obey we must first hear the orders.

Let us give plenty of time to listening, then. What is the Spirit of God revealing to His workers today? What does the master require of His team?

Master, *You have a plan, and nothing will thwart it. What would You say to me? Your servant is listening. Through Christ I pray. Amen.*

Childlike Wisdom

I praise you, Father, Lord of heaven and earth, because you have hidden these things from the wise and learned, and revealed them to little children (Matthew 11:25).

Scripture: **Matthew 11:25-30**
Song: **"I Know Whom I Have Believed"**

A small boy clambers onto the lap of his grandfather with no hesitation or embarrassment. He turns wide eyes to the beloved face, waiting for one of the old man's amazing stories. The boy's heart is ready to accept whatever Grandpa says. He reposes in the complete comfort born of long trust. In this attitude of heart and mind, he sees miracles and wonders everywhere.

A young man returns from the university. He has learned to filter everything through his critical thinking skills. He stands stiffly before his grandfather and shakes his hand. Grandfather's stories meet a knowing smile and a skeptical lift of one brow. He loves his grandpa, but the older man has diminished in his eyes. The young man has learned to doubt and question everything.

The grandfather has much wisdom to offer his grandson. But he is wise enough to know that he must wait for the boy to grow up a little more before he will hear. One day he will regain his childlike wisdom, and then he will again see invisible wonders.

Father, sometimes I think too much! I know You don't expect me to take everything in blind faith, but there are some things that must be believed to be seen. Help me to cultivate a childlike heart. In Jesus' name, amen.

The King's Guard

Men ought to regard us as servants of Christ and as those entrusted with the secret things of God (1 Corinthians 4:1).

Scripture: **1 Corinthians 4:1-5**
Song: **"Why Me, Lord?"**

A wise king needed servants to guard his most precious and secret treasures. "They must be strong," the king said to his counselors. "Unintimidated by the enemy, stalwart in the face of discouragement and fear, and willing to do all that I command."

"Then the applicants must be dreadfully serious?" asked one.

"Oh, not at all," replied the king. "I could not trust one who had no joy. No, I want those who know when to laugh—and laugh well, at that."

"So you desire those who are popular in the taverns?"

"Certainly not! They must be sober of mind—friendly, and yet able to hold close the secrets with which I will entrust them. They must be honest, self-controlled, skilled in arms, and protective of the lowly."

"Oh, king," said an elder counselor, trembling. "I fear that we may not find such servants."

"I say that you will. I have summoned them, you see, men and women of noble character to guard the secret things of the kingdom. I am drawing them to myself, and they will come."

My King, *I am humbled and honored that You have entrusted me with the precious secrets of the soul. Thanks to You, through Christ! Amen.*

The Best Revenge

His intent was that now, through the church, the manifold wisdom of God should be made known to the rulers and authorities in the heavenly realms (Ephesians 3:10).

Scripture: **Ephesians 3:1-13**
Song: **"All My Hope on God Is Founded"**

"I know. Hank will be sorry when he sees me living it up."

"That's not what I meant, Carol. I mean living really well, God's way—forgiving the one who hurt you, praying for him and moving on with your life, with all that you're meant to be here on planet Earth."

"Oh, I know I'm supposed to do all that, but how can I? After the way he betrayed me? Forget it."

"OK," Linda replied quietly. "Then Satan wins."

"What?"

"Either you can let the enemy stomp all over you and make you bitter— useless as a warrior of God—or you can stand up and kick him in the face. You can choose God's way and prove to the enemy what a loser he is."

Carol sipped her coffee. "Well," she finally laughed, "I guess maybe it is time I helped God to prove His point. I'll live so well, I'll make that nasty Satan sorry he ever got in my face."

"That's my little warrior."

O God, sometimes Your way doesn't seem very satisfying. I'd like to exact a little sweet revenge. Help me choose Your way, instead, against those other dubious "rulers and authorities." In the name of Christ my Lord, amen.

Drifting from Doctrine?

As for you, speak the things which are proper for sound doctrine (Titus 2:1, *New King James Version*).

Scripture: **Titus 2:1-13**
Song: **"Blow the Trumpet in Zion"**

As I lay in the rowboat, the sun was warm, the breeze cool, and the clouds drifted along like passing friends. Nothing much was happening, except a gentle rocking. I didn't notice a slow, steady drift to deeper water, along with an ever-growing wind . . .

Some years ago the press attacked former Vice President Dan Quayle, for stating that, all else being equal, it was better for children to be raised by two parents rather than just one. Yes, there are great single parents. But wasn't Quayle right? After all, the role of father and mother was God's idea from the beginning.

My point: Previous generations would have labeled Quayle wholesome and wise, but the popular view has drifted far from such traditional perspectives. Have we in the church drifted too? Maybe we haven't noticed! Maybe we haven't looked out from our small boat as we warm ourselves in the sun. God hasn't changed. But how much have we sought to change Him?

Father, don't let us get too comfortable in our boat. And please keep us from merely drifting with the current of the world. Help us be strong, even in the face of constant peer pressure. In the name of Christ I pray. Amen.

May 18–24. **Daniel Varnell** is a scientist living in Delaware with his wife and three daughters. He serves God and the local church as a teacher and author.

The Goodness of Togetherness

It is not good that man should be alone; I will make him a helper comparable to him (Genesis 2:18, *New King James Version*).

Scripture: **Genesis 2:18-25**
Song: **"In the Garden"**

My dad's side of my family amazes me. Not one divorce can be found in my generation nor the next generation—and none in any previous generation.

Something else unusual about Dad's family: the amount of time spent *as* family. My parents wouldn't even go to a wedding unless children were included. I remember Dad and Mom—together—bringing my brother and me to music lessons. While my brother was being instructed, Dad would walk with me, maybe get a candy bar, or sit in the car with me.

God formed Eve so she and Adam could be together. And *together* they were to "be fruitful and increase in number; fill the earth," (Genesis 1:28). A woman came from a man and they, together, were complete.

Why no divorces in my dad's family? Spouses taking time together, with the children watching. What better way is there?

Dear Father in Heaven, my heart melts as I contemplate the glories of Your grace. I am amazed at Your desire for fellowship with human beings and Your call to us to form community among ourselves. Thank You for the goodness of togetherness! If some are away from family today, I pray for holy bridges over the distance. In the name of Jesus, amen.

In the House

That you shall say, "It is the Passover sacrifice of the LORD, who passed over the houses of the children of Israel in Egypt when He struck the Egyptians and delivered our households" (Exodus 12:27, *New King James Version*).

Scripture: **Exodus 12:21-28**
Song: **"You Are My Hiding Place"**

Twelve-year-old Ruth Becker recalled the terrible night. She watched as an officer grabbed her sister, another grabbed her brother. They placed them in a lifeboat. Her mother screamed, and they let her on, then they were gone. Moments later, Ruth was thrust into Lifeboat #13— and soon the mighty ship *Titanic* sunk beneath the sea.

Ruth's household was divided during that tragedy. But have you noticed in Scripture how God so often saves *by household*? In Egypt, God saved the people of Israel by household. In a boat, God saved Noah's household. Angels went to Lot's household and saved them.

The jailor of Paul and Silas—and the jailor's whole household—came to Christ. At Peter's preaching, God saved the household of Cornelius.

Ruth Becker and her family survived and were eventually reunited. They were a household again and could testify to salvation from ice-cold waves. We too can be households like that. Saved from sin, our whole families can point to the goodness and grace of God.

Father, show each of us where we can be in a godly family that we might together experience Your mercy and serve You.

Let Us Learn!

Prize [wisdom] highly, and she will exalt you; she will honor you if you embrace her (Proverbs 4:8, *Revised Standard Version*).

Scripture: **Proverbs 4:1-9**
Song: **"My Soul Follows Hard After Thee"**

My neighbor, one of the greatest men I've known, passed away a few weeks ago. He fought battles in North Africa, survived a concentration camp in Siberia, and even worked on the Apollo space program. My girls adopted him as a grandfather.

He was passionate about freedom. Having been denied it, he knew its value. He also spoke often about being raised in Poland. In the school system there, if he and his friends didn't apply themselves and learn their lessons, then their parents would have to pay for their schooling. So they had extra incentive to study, to give serious attention to gaining understanding and wisdom.

In today's Scripture, God gives us plenty of incentive to embrace the instruction of a father, to retain the lessons taught us, and to find wisdom in it all. If we do these things, then we will be promoted and honored.

My neighbor found knowledge and wisdom through the lessons taught in his youth and through Jesus Christ. Our heavenly Father brings us lessons in many ways, even amidst the ordinary situations we'll face today. Therefore, let us learn.

God, in prayer, in the Word, and in all things You bring me lessons I need. Give me a heart always ready to learn from You. Through Christ, amen.

In . . . In . . . In . . .

Let the word of Christ dwell in you richly in all wisdom, teaching and admonishing one another in psalms and hymns and spiritual songs, singing with grace in your hearts to the Lord (Colossians 3:16, *New King James Version*).

Scripture: **Colossians 3:12-24**
Song: **"In Him We Live and Move and Have Our Being"**

As the couple embraced, tears streamed down the faces of the Mayan pastor and his wife. They were on a marriage retreat and, for the first time, the pastor saw his wife as a partner in ministry. For the first time she felt included.

A key word in the book of Colossians is "in." Paul wrote to the saints in Colossae, who had hope *in* Heaven, which they learned about *in* the Word, which was told them *in* truth, *in* wisdom, and *in* good works. With Christ dwelling *in* them, they were called *in*to one body to admonish each other *in* psalms, *in* hymns, *in* spiritual songs, with grace *in* their hearts. They were *in* ministry with each other, with Paul and with God.

Look around: with whom are you *in* this Christian journey? You may be overlooking a great partner or your own family. What affects one, affects another—and the whole body of Christ. We are all *in* Christ, members of His body together.

Father, how wonderful to walk with You and my brothers and sisters in Christ. Open my eyes to my partners in Your work. Help me always to walk in loving, respectful relationships with them. In Jesus' name, amen.

Don't Be a Cowbird

If anyone does not provide for his own, and especially for those of his household, he has denied the faith and is worse than an unbeliever (1 Timothy 5:8, *New King James Version*).

Scripture: **1 Timothy 5:1-8**
Song: **"Servant of God, Remember"**

Do you know about cowbirds? They will remove an egg from another bird's nest and destroy it. They lay their own egg in its place and abandon it to the owner of the nest. Sometimes their egg is rejected.

The proper name of the cowbird is *Molothrus ater*. Molothrus refers to a vagabond or parasite—one who surely fails to provide for others.

Paul's instructions to Timothy were sometimes meant to exhort or encourage. But in today's Scripture, Paul simply commands. Sometimes God's Word is candid and direct, because sometimes we need strong medicine. I don't want to be compared to a bird that acts like a parasite. And I certainly don't want to be considered worse than one who denies my Lord Jesus. Therefore, I must provide for others, especially those in the church.

These harsh words point us in the right direction, because they come from one who loves us deeply. He calls us to love others in return. So . . . who should I help today and tomorrow, and how?

Father, let my thoughts and ways be open to Your correction. Pick me up, gently, and point me in the right direction. Help me to be a blessing to someone this day. In the name of Your Son, my Savior, I pray. Amen.

Together Forever

This is a great mystery, but I speak concerning Christ and the church (Ephesians 5:32, *New King James Version*).

Scripture: **Ephesians 5:21–6:4**
Song: **"Draw Me Close"**

At church a woman confided to me that she didn't feel close to God and didn't think God loved her. I was saddened by her sadness. She seemed to walk with one foot in the world and one in church. And she found no joy.

Our Scripture readings this week have highlighted family. Look now at the great picture God lays out for us. Marriage shows how the living church should relate to Christ. Love, covenant, communication, purpose, preparation—all these go into a marriage and a home. Do you feel close to Christ? (You should feel like His bride.)

God had one grand purpose in creating humankind. It wasn't to subdue the earth (that came later); it wasn't to fight back against Satan. No, it was to create a people who would spend time—and eternity—*with* Him. All things, from evangelism to worship, are part of this plan.

With His disciples listening, Jesus closed His earthly ministry before the cross with these words: "Father, I desire that they also whom You gave Me may be with Me where I am" (John 17:24, *NKJV*). He wants to be close to us, forever. Know it. Feel it, right now.

Father, may I see my life from Your perspective. You made me so You could be with me in Heaven, forever. I take a moment now to bask in that amazing truth. How You love me! How I love You! Through Christ, amen.

Running to the Source

Guide me in your truth and teach me, for you are God my Savior, and my hope is in you all day long (Psalm 25:5).

Scripture: **Psalm 25:1-5**
Song: **"Guide Me, O Thou Great Jehovah"**

When my children were young, I often overheard something like this:

"Is *not!*"

"Is *too!*"

"Is *not!*"

"Is *too!*"

These debates usually ended with the children running to me to settle the dispute. They wanted an ultimate answer. My response? "Yes, it's brother's turn to go first."

But sometimes their discussions would concern serious matters, like "Why are there street people?" I didn't always have answers for such harder questions, but I pointed them to the one who did. We would read His Word, pray, and talk about what actions we could take to best please our Lord.

We children of God sometimes foolishly debate questions without running to our heavenly Father for the ultimate truth. Why is this? Don't we value His truth?

Father, give me the confidence of a child in looking to You to provide insight and direction amidst each situation today. In Jesus' name, amen.

May 25–31. **Shelley Houston** is a freelance writer living in Eugene, Oregon, with her husband of 37 years and her extended family.

He Will Lift You Up

When pride comes, then comes disgrace, but with humility comes wisdom (Proverbs 11:2).

Scripture: **Proverbs 11:1-10**
Song: **"Humble Yourself"**

I resigned my job and was cleaning out my desk when my secretary came into my office. "You'll be able to find another job so easily with this position on your resumé," she said. I kindly dismissed her words, but secretly thought she was right.

In the following months, wearing my executive wardrobe, I carried a powerful resumé in my leather briefcase . . . to interview after interview. Two years later, I gave up, feeling like a failure.

Then, for weeks, I cried out to God. (One day I even scared off a salesman coming to the door as I wailed in anguish.) My agony left me broken, like a wild horse finally submitting to its master. Humbled, I finally gave over to God's leading.

And God opened a new career for me: writing. This was my heart's dream, but one I never thought I could afford to pursue. I'm paid little for such offerings and gain less in esteem. But God provides for me and the family as He always has. When we walk in humility, we can experience God leading us to our heart's desire.

Lord, *thank You for loving me so much that You are unwilling to let me wallow in self-importance. Your greatest blessings are waiting on the sidelines. Help me see them more clearly. In Christ's name I pray. Amen.*

What's the Good Word?

How beautiful on the mountains are the feet of those who bring good news, who proclaim peace, who bring good tidings, who proclaim salvation, who say to Zion, "Your God reigns!" (Isaiah 52:7).

Scripture: **Isaiah 52:7-12**
Song: **"Our God Reigns"**

One night, in 1814, Francis Scott Key sat imprisoned on a British ship during an attack on Fort McHenry. Sleepless, he watched the battle, writing notes of his thoughts. Imagine his anxiety as he saw the rockets in the night, fearing not only his own fate but that of his country. As morning broke he strained to see the American flag. Did it still wave over the fort?

Yes! Ecstatic, he penned "The Star Spangled Banner," now America's national anthem, which reflects the good news he received.

What sort of good news are we looking for these days? Every day the battles in our lives raise the question, "Who's winning now?" A wayward child, a broken promise, a lost investment, a life-threatening illness—all can pull us into fearing a chaotic future. But remember this: Jesus Christ already stands as victor. His news is, "Your God reigns!" There is no better news.

Almighty and ever living God, how glad I am to know of Your victory over all forces that oppose You. I praise You to the highest heavens and in all the earth as my king and Lord, my champion to the end. In the name of the Father, the Son, and the Holy Spirit, I offer my worship. Amen.

He Is the One Who Keeps

We are not of those who shrink back and are destroyed, but of those who have faith and keep their souls (Hebrews 10:39, *Revised Standard Version*).

Scripture: **Hebrews 10:35–11:3**
Song: **"Faith in Jesus"**

My husband was recalled to active duty for Desert Storm. Our family became instant celebrities in our little city. Many people reached out to us, but some didn't know what to say. They would often mumble, "Keep the faith," even though they did not believe in God themselves.

Ten years later, I listened to a woman who grew up as a pastor's daughter in Latvia while it was under Russian rule. She and her family suffered many torments because of their faith in Christ. She admitted that at times she wanted to give up. But then she'd recall her young father's words on his deathbed: "Your faith in Christ must endure to the end! Then we will meet again." He understood the supreme importance of their faith as the key to their salvation.

Unlike the faith that was suggested to me—to keep a contrived "faith" in *general*—the Latvian pastor and his family placed their trust in a *person*: the Lord Jesus Christ. May we keep our faith in the same manner, knowing that He is actually the one who keeps us.

Lord God, *let me never be ashamed of the way I walk with You, serve You, and continue to believe in You for all things. Help me to keep the faith as You keep holding me in Your mighty arms. In Jesus' name, amen.*

What to Say?

Give thanks to the LORD, call on his name; make known among the nations what he has done, and proclaim that his name is exalted (Isaiah 12:4).

Scripture: **Isaiah 12:1-6**
Song: **"Great Is the Lord"**

Early this morning I looked out on towering mountains covered with new snow and capped in billowing robes of pinkish clouds. *God's majesty!* I wondered that anyone seeing such wonders could think anything less. And the sad thought came to me: If people see but don't recognize such wonders as the work of a creator's hand, what effect can my simple words of witness have?

Later in the day I heard an international news account of atrocities committed for political gain. As I sat gaping at the television, I realized what the people of the world need to hear. They can see the beauty of the world, it's true. But they experience it tinged with the horror of human sin. Any of us could become deeply convinced pessimists amidst such horrors—if we hadn't come to see the "big picture" of God's redeeming plan. Some day He will put all things right: "The creation itself will be liberated from its bondage to decay" (Romans 8:21). In the meantime, we give thanks for glimpses of His glory, wherever and whenever they come to us. That's what the people need to know, and that's what I can tell them.

Creator and Redeemer, *loosen my tongue and help me proclaim Your perfection in beauty, justice, and holiness. In Christ's name I pray. Amen.*

Memorizing the Map

Though I constantly take my life in my hands, I will not forget your law (Psalm 119:109).

Scripture: **Psalm 119:105-112**
Song: **"Thy Word Is a Lamp Unto My Feet"**

In planning to attend a concert in a city about 50 miles from home, I pulled up a map on the Internet. The city had a complicated downtown with many one-way streets. So I studied the route before I got in my car, and then tucked the map into the glove compartment.

When I left, I thought I had plenty of time to get to the concert. But when I entered the downtown area I immediately became disoriented. I couldn't remember the names of neighboring streets—and that valuable map just wasn't within arm's reach. Soon I was driving in circles.

I finally pulled over and got out the map—which led me straight to the concert. (Late, of course!)

How often do I do the same with God's Word, the "life map" He's given me? Oh, I study the Word, but then I tuck it away, sometimes for days. I set out to live life as I think I remember Him directing, only to find myself straying from the pathway of peace and joy.

What great reasons we have for hiding His Word in our hearts! Not only does God promise to guide our footsteps; He promises sweet companionship along the way.

Dear Heavenly Father, *pull me to your Word daily, that I might know the blessed fellowship of Your presence. How I need Your constant wisdom and encouragement! I pray through Christ my Lord. Amen.*

Endless and Powerful Prayer

Pray in the Spirit on all occasions with all kinds of prayers and requests. With this in mind, be alert and always keep on praying for all the saints (Ephesians 6:18).

Scripture: **Ephesians 6:10-18**
Song: **"Soldiers of Christ, Arise!"**

Dreams are strange, aren't they? Sometimes they're just the result of a too-spicy dinner or a day filled with unresolved problems. But I think God occasionally speaks to me in my dreams. Here's an example: I walked down a hall with many doors on each side. As I walked, something appeared in the distance. A large mattress rolled into a tight bundle filled the entire hall! I couldn't pass, and yet, I must. I ran hard, jumped and dove into the middle of the roll. I pushed and kicked, seeking to worm my way through. But I could not.

Silent darkness came, and then I again walked the same hall and approached the same mattress. "How can I do this, Lord?" I asked. "I tried my best before." Then, as I walked, the mattress dissolved around me. It seemed that God was ready to do battle for me—I only had to ask.

Our text says, "Be alert!" When we arm ourselves for spiritual battle, then proceed without prayer, we walk in our own strength. But God wants to unleash His omnipotence. What better reason to pray in His Spirit?

Dear Lord, I am weak, but You are strong. How can I conquer the impossible before me, except by Your power and grace? Go before me, Lord, and make my path straight. In Jesus' name, amen.

DEVOTIONS®

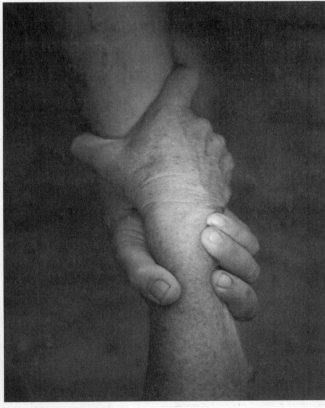

***E*ncourage one another daily.**

—Hebrews 3:13

JUNE

Photo © iStock

Gary Allen, Editor

DEVOTIONS® is published quarterly by Standard Publishing, Cincinnati, Ohio, www.standardpub.com. © 2008 by Standard Publishing. All rights reserved. Topics based on the Home Daily Bible Readings, International Sunday School Lessons. © 2005 by the Committee on the Uniform Series. Printed in the U.S.A. All Scripture quotations, unless otherwise indicated, are taken from the HOLY BIBLE, NEW INTERNATIONAL VERSION®. NIV®. Copyright © 1973, 1978, 1984 by International Bible Society. Used by permission of Zondervan. All rights reserved. Where noted, Scripture quotations are from the following, used with permission of the copyright holders, all rights reserved: *King James Version (KJV)*, public domain.
• *The Lion, The Witch, and the Wardrobe* by C.S. Lewis copyright © C.S. Lewis Pte. Ltd. 1950. Extract reprinted with permission.

Enjoy Each Time

His sister stood at a distance to see what would happen (Exodus 2:4).

Scripture: **Exodus 2:1-10**
Song: **"Thy Will Be Done"**

In his late 30s, our son-in-law felt a call to preach, so he went to school to get his theological education. Thrilled with this turn of events in his family's life, I prayed for God's will, adding a P.S. to my prayer—that God would open up a church nearby.

Shortly before his graduation, he received an invitation to submit his profile . . . to a church in Oklahoma, over a thousand miles away. "No, Lord," I wept. "I can't bear for them to move that far away. When will I ever see our two granddaughters?"

I prayed often that week and was finally able to put this beloved family in God's hands. Then I wrote and told them that, just as I gave our daughter to the Lord when she was born, I was giving her back to Him. I would rejoice with them, no matter where God led.

Moses' mother gave up her son, for a time, and then was allowed to raise him, for a time. Let us be ready to rejoice amid each blessed "time" God gives us.

Lord, help me to enjoy every moment with my family. I pray for Your perfect will for each one—no matter what the sacrifice may be for me. Then let me stand at a distance to see what blessings will occur! In Christ, amen.

June 1–7. **Donna Clark Goodrich,** of Mesa, Arizona, is a freelance writer and instructor at Christian writers seminars.

Is Someone Watching?

Moses was afraid and thought, "What I did must have become known" (Exodus 2:14).

Scripture: Exodus 2:11-22
Song: "You Cannot Hide from God"

Whenever one of our children did something wrong, I could always detect the guilty party. No, I didn't have eyes in the back of my head (as they sometimes thought). But as soon as I asked who was at fault, our youngest—if guilty—would immediately begin to cry. Our middle child would say, "I have to go to the bathroom," or our eldest would take off running, his hands covering his back end.

Moses glanced "this way and that and seeing no one, he killed the Egyptian and hid him in the sand" (Exodus 2:12). He thought he was safe, but later a Hebrew man asked him, "Are you thinking of killing me as you killed the Egyptian?" (v. 14). *Someone saw!*

My mother used to tell me, "God sees everything you do and hears everything you say." Lest this thought make you feel paranoid, however, there is also a positive side. When we help someone in need, when we visit a sick friend, when we prepare a meal or encourage someone who is going through a rough time, we may think no one sees. But God does. Nothing we do is hidden from Him.

Father, remind me today that people are watching what I do and listening to what I say. Let my words and my deeds be acceptable in Your sight. And may people see Your Son, Jesus, in me. Through His name, I pray. Amen.

Reward: Here or There

Moses thought that his own people would realize that God was using him to rescue them, but they did not (Acts 7:25).

Scripture: **Acts 7:23-29**
Song: **"It Pays to Serve Jesus"**

I needed a job. My rent was due, and other bills had to be paid. Then a friend told me of an opening where she worked, and I went for an interview. The work sounded interesting, the pay acceptable, but I would have to sell alcohol and also work on Sundays.

I wrestled with the decision, but then I remembered one of my mother's sayings, "If in doubt, leave it out." I turned down the job, feeling I'd done the right thing.

Moses must have felt he was doing right when he killed the Egyptian who mistreated his fellow Israelites. His own people turned against him, however, saying, "Who made you judge and ruler over us?" Moses ended up fleeing to another country.

But what happened in the end? He found forgiveness—found a wife too—fathered two sons, and later led his people out of Egypt. And my situation? The next week I found a job closer to home, with better wages, and I didn't have to compromise my convictions.

I believe this: If you'll do what is right today, God will reward you—if not in this life, then in the next.

God, today I face many decisions. Help me look beyond material benefits to the peace that comes from doing right. Give me strength to bypass immediate gratification for the promise of eternal reward. Through Christ, amen.

If God Sends You . . .

I have indeed seen the oppression of my people in Egypt. I have heard their groaning and have come down to set them free. Now come, I will send you back to Egypt (Acts 7:34).

Scripture: **Acts 7:30-34**
Song: **"Far Off I See the Goal"**

It was a hard decision. I had over two hundred income tax customers, many second generation. But I felt the Lord calling me to give more time to writing (and encouraging other writers). So I sold the business.

A few years later a former customer said, "I wish you were still doing taxes. " Driving home, I thought, *Why not? The money is good, and I'd be helping people.* Then it seemed as if the Lord were saying to me, "Why do you want to go back to Egypt?"

Moses wrestled with this kind of decision. He left Egypt because his people were being mistreated. And when he stepped in to help, they railed against him. But now God was telling him to go back. His chosen people were being oppressed, they were groaning, and God was saying, "Go back, Moses." And Moses went.

Thirteen years after selling my tax business, I am preparing about 30 tax returns a year, and it feels right. God has sent struggling people my way, folks who need help with life issues as well as taxes. I realize now it's OK to go back to Egypt . . . *if* God sends you.

Lord, I know that my ways are not Your ways. Your Word tells me that whatever state I'm in, I should be content. Help! Through Christ, amen.

Glad Reunion Day

There on the mountain that you have climbed you will die and be gathered to your people, just as your brother Aaron died on Mount Hor and was gathered to his people (Deuteronomy 32:50).

Scripture: **Deuteronomy 32:48-52**
Song: **"Heaven Is Here, Where Hymns of Gladness"**

"They said it'd be any time," my daughter said over the phone. I assured her of our prayers, but when I hung up, I was still concerned for her. She had never been around someone who was dying, and this was her husband's grandmother, whom we all dearly loved.

An hour later came the second call. Grandma Addie was gone, and when we talked to our daughter that evening, I asked her how she had handled it. "Oh, Mom, I'm so glad I was there," she said. "She had a faraway look in her eyes and was nodding and saying, 'Yes, OK, OK.' Then her face lit up, she said, 'Ohhh, yes-s-s-,' and she was gone. It was so beautiful."

When we lose a loved one who has walked with the Lord, Heaven becomes more real to us. This is what God was reminding Moses. Even though there were times when he and his brother Aaron disobeyed God's commandments, at his death he was still considered a "servant of the Lord" (Deuteronomy 34:5). Isn't that how we all would like to be remembered?

Lord of All, may I so live today that when it's time to join those who have gone before me, I may be considered Your servant. In Jesus' name, amen.

Will You Take My Place?

Now Joshua son of Nun was filled with the spirit of wisdom because Moses had laid his hands on him (Deuteronomy 34:9).

Scripture: **Deuteronomy 34**
Song: **"Let Thy Mantle Fall on Me"**

There aren't many people I consider saints, but Claramae Bostwick is one. Not a blood relative, she was known to everyone as "Aunt Clara." My Sunday school teacher when I was a teenager, she also helped plan my wedding ceremony and continued as my friend and mentor for the next 47 years. Now 101 years old, and residing in an assisted living center, her mind is still keen.

She always ends her letters with, "Always live for Him," but one letter that I received a year or so ago really startled me. "You must hang on for when I am gone, Donna. Will you take my place?"

Oh my, take Aunt Clara's place? Who can fill her shoes? A godlier woman I have never met.

Perhaps that's how Joshua felt when he learned he was to be the one to lead the children of Israel into the promised land. Take Moses' place? Fill his shoes? But just as Joshua had the same promises God had given Moses, so I today have the same promises that have sustained Aunt Clara for over a hundred years.

O God, help me be willing to do the work You have for me, even when it means taking up the ministry of one who has led me. I dedicate my gifts to Your kingdom's service—with no strings attached. In Jesus' name, amen.

Standing on Holy Ground

Moses! Moses! . . . Take off your sandals, for the place where you are standing is holy ground (Exodus 3:4, 5).

Scripture: **Exodus 3:1-12**
Song: **"Holy Father, Bless Us"**

Many years ago a lady by the name of Ina Ogdon gave up a brilliant professional career to care for her father, who struggled with a disability. It was difficult for her, one who was accustomed to appearing before thousands, to minister in private to just one person. However, instead of pining away in self-pity, unable to follow her chosen career as a concert singer, she penned the words to the Song, "Brighten the Corner Where You Are."

Moses was a well-educated man, raised as a prince in Pharaoh's palace. But 40 years later he was tending sheep in the desert, a place the Lord told him was holy ground.

Young mother, weary of all the never-ending tasks that fill your day, you're standing on holy ground.

Factory worker, tired of doing the same repetitious routines, hour after hour, you're standing on holy ground.

Retired grandfather or grandmother, wondering if your days of usefulness are over, you're standing on holy ground.

And, as He did with Moses, God is calling you by name today.

Heavenly Father, the place You've called me to may not be of my choosing. Sometimes it feels like a desert. But if it is where You want me, help me to take off my shoes and bring light to my corner. In Jesus' name, amen.

Because I Said So!

God said to Moses, "I AM WHO I am. This is what you are to say to the Israelites: 'I AM has sent me to you'" (Exodus 3:14).

Scripture: **Exodus 3:13-18**
Song: **"O How Happy Are They Who the Savior Obey"**

"Because I said so," my parents often responded when I was a young child questioning them about doing what I was told. Instead of giving me a reason, they just repeated that infamous line one more time.

As a child, truth be told, it rather bugged me! Why should I do something simply because I was *told* to? And further, I vowed in my heart never to repeat that dreaded mantra to my own kids.

A few decades later, of course, "Because I said so" came suddenly from my lips! But something strange had occurred. Now I understood those words from a different perspective. As a parent I realized I wasn't telling my children to do something just for the sake of being told to do it. The emphasis was on the "I"! Just like my parents, I now had the authority to declare something be done. And it was for the child's own good.

God gave Moses a directive. And being a perfect parent, He reminded Moses that He had the authority to commission him to the task.

Dear Lord, *help me to obey You willingly, knowing that all Your commands have my best interest at heart. In the name of Jesus I pray. Amen.*

June 8–14. **Karen Morerod** lives in Kansas with her family. She enjoys bringing God's Word to life through writing and drama.

By All Means!

Then the LORD **said to him, "What is that in your hand?"**
"A staff," he replied (Exodus 4:2).

Scripture: **Exodus 4:1-9**
Song: **"Leaning on the Everlasting Arms"**

When teaching Sunday school or telling others about God, wouldn't it be great to have a visual aid like the one given to Moses? Wouldn't it be great, through God's power, to make an inanimate object come to life? Or to call down some great healing power over a disease or a physical infirmity? Surely people would believe in God after seeing that!

But wait a minute. While God can work His will through whomever He chooses, His question raises an important point. God asked Moses, "What is that in your hand?"

Isn't God asking the same of you and me? "Karen, what is in your hand? What are the gifts and talents I've given you? What special circumstances have I placed before you? And how will you use these things for my glory?"

God can use us—all that we are and have—to do wonderful things in His kingdom. Therefore, let us affirm His greatness, give witness to His faithfulness, and bring people before the throne of His mercy—with every means at our disposal.

Lord, You have blessed me with spiritual gifts to use in advancing Your kingdom and building up Your church. Help me to use these gifts in the most practical ways today for Your glory. In Jesus' name, amen.

Just Keep Witnessing

The LORD said to Moses, "When you return to Egypt, see that you perform before Pharaoh all the wonders I have given you the power to do. But I will harden his heart so that he will not let the people go" (Exodus 4:21).

Scripture: **Exodus 4:18-23**
Song: **"What Are These in Bright Array?"**

Janie and I worked at the same office. We became good friends and talked often of our faith. I soon realized her belief in God was, well, . . . *nonchalant*. She lightheartedly admitted she wasn't too committed to living a God-honoring life. In spite of our differences and my leaving that workplace, we remained close.

Several years after my departure, I sensed God prompting me to talk to Janie about her faith. The urging was persistent, so I called, and we met at a local park one day.

I mustered up some courage and asked: "Janie, what do you think will happen to you when you die?"

"We're all going somewhere, I guess," she said. "But, Karen, I'm not ready to give up certain things in my life right now. So, I guess I'll just take my chances." She has yet to make a firm commitment to living in God's will.

When the Lord asks us to reach out to others, we have no guarantee they'll respond the way we hope they will. But our responsibility is just to be faithful in our witness. God will take control of the results.

Lord, today I ask for the courage to let Your light shine through me—even if Your presence receives a cool reception. Through Christ I pray. Amen.

Forgiven to Forgive

These are the things you are to do: Speak the truth to each other, and render true and sound judgment in your courts (Zechariah 8:16).

Scripture: **Zechariah 8:11-17**
Song: **"Gracious God, My Heart Renew"**

"I'm available if you need help," Kathy said to Denise, who was experiencing all kinds of stress as mother of the bride. Besides the wedding preparations, Denise faced conflict within a close circle of friends over another situation. Sadly, she had already alienated some of those friends with criticism and harsh words.

Kathy phoned to talk to Denise about the situation. But Denise verbally attacked Kathy—and hung up on her! She also asked someone else to take over the wedding tasks that Kathy had agreed to do. A 20-year relationship seemed to have evaporated overnight.

Several weeks passed, and Denise finally called Kathy. While she never said "I'm sorry," Denise seemed apologetic. Kathy paused, wondering how to respond. "Lord, give me the right words," she quickly prayed. Then Kathy knew what she should do: She simply extended grace and forgiveness in order to restore the relationship.

Kathy dealt kindly with her friend because she was so familiar with the undeserved forgiveness of God in her own life. Is it the same for you?

Dear Lord, *Your unmerited favor is the greatest motive for extending grace to others. Help me do it! In Jesus' name I pray. Amen.*

No Rejection Here!

I took you from the ends of the earth, from its farthest corners I called you. I said, "You are my servant"; I have chosen you and have not rejected you (Isaiah 41:9).

Scripture: **Isaiah 41:8-13**
Song: **"The Service of the King"**

John felt called to pastoral ministry in his mid 50s. He gave up a successful business and enrolled in seminary. His career change would mean a huge salary cut, but God's call was clear to him. He graduated and began serving a small but thriving congregation.

The church grew and seemed to be doing well. Then, after several years, some discontented members began trying to force their minister to resign. Overhearing some gossip, John heard about the discord. Specific reasons never came forth, but the tragic undercurrents persisted. After a few months, he resigned.

"I was devastated," he said later. "It was the lowest point of my life; it seemed no one wanted me." Yet John did go on to serve another church, enjoying a fruitful ministry there. (Some years later, the first church closed.)

God calls each of us to serve, using whatever gifts He's given us. Often we will run up against opposition and rejection. But let us constantly hold in our hearts these blessed words: "'You are my servant'; I have chosen you and have not rejected you."

Heavenly Father, *I am so privileged to be Your servant. Help me persevere in this calling, no matter the opposition. In Christ's name, amen.*

Information . . . or Wisdom?

Whoever listens to me will live in safety and be at ease, without fear of harm (Proverbs 1:33).

Scripture: **Proverbs 1:20-33**
Song: **"Step by Step"**

I'm so amazed at the vast amount of information available on the Internet. Is the expiration date on my eyeglass prescription legally binding? What, exactly, is *roseola*? How many planets are there? Where should I plant my hyacinths? How far is Kansas City from Denver? What's the process of refining silver? Can mold from old pancake mix really kill you? It's all there for me, just a click or two away . . .

There's even a Web site to confirm whether something you've read on the Internet is true or not! With all of this knowledge at our fingertips, should we ever be heard replying, "I don't know"?

Having a vast "storage bin" of facts is helpful, but there is something greater than just possessing information. We must learn to put our information to practical use in God's service. This is what the Bible means by "wisdom." And the truest, most reliable source of wisdom is God's Word. Following God's wisdom makes all the difference in how our lives unfold.

O God, I know I can choose to immerse myself in Your wisdom each day. Help me to long for Your words and hide them in my heart. Remind me that "listening" to You in this way will make a real difference in all my attitudes and actions. All praise to You, in Christ's name. Amen.

Knocking—with Knocking Knees

Now go; I will help you speak and will teach you what to say (Exodus 4:12).

Scripture: **Exodus 4:10-16, 27-31**
Song: **"Be Bold, Be Strong"**

I knocked at the assigned door. Linda and I were to visit some guests that had attended a recent church service. Mostly we simply wanted to let them know we were glad they'd visited. But we always anticipated a deeper conversation that might give us an opportunity to talk about Christ.

We'd just completed a series of lessons about witnessing to our faith—but we were still nervous. Been there? As I knocked, Linda whispered, "Dear Lord, please don't let them be at home." Her voice shook, and she clenched her hands together. (This wouldn't be our last visit together—or her last desperate prayer for an empty house!)

Looking back, I remember chuckling and teasing her about her fearful prayer. Thankfully, she was lighthearted through her anxiety.

It helps me to remember this: In those nervy situations, God promises us, as he did Moses, that when He sends us out, *He will go with us.* There's no better confidence builder than the great I AM, whether we're talking to Pharaoh or our neighbors.

Lord, You never promised me an anxiety-free existence. But You did promise Your constant presence amid all circumstances. So help me to rely on You when it's time to speak of Your goodness today. In Jesus' name, amen.

Yes, We Can!

Now get to work. You will not be given any straw, yet you must produce your full quota of bricks (Exodus 5:18).

Scripture: **Exodus 5:10-21**
Song: **"Take Your Burden to the Lord and Leave it There"**

On my first teaching job in the mid-1990s, I was charged with teaching kids how to use a computer keyboard. I entered my classroom to find the computer equipment piled in a heap, and no software in sight. For about two weeks, I taught kids how to type on those old machines. We did the best we could, but we fell far short of the mark. My attitude also fell short.

While it's easy for us to judge the Israelites for their harsh attitudes toward Moses and Aaron, suppose we examine our own attitudes amidst our struggles? When did you last encounter one of those seemingly impossible tasks? And how was your frame of mind?

Today I want to encourage all of us to see the opportunities that come packaged within the tough times. It's then that our witness to God's goodness can shine the brightest. It's easy to be a strong believer when everything seems to be going well. But when the quota of bricks is far too big, can we rely on the one who is greater than every man-made obstacle? (Let me hear you, now: "Yes!")

O Lord, thank You for Your help when the load seems impossible. Help me to do all things as if I'm working for You alone. In Jesus' name. Amen.

June 15–21. **Von Mitchell,** a school teacher and coach in Cedaredge, Colorado, is also a freelance writer and songwriter.

He Is Sovereign

Ascribe to the Lord **the glory due his name** (Psalm 29:2).

Scripture: **Psalm 29**
Song: **"King of Glory"**

I am amazed and humbled by the absolute sovereignty of God. As I read the psalm about how the voice of the Lord "is powerful" (v. 4), "breaks the cedars" (v. 5), and "strikes with flashes of lightning" (v. 7), I recalled an incident that occurred near our home last week.

You see, my wife and I are blessed to live in a beautiful little Colorado town at the base of the Grand Mesa. Just last week, we observed a fire, ignited by a bolt of lightning, which burned down two houses only a couple miles from where we live.

The name of our town? Cedaredge. We did indeed witness the powerful voice of the Lord strike and break the cedars in our little corner of the world.

Many pay homage to the powerful forces of nature around us, but it is the Lord God who deserves glory as the source of it all. Praise God! The same Almighty Lord who shows up in these spectacular natural displays also "gives strength to his people" and "blesses his people with peace" (v. 11). So I ask myself in this quiet moment: Will I live today as His humble servant?

Heavenly Father, I come humbly before You and give You glory. You alone are worthy of all honor and praise. Though Your voice "strips the forests bare" (v. 9), yet I know that You love me and care for every concern in my life. Thank you, Sovereign Lord, in the name of Your Son, Jesus. Amen.

Finding God

If from there you seek the LORD your God, you will find him if you look for him with all your heart and with all your soul (Deuteronomy 4:29).

Scripture: **Deuteronomy 4:25-31**
Song: **"Jesus My Lord, My God, My All"**

This Scripture passage is one of my favorites in the Bible. I love it because it's such a clear promise from God: You will find Him, if you sincerely seek Him.

I remember well the days in my life when I was searching for meaning, searching for truth. I am so thankful that God revealed himself to me as I pursued the answer to my heart's longings. Now, as a schoolteacher, I occasionally have the opportunity to share that experience with kids who are doing some serious searching of their own.

I once heard a wonderful preacher named Bryan Jarrett say, "Transparency before God is the highest form of reverence." I had to think about it for awhile, but then the statement really hit home with me. I don't think God is insulted when we have questions or doubts. He's surely not offended when we are honestly searching for the truth—because He *is* the truth. When we search whole-heartedly, we'll eventually find Him. (But don't take my word for it; take Him at His Word.)

Dear Heavenly Father, thank You for revealing yourself to me when I was searching. I pray today for the kids I've met who are also searching. I pray that You would draw them closer to You each day. I pray this prayer in the name of Jesus, my merciful Savior and Lord. Amen.

Where Would We Be?

I will restore them because I have compassion on them. They will be as though I had not rejected them, for I am the LORD their God and I will answer them (Zechariah 10:6).

Scripture: **Zechariah 10:6-12**
Song: **"Love Found a Way"**

Where would we be without God's compassion? In Old Testament times we read about how the Israelites messed up before God. Many times I have wondered, "How could they? These people saw the sea part. They beheld the glory of God in a pillar of cloud and fire. Their food rained down from Heaven! How could they ever doubt God and turn away to worship idols?"

Then I think about the miracles I've witnessed, and how I too have drifted from God, more preoccupied with some ball game on TV than in spending time with Him. And I am ashamed. You see, God provides my food. His glory guides me by way of the Bible and the Holy Spirit. I've seen relationships restored that seemed as impossible as crossing the Red Sea on dry ground. And I've seen lives changed in ways that defy explanation except to say, "God did it." How could I ever lose sight of God? I am treacherous without excuse. Are you?

Yet we serve a compassionate God who restores us, just as He did the Israelites. His compassions never fail.

Dear God, please forgive me for ever losing fervor for serving You in light of all You have done in my life. Thank You for the Word and Your precious Holy Spirit. I give You thanks. In Jesus' name. Amen.

The Real Lion King

He rescued me from my powerful enemy, from my foes, who were too strong for me. They confronted me in the day of my disaster, but the LORD was my support (Psalm 18:17, 18).

Scripture: **Psalm 18:13-19**
Song: **"Strong Tower"**

Like many people, I love C. S. Lewis's classic book series, The Chronicles of Narnia. In the film adaptation of one of the books, *The Lion, the Witch, and the Wardrobe,* comes an amazing closing scene. A witch is about to kill all that is good in the land of Narnia. It appears that all hope is lost. But then a resurrected Aslan comes a-roarin'! I get chills every time I see it. "It is finished," Aslan says, and order is restored.

Sometimes it seems that evil is about to take over, doesn't it? Maybe a trusted friend has suddenly spoken unkind words against you. Maybe your health takes a nosedive, or a coworker keeps taking advantage of your goodwill. Whatever the case, there is one who comes to "steal and kill and destroy" (John 10:10). He "prowls around like a roaring lion looking for someone to devour" (1 Peter 5:8). But thank God, the Lion of the tribe of Judah is the one true Lord and king. He comes a-roarin' in on the day of our disaster. He is our ever-present help in times of trouble (see Psalm 46:1).

Dear Jesus, *thank You for Your work on the cross when You said, "It is finished!" Thank You for bringing me "into a spacious place" because You "delighted in me" (v. 19). I give You praise for all You have done. Amen.*

Monsoon Time

If any of the peoples of the earth do not go up to Jerusalem to worship the King, the LORD **Almighty, they will have no rain** (Zechariah 14:17).

Scripture: **Zechariah 14:12-19**
Song: **"Grace Like Rain"**

For weeks we had no rain. The wind would blow, and occasionally it would cloud up, but no rain. It was a definite dry spell—one we're not so used to where we live. Then, as if on some mysterious cue, it finally rained!

We were overjoyed. It seemed that our greenery sprang to new life overnight. The air was filled with that beautiful, clean smell and, for once, the temperatures cooled down. All of nature rejoiced (including the two residents of our household).

We go for stretches of time with "no rain," don't we? I mean that we tend to dry up, spiritually—and even become a little crusty—as we move away from the Lord with questionable priorities. I don't have any geographical explanation for this arid condition of our hearts, but it sure seems as if Scripture does: Maybe we dry up because we spend so little time worshiping the king.

Friends, if that's all it takes to unleash the clouds of Heaven in our souls, then let's worship God with all our hearts today. Take a moment and lift up a thankful heart for all He's done in your life. Bring on the monsoon.

Father, please forgive me for not spending more time worshiping You. You alone are the source of my soul's renewal. In Jesus' name, amen.

Keep the Faith

"Ever since I went to Pharaoh to speak in your name, he has brought trouble upon this people." . . . Then the LORD said to Moses, "Now you will see what I will do to Pharaoh: Because of my mighty hand he will let them go" (Exodus 5:23; 6:1).

Scripture: **Exodus 5:1-9, 22, 23; 6:1**
Song: **"Here Am I, Send Me"**

The Lord was calling the Israelites to draw closer to Him, and Moses had just delivered God's order to Pharaoh: "Let my people go." But this Egyptian ruler, who had significant power at the time, decided to make things even rougher yet on God's people.

Has that ever happened to you? You decide to tithe . . . but the car breaks down. You set up family devotions for 8:00 every night . . . but hectic schedules prevent you from following through. You want to draw closer to God . . . but countless obstacles rise up in your way.

Well, keep the faith. Our hope comes in God's answer to Moses in our Scripture passage for today. We may encounter difficulties when we move to draw closer to God. (The forces of evil certainly don't want to see us get closer to the Lord.) But take heart! Our Savior has overcome the world (John 16:33) and will help us do the same.

My Lord God, I pray that You will help me press in and draw closer to You. Help me overcome any of the obstacles that will surely get in the way. Remind me, again and again, that with You all things are possible. In the name of the Father, the Son, and the Holy Spirit, I pray. Amen.

Legacy? Begin Now!

Moses took the bones of Joseph with him because Joseph had made the sons of Israel swear an oath. He had said, "God will surely come to your aid, and then you must carry my bones up with you from this place" (Exodus 13:19).

Scripture: **Exodus 13:17-22**
Song: **"Faith of Our Fathers"**

The great 19th-century evangelist D. L. Moody determined to impart a legacy of faith that would reach beyond the grave. He said, "Some day you will read in the papers that Moody is dead. Don't you believe a word of it! At that moment I shall be more alive than I am now. I shall have gone up higher, that is all—out of this old clay tenement into a house that is immortal, a body that death cannot touch." On his deathbed he made assignments for work still to be done. That work continues, a hundred years later, at the Moody Bible Institute in Chicago, Illinois.

Joseph, while on his deathbed, gave an assignment to his brethren, promising the help of God. This patriarch lived a legacy of faith until his dying day, constantly showing confidence in his promise-keeping God. That is the kind of legacy I, too, would like to leave behind some day. But I can begin now, today, with the smallest step of faith. Thanks be to God!

Father, grant me the fortitude to live out a legacy of faith that brings honor to Your name. I pray in the precious name of Jesus. Amen.

June 22–28. **Kathy Hardee**, a writer in Mendota, Illinois, is married with two children and one grandchild. She strives to glorify God through her writing.

Destined for Glory

I will harden Pharaoh's heart, and he will pursue them. But I will gain glory for myself through Pharaoh and all his army, and the Egyptians will know that I am the Lord **(Exodus 14:4).**

Scripture: **Exodus 14:1-9**
Song: **"Glorious Is Thy Name, O Lord"**

Steve and I had been dating for four years and were engaged. He was working toward his medical degree, and I was starting nursing school in the fall.

Our lives seemed to be moving forward at a comfortable pace . . . until the car accident. Just past midnight a drunk driver sped through a red light and smashed into the side of our car. Steve was unharmed, but I suffered broken bones, needed several surgeries, and faced months confined to a wheelchair. Yet I'll never forget the sense of God's presence with me during those long hospital nights and quiet mornings. Through pain I found a peace with God I hadn't experienced before.

Within a month after the accident, Steve and I broke up, and I decided not to pursue nursing. What many considered a "bad news" situation, God redeemed for my good—steering me onto a new and better path. Yes, God used a drunk driver to show me—and the hardness of Pharaoh's heart to show the Israelites—the glory of His power and presence.

Dear Lord, thanks for always working for my good. I trust Your plan for my life, and I give you all the glory for the results. In Jesus' name, amen.

Point Them to God

Moses answered the people, "Do not be afraid. Stand firm and you will see the deliverance the LORD will bring you today" (Exodus 14:13).

Scripture: **Exodus 14:10-14**
Song: **"The Battle Is the Lord's"**

"Mom, I think I'm pregnant," my daughter said one morning before school. My heart broke. In that moment, all the wonderful dreams I'd cherished for my daughter seemed to vanish. It was hard to see how God could work this out for good. I could have said any number of hurtful things, but I saw the fear in her eyes. All I could do was love her and assure her that God would see us through.

When the Israelites turned on Moses at the first sign of trouble, he looked beyond their anger. Pharaoh's army was indeed chasing them with a vengeance. And, yes, things looked bad. "What have you done to us by bringing us out of Egypt?" the people cried.

Moses could have said, "Have you so soon forgotten the misery of Egyptian bondage? You stubborn and forgetful people!" But he didn't say any of those things. He saw the fear in their eyes. He was moved to compassion. All he could do was assure them that God would see them through. (And that is what God did.)

Great God of Glory, help me to see hurting and fearful people as You see them. Use me to point them to You—the one who fights for and protects His own. In the name of Jesus, Lord and Savior of all, I pray. Amen.

Our Fortress

The LORD **Almighty is with us; the God of Jacob is our fortress** (Psalm 46:11).

Scripture: **Psalm 46**
Song: **"A Mighty Fortress Is Our God"**

The alarm rang, and Mrs. Anderson rushed us into the hallway. We sat in a row next to our lockers, legs crossed, heads down, arms wrapped over our heads. The tornado ripped off the gymnasium roof, shattered windows, and frightened several hundred children and their teachers. But we were huddled in the hallway, the safest place in the school.

Today's Scripture tells us about the safest place in the world. When calamity shakes the earth and nation rages against nation, we have a place to go. That "place" is Almighty God. He is waiting. Strong. Secure. Fortified. No enemy is allowed entrance. No harm will come to those dwelling in His presence.

I sometimes forget that God is not only my heavenly Father, He is my fortress. The Lord is my strong tower. When I run to Him, I am safe.

Inspired by this psalm, Martin Luther wrote the hymn, "A Mighty Fortress Is Our God." Whenever he heard discouraging news, he had been known to say, "Come, let us sing the 46th Psalm." May that be the song filling our hearts today.

Lord, I run to You. Please wrap me in the arms of Your love and renew me in the power of Your strength. Thank You, in Jesus' name. Amen.

A Grandmother's Legacy

Trust in the L ORD **with all thine heart; and lean not unto thine own understanding. In all thy ways acknowledge him, and he shall direct thy paths** (Proverbs 3:5, 6, *King James Version*).

Scripture: **Proverbs 3:3-10**
Song: **"Trust and Obey"**

With every note or greeting card I send, I include a verse of Scripture. I hope those words from the Lord will bring encouragement to the person receiving them. I often spend more time contemplating which verse would be best than I spend writing the note.

I learned this habit from my grandmother. On every birthday card, book, or Bible she gave me—and there were many—I'd find a verse or two written in her perfect penmanship. But Grandma didn't spend much time deciding which verses to write. Nine times out of ten, she inscribed Proverbs 3:5, 6, always in the *King James Version.*

Grandma must have known that if I spent all my days obeying just those two verses, I would live a joyful and successful Christian life (also see Psalm 1:1-3).

Has God written a verse on the tablet of your heart? Suppose you were to share with others those precious words of encouragement from the Lord?

Dear Lord, help me to trust You today with more of my heart—and to lean only on Your wisdom and understanding—so that my footsteps will always be following Yours. And as You guide me, may I ever be open to sharing Your wisdom and goodness with others around me. I pray this prayer in the name of Jesus, my Savior and Lord. Amen.

Problem Solved

Who among the gods is like you, O Lord? Who is like you— majestic in holiness, awesome in glory, working wonders? (Exodus 15:11).

Scripture: **Exodus 15:1-13**
Song: **"Victory in Jesus"**

Shirt-tags drove my 2-year-old grandson crazy. He often came running to me, pulling on the collar of his shirt, crying, "Bugging me, Gram. Bugging me." I'd scoop him up in my arms, give him a hug and assure him that I'd take care of his problem. Although shirt-tags might seem a huge problem to a 2-year-old, to me it was no big deal. One snip; problem solved.

The ancient Israelites faced a much more formidable foe. When they looked up, there were the Egyptians, marching after them, and God's people were terrified. They cried to the Lord and complained to Moses: "Why didn't you just let us stay and serve the Egyptians?"

But their problem was puny to an all-powerful God. After He delivered them, they expressed their astonishment and praise as they sang: "You blew with your breath, and the sea covered them. They sank like lead in the mighty waters" (v. 10). Pharaoh's great army was no match for the breath of God. One blow; problem solved.

Heavenly Father, thank You for reminding me: All of my problems are small compared to Your omnipotent power. Help me to praise You now, even as I wait on You. In the name of Your Son, my Savior, I pray. Amen.

God Used . . . *Whom?*

I will harden the hearts of the Egyptians so that they will go in after them. And I will gain glory through Pharaoh and all his army, through his chariots and his horsemen (Exodus 14:17).

Scripture: **Exodus 14:15-25, 30**
Song: **"Glorify Thy Name"**

This is what I want on my headstone: *Kathy Hardee—A Champion for God's Glory.* That's why I became excited one morning after reading Romans 9:17, "I raised you up for this very purpose, that I might display my power in you and that my name might be proclaimed in all the earth."

"Yes, Lord," I prayed, "that's what I want for my life. Display Your power and glory in me!" When I finished praying and looked back at the page, I realized I'd missed the first part of the verse, "For the Scripture says to Pharaoh . . ."

I had to reread that phrase several times? Unbelievable! God spoke these words to the great enemy of Moses and God's people?

Of course, God wasn't surprised by Pharaoh's attack on the Israelites. Nor did Pharaoh rise to a place of leadership purely of his own volition. God raised him up for His own purposes. God uses whomever He pleases to accomplish His plan and glorify His name.

I just hope He uses me, starting this very moment . . .

Dear God, I'm awed by the thought that You, the creator of the universe, might work in me to glorify Your name. Even so, use me, Lord God, use me today for Your purposes. I pray in Jesus' holy name. Amen.

Not Safe!

The Mighty One, God, the LORD, **speaks and summons the earth from the rising of the sun to the place where it sets** (Psalm 50:1).

Scripture: **Psalm 50:1-6**
Song: **"I Sing the Mighty Power of God"**

The *Seattle Post-Intelligencer* reported in 1997 that wild animal attacks were on the rise, including attacks by American bison in Yellowstone National Park. The article said, "In the last 15 years, more than 56 people have been injured and two killed by these seemingly placid beasts. . . . Nearly all attacks result from provocation, often when someone approaches to get a good photo."

Approaching great power with unthinking nonchalance—it made me think: although God is my friend, He is also the creator and sustainer of the universe. He, of all that is powerful, deserves the utmost respect.

In one of my favorite passages in C. S. Lewis's *The Lion, the Witch, and the Wardrobe,* beavers explain to the human children that Aslan, the Christ figure, is a lion. When Lucy asks, "Then he isn't safe?" Mr. Beaver responds, "Who said anything about safe? Course he isn't safe. But he's good. He's the King, I tell you."

God of the Universe, Your powerful wildness demands my veneration. I bow in reverence and acknowledge Your kingship over my life. In the name of Jesus, Lord and Savior of all, I pray. Amen.

June 29–30. **Bonnie Doran** lives in Denver, Colorado, with her husband of 24 years. She works part-time as a bookkeeper for her church.

Out of Water

Repent, then, and turn to God, so that your sins may be wiped out, that times of refreshing may come from the Lord, and that he may send the Christ, who has been appointed for you —even Jesus (Acts 3:19, 20).

Scripture: **Acts 3:17-25**
Song: **"The Waves of Salvation"**

I participated in a 9 kilometer race several years ago. The course followed a dirt path around Boulder Reservoir on a warm morning in May.

The inaugural race during the previous year had been rather sparsely attended, so the large number of participants for the second annual race caught the planners by surprise. By the time I reached the water stations, along with the back of the racing pack, the stations were dry— and so was I! Although I'd carried some water with me, I couldn't wait to cross the finish line where a friend waited with an ice-cold bottle of refreshment.

My own efforts at spiritual growth sometimes feel like that hot, dusty race course. I try to do everything in my own strength and wonder why I'm so tired and discouraged. Yet God calls to me (and you) every day: "Come, all you who are thirsty, come to the waters; and you who have no money, come, buy and eat! Come, buy wine and milk without money and without cost" (Isaiah 55:1).

Source of Living Water, *let me submerge myself in Your ocean of strength and love before I put on my running shoes for the course You've set for me. In the precious name of Jesus I pray. Amen.*

My Prayer Notes

DEVOTIONS®

I am the LORD your God.

—Deuteronomy 5:6

JULY

Photo © iStock

Gary Allen, Editor

DEVOTIONS® is published quarterly by Standard Publishing, Cincinnati, Ohio, www.standardpub.com. © 2008 by Standard Publishing. All rights reserved. Topics based on the Home Daily Bible Readings, International Sunday School Lessons. © 2005 by the Committee on the Uniform Series. Printed in the U.S.A. All Scripture quotations, unless otherwise indicated, are taken from the HOLY BIBLE, NEW INTERNATIONAL VERSION®. NIV®. Copyright © 1973, 1978, 1984 by International Bible Society. Used by permission of Zondervan. All rights reserved. Where noted, Scripture quotations are from the following, used with permission of the copyright holders, all rights reserved: *New American Standard Bible (NASB), © The Lockman Foundation, 1960, 1962, 1963, 1968, 1971, 1972, 1973, 1975, 1977, 1995. The New King James Version. Copyright © 1982 by Thomas Nelson, Inc. The Revised Standard Version of the Bible (RSV), copyrighted 1946, 1952, © 1971, 1973.*
• *Mere Christianity* by C.S. Lewis copyright © C.S. Lewis Pte. Ltd. 1950. Extract reprinted with permission.

Joy: More Than a Feeling

I will clothe her priests with salvation, and her saints will ever sing for joy (Psalm 132:16).

Scripture: **Psalm 132:11-18**
Song: **"Joyful, Joyful, We Adore Thee"**

In the story of Batman, one of the villains is the Joker, so-called because a surgical mistake left him with a permanent, grotesque smile. And that smile is anything but genuine.

Unlike the Joker, I don't walk around town with a grin glued to my face. Circumstances can depress me. I allow minor irritations to balloon into personal affronts. I answer one too many telephone calls from solicitors. Or I try to cope with the day's demands with only a few hours of sleep (and way too much caffeine).

Sometimes I feel far from the teensiest bit of joy, let alone being able to show it in word and deed. However, I do have a deep satisfaction in God that transcends temporary happiness. God has proved faithful in keeping His promises to me and my family down through the years. I know I can rely on Him . . . even when I don't feel like it.

__My Lord and King,__ sometimes I feel I have the emotional excitement of a teaspoon! But I thank You for Your goodness to me, day by day—and for Your promise of eternal joy still to come. Please keep my heart singing today—and if I need a nap, give me some time for that wonderful joy as well! I pray in Jesus' name. Amen.

July 1–5. **Bonnie Doran** lives in Denver, Colorado, with her husband of 24 years. She works part-time as a bookkeeper for her church.

Heavenly Amnesia

I will forgive their wickedness and will remember their sins no more (Hebrews 8:12).

Scripture: **Hebrews 8:6-12**
Song: **"Love Lifted Me"**

As I grow older, it seems my short-term memory needs more and more help. One little trick has been around for ages, and it apparently works for most people—tying a string around a finger. However, I've never tried this because I can't tie a bow with one hand (and I'm afraid the string might get caught in my computer's keyboard).

My method? I usually try, as soon as possible, to write down what I want to remember. Problem is, later on, I often can't decipher my own hurried handwriting!

One weight-loss program uses what they call an "anchor." A member uses an object, such as a key ring, to spark the remembrance of former successes and to be encouraged to continue following the program.

Well, here's my point: God untied the string and lost the anchor regarding our sins. He has not only forgiven us, but forgotten we ever disobeyed Him.

It may seem strange that Almighty God chooses long-term (lasting for eternity) memory loss. But that's the power of His love. And that heavenly amnesia is the source of all my praise.

Lord God, I thank You for the power of Your awesome love. You forged the true meaning of "forgive and forget." Help me do the same toward others who may wrong me this day. I pray in Christ's name. Amen.

A One-Way Pact

This is my covenant with them when I take away their sins (Romans 11:27).

Scripture: **Romans 11:25-32**
Song: **"O the Deep, Deep Love of Jesus"**

I never learned all the nuances of proper etiquette. I know, however, that receiving a wedding invitation means I need to buy a present for the happy couple. A potluck implies I'll bring a dish to share. If I've helped someone move, I hope I can ask them to help me when I'm loading my own truck. And when someone invites me to dinner, it's politely expected that I'll reciprocate before too long.

These unwritten rules of social interaction remind me of the old adage, "You scratch my back, and I'll scratch yours." Approached in the right way, this rule of thumb can create a friendship based on mutual assistance. Used wrongly, it can also create excess guilt if we're wired to feel obligated every time someone does us a favor.

God doesn't dump guilt on us when He draws up a contract. His back-scratching pact works only one way. We can't do anything to earn it or deserve it, but He lavishes His love on us anyway. His promise of forgiveness doesn't depend on how well we perform, but entirely on His mercy. Hallelujah!

Dear Lord, *thank You for Your great love in spite of my unloveliness. I respond in reverence and awe to the pure grace of Your salvation. I pray this prayer in the name of Jesus, my merciful Savior and Lord. Amen.*

Spirit of the Law

All the Law and the Prophets hang on these two command-ments (Matthew 22:40).

Scripture: **Matthew 22:34-40**
Song: **"My Country 'Tis of Thee"**

My new stove has a Sabbath setting. I can program it to bake up to 73 hours ahead of time. Apparently the European manufacturer wanted to assist Orthodox Jews and others in their observance of the Old Testament law. (No cooking allowed on the Sabbath!)

The Pharisees insisted on strict adherence to the law and debated endlessly on how its regulations should be observed. Jesus turned their tome of regulations into two: Love God and love your neighbor. That proclamation must have come as a shock.

But we, too, like to measure our spiritual progress by tangible means. Did we pray for 20 minutes today? Read our three chapters in the Bible? Tithe exactly 10 percent? Often we want to get out the clipboard and check off our activities on a kind of spiritual to-do list.

Love for God and others can't be measured that way, though. My husband, John, tried to help a neighbor with car trouble. When they were unsuccessful in fixing the problem, John offered the use of his truck for the evening. At that moment, was his generosity closer to God's ideal than attending a church service or singing in a choir?

Lord, help me demonstrate love for You and for my neighbor with a sincere heart. Keep me true to the spirit of Your law! In Jesus' name, amen.

Freedom

I am the LORD **your God, who brought you out of Egypt, out of the land of slavery** (Deuteronomy 5:6).

Scripture: **Deuteronomy 5:1-9, 11-13, 16-21**
Song: **"O Lord of Life, and Love, and Power"**

My husband created a design based on the abstract art of Piet Mondrian. A grid of heavy black lines enclosed squares of primary colors on a white background. One green square lay outside these lines. He titled it "Out of Bounds." Friends suggested other titles, such as "Thinking Outside the Box" and "Freedom."

God brought the Israelites out of slavery—but not out of bounds. They had freedom, but that freedom was tempered with certain clear-cut rules of conduct. Not "The Ten Guidelines" or "The Ten Suggestions," but "The Ten Commandments."

Yes, they were rules, but God intended them as a blessing, not as a burdensome list of do's and don'ts. We do the same with the people we love. For example, when we admonish a toddler, "Don't touch the stove—it's hot," we lay down a rule for the child's own good.

We have been brought out of slavery to sin into the freedom Christ bought for us on the cross. That freedom doesn't give us license to do anything we want. It does give us the power—and the gratitude—to do what pleases God.

Lord, I stand amazed at the price You paid for my freedom from sin. Thank You for giving me the desire to serve You gladly. In Jesus' name, amen.

Successful Mediocrity?

However many years a man may live, let him enjoy them all. But let him remember the days of darkness, for they will be many. Everything to come is meaningless (Ecclesiastes 11:8).

Scripture: **Ecclesiastes 11:7–12:1**
Song: "Joyfully Sing"

Would you rather be great . . . or just happy? Writer Henry Longfellow once said: "Most people would succeed in small things if they were not troubled with great ambitions." The idea makes me think of a friend of mine who once told me: "You know, Carol, I actually began to relax and enjoy my life—when I finally accepted that I was going to be a fairly mediocre person."

Bottom line: I am not under some cosmic mandate to be "great" in life. But I am called to see all of my life as resting in God's hands—my existence begun by Him and my life headed back to Him. The important thing is to live each day with the creator's reputation in view, rather than my own.

With this outlook, I know that I can enjoy each moment of my life. But, as Solomon (the writer of Ecclesiastes) reminds us, God is in charge of the Success or Failure Department. As He guides me, my so-called mediocrity will become an eternal success.

Lord, help me enjoy each day as it comes and to live it to the fullest. May I give thanks to You amid every situation. In Jesus' name, amen.

July 6–12. **Carol Wilde** is a pastor's wife and freelance writer living in Moultrie, Georgia. For exercise, she loves walking her Yorkshire terrier, Robbie Burns.

He's Still There

Will the Lord reject forever? Will he never show his favor again? . . . [But] I will remember the deeds of the LORD; yes, I will remember your miracles of long ago (Psalm 77:7, 11).

Scripture: **Psalm 77:3-15**
Song: **"Seek the Lord Who Now Is Present"**

I've been to plenty of meetings where people were "seeking God." I've heard many sermons, too, about what it takes to find God, and what needs to be done to stay close to Him. All of it seems like so much hard work. Really, a bit discouraging.

No doubt there is a place for discipline in pursuing spiritual growth. But it is not the starting point. For God is the one who first began the search, and He has found us.

The psalmist fears that he has grown far from God's presence, that somehow God has chosen to reject Him. Then he remembers: God's presence is woven into the fabric of his personal and communal history. He can discern God by reading back through his own life's story, by journeying back through the halls of memory and tracing the gracious hand that reached out to guide and bless, sometimes miraculously. I love how C. S. Lewis once summed it up: "While in other sciences the instruments you use are things external to yourself, . . . the instrument through which you see God is your whole self."*

O Lord, keep me alert to Your blessings at all times. Yes, help me to see Your hand at work in the most mundane unfolding of each day. In the precious name of Jesus I pray. Amen.

Remember God's Wonders

Remember the wonders he has done, his miracles, and the judgments he pronounced (Psalm 105:5).

Scripture: **Psalm 105:1-11**
Song: **"Happy the Souls to Jesus Joined"**

Have you found that it takes a good memory to be truly happy? How hard it is for us to accept: Happiness comes after the fact; it is a result rather than a goal. Usually it is the result of striving for a goal that focuses attention away from our own selves and circumstances.

To become totally involved in pursuing our passions, rather than our happiness, brings us to the point, later, in which we realize that we have reached a state of peace and contentment. The poster on my husband's office wall, with words by Nathaniel Hawthorne, puts it so well:

Happiness is like a butterfly;
    The more you chase it,
    The more it eludes you.
But when you turn your attention
    to other things, it comes,
    And sits softly on your shoulder.

As I go about my day today, I would like to let happiness land where it will, in its own time and place. Each instance will create a memory for me of God's goodness.

Dear God, *help me to dedicate myself to doing Your will—and to make some good memories today! In Jesus' name I pray. Amen.*

Mistakes? Learn!

Not since the days of the judges who led Israel, nor through-out the days of the kings of Israel and the kings of Judah, had any such Passover been observed (2 Kings 23:22).

Scripture: **2 Kings 23:1-3, 21-23**
Song: **"The Mistakes of My Life"**

Oops! What a mistake! God's people had simply forgotten—for many long years—to abide by His Word. They'd even let the all-important Passover celebration slip into oblivion.

Individuals, even whole nations, do "mess up," regularly. So, have I got you thinking about all your own mistakes at the moment? Rather than wallow in guilt, probably the best thing we can do now is to "reframe" our mistakes. That is, instead of seeing them as terrible disasters, we begin to view them as normal and natural results of the courage to make decisions and take risks. For the Christian, that is simply a good definition of determining to live by faith, each day.

Actually, a mistake can serve as a welcome call to slow down and look more closely at the direction we're traveling. What adjustments can we make? How can we avoid this in the future?

Dear Heavenly Father, remind me today that my mistake need not grow into a moral frame-up in the court of personal self-condemnation. Help me remember that, like any other human experience, I can invite a mistake to become my teacher. I pray this prayer in the name of my precious Lord and Savior, Jesus Christ. Amen.

It Actually Worked Out!

They left and found things just as Jesus had told them (Luke 22:13).

Scripture: **Luke 22:7-13**
Song: **"Still, Still with Thee"**

Peter and John were given a set of clear-cut, but rather elaborate, instructions to follow. Did they believe, at the outset, that everything would fall into place?

Actually, I think they simply had to step out in faith. I see them having to take a risk. But then what joy when they found that the plan had unfolded "just as Jesus had told them"!

Could I live like that? Suppose I choose to live a life of faith (which will involve plenty of risky decisions), and I thereby miss out on all kinds of fun, fulfilling, satisfying experiences? Surely I would regret such a decision! That thought has crossed my mind occasionally. Are God's plans for us always in our very best interest? Couldn't we devise a more self-fulfilling life on our own?

But to be convinced of God's good will toward me is the only way I can be moved to live a life of holy risk—of faith in God. Here's something that helps: to come to the blessed place in which I finally see that "what God commands" is exactly the same as "what is the very best for me."

O Lord, I celebrate Your involvement in the unfolding drama of my life's adventure! Help me to step out in faith, quickly, when You call me to do Your will. In Your precious name I pray. Amen.

For Joy: Remove the Sin

It is actually reported that there is sexual immorality among you (1 Corinthians 5:1).

Scripture: **1 Corinthians 5:1-8**
Song: **"Print Thine Image, Pure and Holy"**

The silly little cartoon showed Moses speaking, just returned from Mt. Sinai with the Ten Commandments in his hands. He's reporting to his people about his encounter with God on the mountaintop. He says: "It was hard bargaining—we get the milk and honey, but the anti-adultery clause stays in."

Of course, the topic of sexual immorality is serious business, as the apostle stressed to the Corinthians. But the practical question remains: Must a life of faith be a series of hard-bargaining rounds, as the cartoonist believes?

It's true that some things are clearly wrong, and a number of "anti" clauses must stay put (the real Moses would never have questioned that). Yet some people view God as quite disappointed when His creatures seem to be having a little fun.

That's a contrast to my sense of who God is. For example, I've been surprised to find out how much joy flows from the pages of Scripture—pure fun: singing, dancing, shouting, playing, making music. Surely God smiles at our joy. And that, of course, is why He commands against every self-destructive behavior.

Dear Father in Heaven, *help me to see Your commands as an invitation to live a happier life. In the name of Christ I pray. Amen.*

Help Me Focus!

Observe the month of Abib and celebrate the Passover of the LORD your God. . . . For six days eat unleavened bread and on the seventh day hold an assembly to the LORD your God and do no work (Deuteronomy 16:1, 8).

Scripture: **Deuteronomy 16:1-8**
Song: **"Listen to the Blessed Invitation"**

On television one evening, my husband and I watched a Japanese tea ceremony and marveled at the "attitude of awareness." The participants in the ceremony sit still and silent on a straw mat, facing each other, waiting for the hissing sound of boiling water in the pot before them. They listen to the water seethe. Then one man drops in the tea, whisks it, and presents the pottery bowl to his friend. The receiver looks at the bowl, inspects it, feels it, comments about its beauty, and then slowly drinks. Everything is done slowly; awareness reigns. Of course, they are not just drinking the tea, but, if it doesn't sound too strange, they are "being there with" the tea.

I believe the Lord calls for a similar kind of attentiveness when He commands the Israelites to observe an entire month—and one day per week—with special devotion to Him. Perhaps with these commands, they will learn the habit of staying attuned to His presence, even in the "ordinary" days`.

Dear Father, can I even do one thing without a multitude of other things screaming for my attention? Help, Lord! Give me special times of peace and quiet that I might focus on Your loving presence. In Jesus' name, amen.

No Generation Gap

Shout for joy to the LORD. . . . For the LORD is good and his love endures forever; his faithfulness continues through all generations (Psalm 100:1, 5).

Scripture: **Psalm 100**
Song: **"Great Is Thy Faithfulness"**

Our family gathered at the dining room table to decorate pumpkins one autumn Sunday evening. Grandson Nathan (about 7 years old) took time out to lead us in song. His arms waving wildly, he caught his reflection in the window and smiled at himself, pleased with his conducting skills.

During his college years, Nathan directed from the back of his dad's church, manning the sound system. Now a graduate, he plans to work on a master's degree while living in Israel. Some form of ministry in his future proves God's faithfulness through at least five generations of our family. Nathan's father, grandfather, great-uncle, and great-great grandfather served in pastoral ministry.

Tracing our spiritual heritage back through the generations is an exciting and God-honoring activity. (Try it, even though it may take some research!) God's faithfulness extends backward and forward, while rewarding us with a grateful heart.

Faithful God, I am so grateful for Your kindness to me through years past. And I sing Your praises as I move into the future. In Christ's name, amen.

July 13-19. **Ann L. Coker,** Terre Haute, Indiana, directs a crisis pregnancy center. She's married to her favorite preacher and has 4 children and 12 grandchildren.

Return to the Lord

Blow the trumpet in Zion, declare a holy fast, call a sacred assembly (Joel 2:15).

Scripture: **Joel 2:12-16**
Song: **"Come, Thou Fount of Every Blessing"**

From various e-mails I began to see that many people around the world are serious about revival. One e-mail alerted Messianic Jews to blow their shofars at an appointed time—to call the nation to repent. A second e-mail came from prayer groups around the world announcing a Global Day of Prayer planned in key cities. A third e-mail, from my friend and her husband, told about their decision to hold days of fasting during each week. This will help them prepare for their upcoming short-term mission trip to China. They're inviting others to join them.

Blowing shofars, gathering to pray, and even fasting doesn't guarantee revival. But these are surely steps in the right direction. However, let's remember, God is as close as our next breath. I like the way writer Tim Stafford put it: "You can worry that your relationship with [God] has gone cold. . . . You can think it will take a lot of time, a month or so of spiritual discipline, to get going again with Him. Then you sit down and discover, in just minutes, that you don't have to do a thing—except take some time. Be alone with him. In what feels like no time you are caught up again in your love."

Dear Father, *I am prone to wander. Change my heart, O God; renew me by Your Spirit; help me make the return trip home. In Jesus' name, amen.*

Serving *Is* the Reward

This service that you perform is not only supplying the needs of God's people but is also overflowing in many expressions of thanks to God (2 Corinthians 9:12).

Scripture: **2 Corinthians 9:6-12**
Song: **"In the Service of the King"**

We hear it repeatedly. The one who visits a shut-in feels she's the one receiving the blessing. A carpenter or bricklayer helps with renovation of houses damaged after a hurricane, and he returns with a renewed sense of thankfulness. We give of ourselves in service, and yet we are the ones who receive such joy in return.

A couple from our church has taken several mission trips to Haiti. They offer their professional skills, dentistry and pharmacy, to meet the medical needs of the village folk. But hearing this couple tell their story, I sense that they were on the receiving end. They overflow with gratitude for the opportunity to give in Christ's name.

When we help supply what others need, whether they "deserve" it or not, we are truly serving in the name of Jesus. The rewards we receive are eternal, but we are also rewarded *in the very act of service.* Just talk with those in ministry and ask about the personal benefits. Then look around you and plug into some of your church's outreach efforts.

Lord, I want to serve You and Your people with a grateful heart. May my service honor You as I seek to help meet needs around the corner and around the world. May my reward be found in You alone. In Jesus' name, amen.

Right Answer, Wrong Response

John came to you to show you the way of righteousness. . . . And even after you saw this, you did not repent and believe him (Matthew 21:32).

Scripture: **Matthew 21:28-32**
Song: **"Just As I Am"**

At the crisis pregnancy center where I work, most of our clients are single yet sexually active. The peer counselors tell them about the physical, emotional, and spiritual benefits of abstinence. Some will quickly agree to wait until marriage, yet we see most of these girls again. Broken vows reap the consequences of pregnancy and/or sexually transmitted diseases.

Those clients who keep a commitment to wait express a sense of regret, remorse, and guilt about their former lifestyles. I think their sense of guilt is a good thing, however. It leads to repentance and right actions. For these girls and guys, there is hope.

There is only hope when we agree with God about our sinful and self-destructive attitudes and actions. When the truth bears down on our consciences, we accept the truth. Then, and only then, do we have hope.

In other words, we can have the right answer but the wrong response. Unless we act out our decision to follow Christ, we continue to run around in circles of confusion.

Heavenly Father, *I know that You are pleased when my actions agree with my words. Help me not to turn a deaf ear to You but to act according to Your perfect will. I pray through my deliverer, Jesus. Amen.*

Caught in the Expectation Trap?

Do not be conformed to this world, but be transformed by the renewing of your mind (Romans 12:2, *New American Standard Bible*).

Scripture: **Romans 11:33–12:2**
Song: **"May the Mind of Christ, My Savior"**

Freshmen girls asked me to lead their late-night devotional. I talked about the difference between *conforming* and being *transformed*. We can conform to the good life but in a wrong way.

This was a Christian college; these girls came from Christian homes and attended church. Such teens can easily abide by the rules of house or dorm, doing what's expected. But have their minds been transformed?

All of us believers must choose whether to be transformed from within or simply to conform to outside pressures. Christ makes the inner transformation possible.

Counselors at the crisis pregnancy center look for red flags in their clients. Surprisingly, one group of risk factors actually involves *good* behavior—attending church, getting good grades, being athletic, and having a college scholarship. In the environment of success, these girls may rationalize that this is not the time to have a baby. Thus, they merely conform to the world. Their basic need is to be transformed by kingdom values.

O God, You have revealed Your perfect and acceptable will. Show me the areas where I need to move away from mere conformity. Instead, transform me, renewing my mind daily. Through Christ, I pray. Amen.

Two Teachers or One?

So that with one accord you may with one voice glorify the God and Father of our Lord Jesus Christ (Romans 15:6, *New American Standard Bible*).

Scripture: **Romans 15:1-6**
Song: **"Our God Has Made Us One"**

Never have I seen such a smooth process of speaker and interpreter working together. My husband, Bill, was speaking on holiness at a seminary in Malang, Indonesia. The interpreter was a student who had previously studied in the United States. As soon as Bill completed one sentence, the student spoke the translation. Actually, they seemed to speak with one voice. They even found Scripture passages and read together without hesitation.

The Lord was glorified as students and faculty heard the message in their own language. We knew God was in control, for a clear sense of His presence prevailed in that auditorium. We could have sung: "Our God has made us one; His glory is displayed."

We know that God's glory filled the tabernacle in the wilderness. And on the Day of Pentecost the disciples were of one accord. Those who listened to the disciples' message heard it in their own and varied languages. Even today, can we not expect God to move among us when we serve Him with one mind and voice?

Lord, I want You to move within me and show me Your glory. You desire this even more than I do! So I humbly ask that You begin the change in me. Bring me into one accord with Your will and Word. In Jesus' name, amen.

Say It; Do It

Moses said to the assembly, "This is what the LORD has commanded to be done" (Leviticus 8:5).

Scripture: **Leviticus 8:1-13**
Song: **"Lead Us, O Lord"**

The minister of a rural church called the children up front. He asked them, "Who is your neighbor?" All together they answered with names of their friends who live nearby. Then the tougher question, "How are you supposed to treat your neighbor?" Silence. The 4-year-old son of visiting missionaries spoke loud and clear, "I have to share." That was a typical first answer. "And what else?" Again the visitor was the first to respond, "I have to forgive." That answer went deeper.

Why was he ready to respond? He was taught that precept over and over, and he practiced it. He also saw that it worked for his good. He heard it said by his parents, and his part was to obey. Saying it was as good as doing it.

How does this simple lesson connect to the story in Leviticus about the anointing of priests? Over and over, Moses heard God speak His commands. Over and over, Moses and the Israelites were instructed to obey. When they did obey, they benefited. When they disobeyed, well . . . that's another story.

Father, I cannot address You as Sovereign Lord without acknowledging Your rule over me and all things. Through Your Word, I know who You are and how You want me to live. May all I do be a testimony to the joys of obedience. In the name of Your Son, my Savior, I pray. Amen.

Headline News Makers

News about him spread through the whole countryside (Luke 4:14).

Scripture: **Luke 4:14-19**
Song: **"Pass It On"**

The aftermath of 9-11 brought the name of a man, and his organization, to the forefront of newscasts throughout the whole world. We do not need to mention his name, but most people could tell you if asked. People also remember where they were when the infamous news-creating act of this man's organization was thrust upon the world.

Our verse today speaks of another man, a man in the process of founding a life-changing opportunity for every man, woman, and child that would ever live. News of him also spread throughout the whole country. But that man, and the news of him, centered in love and truth. His words and actions produced life rather than death. And people praised Him for the power and the truth that flowed from Him as He taught in their synagogues.

Two men, two news-creating circumstances. Yet, what contrasting realities! What differing effects! It makes me wonder: What kind of "news" will I bring to my own world this day?

Heavenly Father, help me to spread only goodwill in my world and to pass along the wonderful news of Your salvation to others. And keep the fire of Your presence real in my life. In the name of Christ I pray. Amen.

July 20–26. **Mary Louise DeMott** is a wife and grandmother who loves to teach and write about the most important thing in her life—her Lord and Savior.

Needing to Forgive?

"Lord, how many times shall I forgive my brother when he sins against me? Up to seven times?" Jesus answered, "I tell you, not seven times, but seventy-seven times" (Matthew 18:21, 22).

Scripture: Matthew 18:21-35
Song: "The Joy of the Lord Is My Strength"

A recent family misunderstanding caused many hurt feelings, much weeping, and frequent cries of "You don't understand!" The situation could have been avoided with better communication. And, of course, much forgiveness could have helped heal the many wounded hearts in this battle.

Our verse today challenges me in my relationships with others. It is so easy to "say" I forgive you without truly meaning it. The reality is that my enemy, and yours, does his best to use such unforgiveness as a wedge between us and our Lord.

Here's something that helps me. I find a verse that speaks to my heart. Then I meditate upon it (sometimes for days) until I arrive at true forgiveness and peace. Nehemiah 8:10 is such a verse: "The joy of the Lord is your strength." I have found that as I begin to praise the Lord, I am reminded how much He has forgiven me. That tends to melt my heart toward anyone whom I feel has wronged me.

Father, help me to remember all that You have forgiven me when I am distressed about a perceived wrong. In the name of Jesus I pray. Amen.

Know, Do, Live

**"What is written in the Law?" . . . "You have answered correctly,"
Jesus replied. "Do this and you will live"** (Luke 10:26, 28).

Scripture: **Luke 10:25-37**
Song: **"Thy Way, Not Mine, O Lord"**

A mother whale gives birth to her baby under water. It seems that God has given her an inborn knowledge that her baby must be helped to the surface for that first life-giving breath of air. By the time that baby has grown to adulthood, it will have learned to take a huge gulp of air that will give it almost an hour of underwater swimming. We might say the baby whale is blessed to have a "knowledgeable" mother give birth to him.

Knowledge is important, but Jesus stresses something much more important—that Christians should both *know* and *do* His Word. The Parable of the Good Samaritan simply reinforces the idea by means of a practical example.

You see, we can't claim allegiance to powerful spiritual precepts without "getting our hands dirty" with their interpersonal implications. Love is, ultimately, an action word! As Bible commentator William Barclay said: "It will always be true that the outsider will have no use for an alleged faith which is demonstrably ineffective. Long ago, Nietzsche, the atheist philosopher, issued the challenge: 'Show me that you are redeemed, and then I will believe in your Redeemer.'"

Lord, help me not only to love the concepts of the Bible but also to love doing them. Guide me in ministry this day! Through Christ, amen.

Send Out Workers

The harvest is plentiful but the workers are few. Ask the Lord of the harvest, therefore, to send out workers into his harvest field (Matthew 9:37, 38).

Scripture: **Matthew 9:35-38**
Song: **"Send the Light"**

The evening service was especially moving to our minister and his wife. Their son, Logan, and Kendra, his wife, were the speakers. That evening they told about New Tribes Mission. They had just graduated from the first section of training and were preparing to begin the final two years.

Those two years would be harder and more intense than anything they had experienced so far. Furthermore, they were told they couldn't work at a "paying" job; they would have to raise their own support. This would help prepare them for their years of missionary service.

It was obvious to all of us that this young couple found it difficult to ask for support. But it was also obvious to us that God wanted this work done in His kingdom. What a blessing to be part of such a great endeavor!

Each of us must "support" through finances and prayer, if we cannot "go." Some do not have finances, but all should be participants in prayer for missionaries doing God's work. Let us be God's hand extended to a lost and dying world.

Lord, help me to support financially—and with daily prayer—those You send to places I can't go with the gospel message. In Jesus' name, amen.

He Watches Over You!

When the Lord saw her, his heart went out to her and he said, "Don't cry" (Luke 7:13).

Scripture: **Luke 7:11-17**
Song: **"His Eye Is on the Sparrow"**

Tears filling his eyes, the weary man sat outside the main gate to the White House. His ragged clothes gave evidence of a long journey. A young boy stopped and asked why he was crying. The man's son was to go in front of a firing squad and be killed for desertion. "The guards will not let me see the president," said the man as he rubbed his eyes. "Mr. Lincoln is so kind that, if he heard the full details, I feel sure he would pardon my son."

"I can take you to the president," said the young boy.

"You?" asked the old man, surprised.

"Yes, he's my father. He lets me talk with him whenever I want to."

True to his word, president Lincoln's son brought the man to the Oval Office. And, indeed, when the president heard the full story, he pardoned the condemned soldier.

Lincoln, known for his great compassion, is only a shadow picture of our great God and His compassion for every man, woman, and child that has ever lived. Even now, He invites you to open Your hurting heart to Him.

Dear Father in Heaven, when I am hurting and discouraged, You are there. You care for me and constantly oversee my needs. Let me always trust You, even in the times when my tears are flowing freely. I pray this prayer in the name of Jesus, my merciful Savior and Lord. Amen.

God's Bidding

I tell you the truth, whatever you did for one of the least of these brothers of mine, you did for me (Matthew 25:40).

Scripture: **Matthew 25:31-40**
Song: **"Do Something for Jesus"**

One of the most moving experiences of my life happened one Christmas season. A heavy workload had kept me from completing my shopping. During one lunch hour I raced into a store, planning on grabbing lunch afterwards.

Finished shopping, I spotted a checkout line where I would be next. Others crowded behind me, and then . . . the clerk's phone rang. Turning away, she whispered, but I heard desperation in her voice as she said, "My tire went flat on the way to work, and I'm almost out of gas. I'm out of money until Friday; no, I can't get to church tonight. Please, can you help?" A look of desperation, and then she whispered, "That's OK, I'll find someone." As the young lady rang up my purchase, I saw her fighting to keep tears from falling.

I've never felt God speak to my spirit so clearly. I grabbed what money I had and pressed it into her hand. "I believe God wants me to give you this," I whispered. Turning, I hurried out the door, hoping I had done God's bidding.

Dear Father, please help me stay alert to Your voice, and let me act on what You are telling me to do. Let me be Your hand extended to one of Your hurting creatures in my world. In the name of Christ I pray. Amen.

He's Coming!

Have the trumpet sounded everywhere (Leviticus 25:9).

Scripture: **Leviticus 25:8-21, 23, 24**
Song: **"The King Is Coming"**

The first time I heard the song "The King Is Coming," I felt chills. I was at a concert, and as the houselights darkened for the second half of the program, the Gaither Trio stood there ready to sing a new song. But before the music started, shockingly, from the back of the auditorium a blaring trumpet fanfare sounded. The Gospel Brass came up the center aisle, playing. As they neared the front the Gaithers began singing:

> "The King is coming, the King is coming,
>   I just heard the trumpet sounding,
> And now His face I see."

The audience stood in awe. What a beautiful experience it was for all of us.

I've never forgotten that moment, and every time I read about the trumpets sounding in the Bible, I recall that concert so many years ago. It intensified the reality of my coming king. For one day God's trumpets will sound everywhere, and all peoples will bow down to the Lord of lords.

Almighty and everlasting Father, help me always remember that Your Son is coming back again at any moment. May I stay ready—and looking up. In the name of the Father, the Son, and the Holy Spirit, I pray. Amen.

My Portion: The Best

I cry to thee, O Lord; I say, Thou art my refuge, my portion in the land of the living . . . for thou wilt deal bountifully with me (Psalm 142:5, 7, *Revised Standard Version*).

Scripture: **Psalm 142**
Song: **"Jesus, My All in All"**

My grandfather loved telling about "the good ole days." One summer day he told me of working in the watermelon fields of Oklahoma. He said he walked to the field in the dark of the day and chose a large watermelon. He carried it to the creek and placed it deep in the stream. The sun rose high overhead, and the heat and humidity pressed hard upon him as he worked.

"By noon, I was all but dead," he said. He dragged to the river and plunged into the cool water to retrieve his melon. After cracking it open on a rock, he'd used his pocket knife to slice out the middle. He said that the juicy, red sweetness ran down his chin and throat to cool him inside and out.

"But Grandpa, you ate just the middle?" I asked.

"It was my portion," he said, smiling. "When you work in a melon field, you eat the very best of the melon."

God provides similarly for His tired workers. He refreshes with the very best—himself.

O Lord, refresh my commitment to serve You today, even when I feel pressed down. Let the joy of my salvation sustain me. In Christ, amen.

July 27–31. **Shelley L. Houston** lives in Eugene, Oregon, with her husband of 37 years. She writes for various secular and Christian publishers.

Maudlin Murmurings

Moses said to Aaron, "Say to the whole congregation of the people of Israel, 'Come near before the LORD, for he has heard your murmurings' " (Exodus 16:9, *Revised Standard Version*).

Scripture: **Exodus 16:1-12**
Song: **"Guide Me, O Thou Great Jehovah"**

It was hot. The moving truck we'd rented had no air conditioning. I was six months pregnant, and our two toddlers squirmed nonstop between us. Half of the 16 hour trip lay ahead.

"Could things be any worse?" I complained to my husband . . . just before the truck broke down. Hours later, a mechanic told us it would be a three-hour repair. He suggested we walk to a restaurant two miles away, since there was no cool place to wait. On the way out of his yard, I tripped on an old car part and gashed the top of my foot.

We had to walk under a freeway overpass. The shaded concrete felt cool as we sat to spell ourselves. Soon, my husband wanted to go, but I balked.

"I'm not moving . . . ever. I'm going to sit here until I die," I moaned, watching the blood ooze from my foot.

I felt justified in my complaining that day, just as the Israelites must have felt in the wilderness so long ago. But the truth is, our merciful God knew where we were. He heard not only my words but my aching heart.

Lord God, forgive my moaning, my whining, and my wanderings. But thank You for caring when I hurt and knowing what to do when I cry out with a deep need. I pray through my deliverer, Jesus. Amen.

Bread of Heaven

Truly, truly, I say to you, he who believes has eternal life. I am the bread of life (John 6:47, 48, *Revised Standard Version*).

Scripture: **John 6:41-51**
Song: **"Bread of the World"**

"Bread is sacred in France," our French exchange student explained to our family. "Children are never allowed to play with their bread, and a loaf of bread is placed carefully on the table, right side up, so as not to cause it to be dishonored."

"Why is that?" I asked.

"During WWII there was a shortage of bread, and so our grandparents have taught us not to waste. But also, bread is traditionally thought to be the body of Christ."

I was stunned by his reply, since he and his parents were atheists. His words about a national tradition had an empty ring to me, as they seemed to mimic a time of heartfelt reverence for Christ. The difference between the two eras was faith. One generation believed, the next two only go through the motions of respect out of tradition.

This all caused me to wonder. To what extent do we honor the Christ, the bread of life? Do our own children understand the sacredness of the bread, the body of Christ? And more importantly, do they know and believe in the Christ whom it represents?

Heavenly Father, fill me with Your presence today. Make me aware of Your nurturing Spirit who teaches us and our children to believe. Thank you, Father, in the name of Your Son, the bread of life. Amen.

Relying on the Spirit

Simon Peter answered Him, "Lord, to whom shall we go? You have the words of eternal life" (John 6:68, *New King James Version*).

Scripture: **John 6:60-68**
Song: **"No Not One"**

I live in a small town, but we do have our own airport. However, since so few people use the service, only one carrier can afford to operate flights from here. So when I want to take a flight from home, I must use this carrier.

When Simon Peter confessed Jesus as his Lord, he made a statement that seems similar, at first blush, to my situation of having only one air travel provider. But that's not what Peter was saying when he asked, "to whom shall we go?" It's not that there was no one else who claimed to have knowledge of true religion. Many people in Jesus' time offered answers to the people's spiritual needs. And there were even numerous pretenders in those days claiming the title of Messiah.

Peter realized, instead, that what Jesus provided was the true Way—Jesus himself as the sacrifice for sin. Peter might not have understood the full significance of Jesus' blood and body yet, but he surely knew that Jesus' very words held the key to eternal life. In Peter's time, and in our own, there truly is no other way.

Lord, I thank You for Your great gift of salvation by the sacrifice of Jesus' body and blood. He has released us from the sentence of death and from the power of sin. May I live out this truth today! In Jesus' name, amen.

Look to the Rock

Let any one who thinks that he stands take heed lest he fall (1 Corinthians 10:12, *Revised Standard Version*).

Scripture: **1 Corinthians 10:1-11**
Song: **"Rock of Ages"**

I went on vacation recently and visited a church in another state. It was a large, well-established congregation. The sermon theme was the necessity of doing good works, a theme repeated in the bulletin and on posters in the halls. But to this church "good works" meant providing services and programs *for each other*—such as mowing the church lawn, hosting ladies luncheons, leading men's retreats, and offering child care. There seemed to be no thought of the church having any ministries in their community at large nor in global missions.

My visit to this seemingly self-serving church caused me to rethink my own service to God. A minister once urged our congregation to think of our church not as a country club where we come to fellowship, but as a hospital where the weak and wounded can be received, comforted, and healed. I realized that lately my own "service to God" consisted of meeting my own needs, mainly for social interactions.

How easily our religion slips into pleasure-seeking idolatry, with our own needs as the focus. May we keep our eyes on the rock, our Savior, so that we don't fall.

O God, please forgive my sin of "self service." Lead me into paths of true service for Your glory. In Christ's holy name I pray. Amen.

DEVOTIONS®

I lift up my voice to the LORD . . . . Set me free . . . that I may praise your name.

—Psalm 142:1, 7

AUGUST

Photo © Comstock

Gary Allen, Editor

Holy Vacations

Keep yourselves in God's love as you wait for the mercy of our Lord Jesus Christ to bring you to eternal life (Jude 21).

Scripture: **Jude 1:14-23**
Song: **"What a Friend We Have in Jesus"**

When our children were growing up we took many modest vacations. The family sometimes planned all year for a special time away, but we often took short trips of a day or two as well. These times built great memories and relational bridges among us.

There were many other children in our neighborhood, but we never included them in our vacations. Why? They weren't a part of our family. Members are privileged to whatever bonuses the family offers, from extras—like vacations—to basics, like room and board.

God fashioned the family after the structure of His relationship with us. We Christians also benefit from being seated in His circle, a position that those who "follow their own ungodly desires" (v. 18) cannot enjoy. As we spend time with our Father, we develop a stronger relational bond along with great memories that we can share with the rest of the family. So, today, let's take some "vacation time" with our Father.

Heavenly Father, may I see and hear You with new ears and heart. Refresh my cold soul with the warmth of Your love, like an Arizona sun on our Alaskan backs. I love You, Father, in Jesus' name. Amen.

August 1, 2. **Shelley L. Houston** lives in Eugene, Oregon, with her husband of 37 years. She writes for various secular and Christian publishers.

Troubling the Servants?

Why have you brought this trouble on your servant? What have I done to displease you that you have put the burden of all these people on me? (Numbers 11:11, 12).

Scripture: **Numbers 11:1-6, 11-15**
Song: **"Father, Make Us One"**

Do you ever get your way at church?

Many decades ago, I thought my church was out of touch with what was relevant to life, especially concerning standards of dress. I decided to help them out of the "stone age" by wearing pants to church on a Sunday night. This action didn't have the effect I hoped—Mom cried, and a woman verbally shamed me. However, in time, the church did consent to women wearing pants to services.

A victory? Not mine. I have learned there is little worth fighting about in church. However, I continue to be amazed at the large number of Christians who selfishly torpedo the work of God over disappointments about their fairly trivial preferences. Things like the style of music, architectural aesthetics, parking lot spaces, or a myriad of other personal opinions are raised to church-splitting levels.

Some members tend to "bury" the true servants of the Lord in trivialities and foil their worthy efforts to witness to the message of God's grace. (So tell me: How are we different from the meat lovers' grumblings in the desert?)

O God, forgive my foolish ways. Cause me to see my brother's needs as more important than my own. Help me respond to the higher calling of Your work in me, on behalf of others. In Jesus' name, amen.

It's a Privilege

They forgot what he had done, the wonders he had shown them (Psalm 78:11).

Scripture: **Psalm 78:5-17**
Song: **"Trusting in Thee"**

"Don't you remember?" my friend said. "We talked about this before."

I did remember . . . vaguely. That is, I remembered talking, but I couldn't remember the particulars. "Sort of," I said. "But could you refresh my memory?"

Forgetfulness, I'm learning, is a natural by-product of growing older. I once could recall all sorts of random trivia. Now I'm lucky to remember what I ate for dinner yesterday. Usually, forgetfulness is merely inconvenient or embarrassing. In matters of faith, however, forgetfulness can be disastrous.

Many mornings I study the Bible, only to forget what I've learned by noon. Or God answers a prayer in a remarkable way, and within weeks I've forgotten about it. Perhaps one of the main reasons God gave us the Bible is so that we could go back over it, again and again, and refresh our memories. What a privilege He gives us!

Lord, my memory dims with each passing year, and I forget things I want to remember. Should I forget all else, help me to remember You and Your faithfulness. Help me to remember what You've done, both in the grand scope of history and in my own personal history. In Jesus' name, amen.

August 3–9. **Sarah Overturf** lives in Longmont, Colorado, with her husband and three children. She is a writer and a school librarian.

Lost, Not Forgotten

Although they have sold themselves among the nations, I will now gather them together (Hosea 8:10).

Scripture: **Hosea 8:1-10**
Song: **"Bringing in the Sheaves"**

I love browsing antique stores and rummaging through the old artifacts that speak of lives lived and passed. But I'm always saddened when I come to the inevitable box of black and white photographs. I look at the pictures of families, young couples, children, and babies, and I think, "Someone should have these." But how do you identify the "someone" who's connected to these lives? We live in a scattered society where we rarely know the names of our forbears, let alone their faces.

In God's family, however, there are no unknowns. There is no box of people He can't place. He knows our names, and He knows our faces. Even when we stray far away from His care, He does not forget us. He is ever waiting to gather us back to himself, to reclaim us as His own. "This one here—he is mine. And that one there—she belongs to me."

Are you praying today for someone who is "lost"? Keep praying. That person may be lost, but he or she will never be forgotten.

Father, thank You for bringing me back to yourself. Thank You for claiming me, for calling me Your child and allowing me to call You Father. Thank You for reminding me that though I may be forgotten in this world, I matter to You for eternity. Amen.

Too Much to Ask?

He has showed you, O man, what is good. And what does the Lord require of you? To act justly and to love mercy and to walk humbly with your God (Micah 6:8).

Scripture: **Micah 6:1-8**
Song: **"He Has Shown Thee, O Man"**

I wasn't asking for much. Laundry folded. The dishwasher emptied. Bathrooms tidied. And no bickering. What I got instead were grumblings, sharp words, and shoddy work. Was it too much to ask for a few simple tasks to be completed with good attitudes?

Yet I have to admit that sometimes my own attitude and work can be less than exemplary. I groan when the phone interrupts an important project. I scowl at the dryer when it buzzes—again. Sometimes I wonder whether God looks at me and says, "Is it too much to ask—?"

Really, God doesn't ask that much of us. Just three things: justice, mercy, and humility. What would my life look like, I wonder, if I kept those three things at the fore of my thoughts? What if my children saw actions from me today that were truly just? What if my coworkers heard words of mercy from me? What if my neighbors saw me walking humbly? I wonder what good such a life might do. Surely finding out is not too much to ask.

Lord, You have shown me what is good and what You require of me. Help me now to live it in the most practical ways. May my life be marked by these three things: justice, mercy, and a humble walk with You. I pray this prayer in the name of Jesus, my Savior and Lord. Amen.

Understanding Comfort

This is why I weep and my eyes overflow with tears. No one is near to comfort me, no one to restore my spirit (Lamentations 1:16).

Scripture: **Lamentations 1:16-21**
Song: **"The Comforter Has Come"**

My neighbor looked at me through her filmy blue eyes. "There aren't many left," she said.

I nodded as though I understood, but I didn't. Not really. She was near the end of her life. Her husband, her siblings, and most of her friends were gone. I was in a very different place, busy with little kids at home. I had no idea what it was like to be one of the last in an ever-shrinking circle of relationships. But my neighbor didn't need me to know that. She just wanted someone to know that she was in a hard and lonely place. I didn't have to be nearing the end of my own life to give her understanding. I could be right where I was.

When someone is going through a hard time, often what they need most is just someone who is near. A listening ear, the touch of a hand, a hug, an arm around their shoulders—these things bring both comfort and restoration to their spirits. And the only cost is a little of our time.

Father, Your Holy Spirit is the Comforter within me. And yet You often choose to bring Your comfort through Your people. Help me to be a channel of comfort today. Help me see who is hurting and to be a human touch for Your heavenly warmth. I pray in the name of Christ. Amen.

Test Time

Let us examine our ways and test them, and let us return to the Lord (Lamentations 3:40).

Scripture: **Lamentations 3:39-50**
Song: **"I Am Thine, O Lord"**

Tests must be the bane of nearly every student who has ever sat at a desk. All that studying, all that work, and for what? Well, beyond basic knowledge, tests get us ready for life.

Tests don't end when school does. From the time we wake (will I hit snooze or get up and pray?) to the time we go to bed (will I go to bed angry, or will I make things right?), we're faced with one test after the other. Are we kind when others are rude? Are we gracious when someone else gets credit for a job we did? Are we patient, even when our last nerve is stretched thin?

Sometimes we fail at something we try, but there is zeal and passion in our motives. Sometimes we say the sweetest things, but our hearts are darkened with bitterness or envy. How will we know, unless we examine ourselves?

We won't pass every test with flying colors, but when we're consistently examining ourselves, we'll find that our tests bring us nearer to God. And that's better than an A any day.

Dear Father, I need Your wisdom to examine both my ways and my heart. I don't see motives as clearly as You do, and I want them to be pure. I want the things I do, and the reasons behind them, to bring me nearer and nearer to You. In Jesus' name I pray. Amen.

Pardon Me

Who is a God like you, who pardons sin and forgives the transgression of the remnant of his inheritance? You do not stay angry forever but delight to show mercy (Micah 7:18).

Scripture: **Micah 7:14-20**
Song: **"Grace Greater Than Our Sin"**

Anger covers quite a spectrum, including everything from being a little miffed to being blood-boiling, steam-rising furious. Anger is one of the strongest emotions we feel, and its energy powers many of our attitudes and actions. Strangely enough, it also seems to power some of God's actions.

What angers God? Sin. But because God also loves us, He does something about it. Through His anger comes a remarkable gift: pardon. He says, yes, what you did was wrong. But the debt has been paid. My Son paid it for you.

Scarcely a day goes by that we don't feel some form of anger. We can't keep anger from bubbling up, but we can choose what to do with it when it rises within us. We can fuel it, or we can let it lead to pardon and mercy.

Thankfully, God's anger doesn't last forever. He delights in pardoning us. And what a joy it is for us to receive and share both His pardon and His delight.

*Who is a God like You, **Lord**? Anger that leads to mercy—what an incredible gift! Help me when I am angry to remember to show mercy to those around me. Help me to pardon others as You have pardoned me. In the holy name of Jesus, my Lord and Savior, I pray. Amen.*

Running Scared?

Only do not rebel against the LORD. And do not be afraid of the people of the land, because we will swallow them up. Their protection is gone, but the LORD is with us. Do not be afraid of them (Numbers 14:9).

Scripture: **Numbers 14:1-12**
Song: **"Have Faith in God"**

I was jogging through my neighborhood one winter night, bundled against the cold in a jacket, gloves, and a head warmer. Suddenly I heard footsteps behind me. Running footsteps. But they weren't passing, they were following me.

My already rapid heart rate raced as I tried to think of a plan. Ring someone's doorbell? Stop? Turn? Scream?

Ahead, a man was wheeling his trash can out to the curb. Surely here was help. But he only glanced quickly in my direction before going inside.

Then I felt something. Something I hadn't noticed before. My hair was bouncing against the head warmer as I ran. And the head warmer covered my ears, muffling the sound. There were no footsteps; it was only hair.

Isn't that how it often is with fear? Something that seems so terrifying turns out to be nothing. Sometimes there are real giants in the land, but sometimes they are only giants because we've let some unworthy thing grow too big in our own minds.

Lord, this world is filled with frightening things. Help me to remember that when You are with me, I have nothing to fear. Through Christ, amen.

Imperfect, but Honored

Take Aaron and Eleazar his son, and bring them up unto mount Hor (Numbers 20:25, *King James Version*).

Scripture: **Numbers 20:22-29**
Song: **"There's a Wideness in God's Mercy"**

The death of Israel's first high priest is typical of the death of many great, but flawed leaders. Three key words sum up Aaron's life.

Stripped: At his death, Aaron was divested of his honorable position and distinctive garments. He died humbly on a lonely mountaintop. Like Aaron, many of God's servants die peacefully, but sin leaves a dark cloud over their lives.

Gathered: Aaron was not "cut off" from his people like a rebellious sinner, but "gathered" to them like a repentant one (v. 26). God restored Aaron, and the passing of such a servant deserves a place of honor in the hearts of his countrymen.

Mourned: While his vital position was filled, Aaron's absence left a conspicuous hole (v. 29). After all, he and Moses were the original leaders of the Exodus. Like so many of God's servants, Aaron was valued more in death than in life. Death has a way of putting an imperfect career in its true light.

Dear Lord, help me to honor the good that Your grace has accomplished in the imperfect lives of those who have loved You. In Jesus' name, Amen.

August 10–16. **Richard M. Robinson** is a Baptist minister in Denver, Colorado. He enjoys singing in a gospel quartet, writing, and collecting vintage Mac computers.

How History Comes Alive

Blow up the trumpet in the new moon, in the time appointed, on our solemn feast day (Psalm 81:3, *King James Version*).

Scripture: **Psalm 81:1-10**
Song: **"O Praise Our God Today"**

Israel's celebrations were to be tributes to a loving God. Their religious holidays rested on historical reference points, especially their slavery in Egypt (vv. 5, 6) and survival in a barren wilderness (v. 7). Over time, this glorious history became academic and ordinary to the people. But holidays need history, or they will lose their power to inspire. To counteract this tendency, Asaph called up images from the past, as when their ancestors were released from heavy burdens and menial work (v. 6).

Short of a time machine, a little sanctified imagination is the next best thing to being there. After all, we should learn history to leap into it. So be creative.

Joseph Bayly, in his poem, *Psalm of Laughter for Easter*, compared history's greatest event with life's happiest moments. To jump-start his joy, he imagined this:

> *Christ died and rose and lives.*
> *Laugh like a woman who holds her first baby.*
> *Our enemy death will soon be destroyed.*
> *Laugh like a man who finds he doesn't have cancer.*

It's true! A little imagination makes history come alive.

Dear Lord, *sanctify my imagination as I study Your Word. Let it produce celebrations of joy in my life. Through Christ I pray. Amen.*

How Will You Respond?

It is a people that do err in their heart, and they have not known my ways (Psalm 95:10, *King James Version*).

Scripture: **Psalm 95**
Song: **"Search Me, O God"**

The Exodus Generation were eyewitnesses to history's greatest miracles. As the Lord declared, they "saw my work" (v. 9). But lacking the faculty of spiritual eyesight, they stumbled in unbelief like blind men. They were incredibly wrong-headed in their assessments and conclusions of God's dealings.

The real problem was their erring hearts. Verse 10 is quoted in Hebrews 3:10 with one addition: "They do always err in their heart." Chronic wrong thinking stems less from defective logic and more from diminished love. If they had only known God's heart, they would have understood His ways.

It's all in how you respond. In verses 1-7, hearts melt like butter. But in verses 8-11, they harden like clay. Some receive and others reject, but the love is the same.

This psalm ends in death. Hardened and hopeless, the erring ones must die in the wilderness (v. 11). As Thornton Wilder observed, "There is a land of the living and a land of the dead—and the bridge is love, the only survival, the only meaning."

*"Search me, **O God,** and know my heart: try me, and know my thoughts: and see if there be any wicked way in me, and lead me in the way everlasting" (Psalm 139:23, 24). In Jesus' name, amen.*

A Tale of Two Trees

Blessed is the man that trusteth in the LORD, and whose hope the LORD is (Jeremiah 17:7, *King James Version*).

Scripture: **Jeremiah 17:5-10**
Song: **"Find Us Faithful"**

To borrow a few lines from a classic Dickens story: "It was the best of times, it was the worst of times, it was the age of wisdom, it was the age of foolishness . . . it was the spring of hope, it was the winter of despair . . ."

The prophet Jeremiah would certainly agree. In his day, society was a study in contrast. The majority were morally decayed and spiritually stunted, the outgrowth of a godless culture. However, the faithful remnant experienced revival in the midst of national decline.

This disparity comes through in the prophet's picture of two trees. The unbelieving majority were like a "heath in the desert" (v. 6). Resembling the Dwarf Juniper, they were as Matthew Henry described, "a naked tree, a sorry shrub, the product of barren ground, useless and worthless." But there was a godly minority that spiritually prospered like "a tree planted by the waters" (v. 8). The happy result: they were stable, preserved, and fruitful.

Even in the worst of times, surrounded by fools with spirits chilled into despair, you can be God's paradox, flourishing by faith.

Dear Heavenly Father, may I trust You more fully today. And keep me rooted in Your Word so that I may show others the secret of abounding in You. In the name of Jesus, Lord and Savior of all, I pray. Amen.

Diluting the Savior?

He saith unto them, But whom say ye that I am? (Matthew 16:15, *King James Version*).

Scripture: **Matthew 16:13-18**
Song: **"Our Great Savior"**

Back in 2001, a Kansas City pharmacist was charged with diluting the cancer treatment drugs, Gemzar and Taxol, in order to make a larger profit. Americans were shocked and outraged. Robert Courtney admitted to diluting the drugs over a five-month span.

Commentator Michael Owenby observed, "This man held life-saving power in his hands, and for the sake of personal gain diluted it to the point where it could not help people. We can do the same with God's life-saving truth."

With life and death implications, Jesus asked His disciples, "Whom do men say that I, the Son of man, am?" (v. 13). If they presented anything less than the truth, the gospel would be turned into a powerless placebo for dying sinners. This is the worst criminal act in the world.

Peter's bold, clear answer was the pure truth: "Thou art the Christ, the Son of the living God" (v. 16). This is the only cure for the cancer of sin. And if we are to save souls and escape Heaven's censure, we dare not dilute the Savior!

O Holy Father, keep me from ever carelessly or knowingly misrepresenting Jesus, the Son of God, to a sin-sick world. He is fully man, fully God, incarnate to save us by His cross. And I pray in His precious name. Amen.

Is It Worth It?

He that sat upon the throne said, Behold, I make all things new. And he said unto me, Write: for these words are true and faithful (Revelation 21:5, *King James Version*).

Scripture: **Revelation 21:1-7**
Song: **"When We All Get to Heaven"**

As the Bible ends with John's final glimpse into the eternal future, it again answers one of life's biggest questions: "Is it worth it?" Yes, life is hard, often unfair, and sometimes tragic. But take heart, a new world is coming (v. 1). Overcomers down here won't be underwhelmed up there. That era will be as far ahead of our age as we are to worms crawling in the mud!

John's picture actually defies description. In describing these visions, Don Fleming wisely observes: "They are not pictures of the physical characteristics of the new heaven and the new earth. The heavenly city is not an improved version of the present earthly city . . . the present world is to be completely replaced by a new order."

God means it when He says, "Behold, I make all things new" (v. 5). Think of it. Everything and everyone made new, made pure, made perfect forever. And best of all, "God himself shall be with them, and be their God" (v. 3).

Is it worth it? You be the judge.

Dear Father, it's really true, "the best is yet to be." Thank You for all my present blessings, but I am most grateful that You saved the best for last! In the name of Jesus, my Savior, I pray. Amen.

Does Anger Really Work?

Moses lifted up his hand, and with his rod he smote the rock twice: and the water came out abundantly, and the congregation drank, and their beasts also (Numbers 20:11, *King James Version*).

Scripture: **Numbers 20:1-13**
Song: **"Teach Me Thy Way, O Lord"**

Scripture declares that maturity, experience, and position aren't in themselves sufficient against temptation. Some of the Bible's greatest heroes have sinned after reaching an advanced age. Noah, David, Solomon, and Hezekiah are all prime examples of failing after much success. And the list includes Moses.

When God told Israel's greatest prophet to bring water out of the rock by speaking to it, Moses never even hinted that he would do otherwise. But because he was slandered and provoked by the people, Moses secretly simmered in anger.

Feeling belittled and humiliated by a new generation not half his age, he decided to strike back—literally. Whack! Whack! Two dramatic blows, and water gushed out. But now Moses' career was about to dry up.

The whole sad episode was caused by anger. As James reminds us, "the wrath of man worketh not the righteousness of God" (1:20). All Moses really needed to do was "Speak softly and carry a big stick."

Dear Lord, *help me to be patient and forgiving with others. Remind me that meekness is a virtue that You look for and use. In Jesus' name, amen.*

The Lord Is at Hand

I will walk among you and be your God, and you will be my people (Leviticus 26:12).

Scripture: **Leviticus 26:3-13**
Song: **"O Master, Let Me Walk with Thee"**

Sometimes, life becomes truly hectic. Pressures of family, job, community, and church bear down. You hunger for quiet minutes, maybe with a friend over coffee.

Well, good news. That friend is nearby. Jesus' final instructions to His disciples closed with these words: "Surely I am with you always, to the very end of the age" (Matthew 28:20). You might call that promise the fourth dimension of the great commission.

We know well the first three dimensions. Go and make disciples (recruit new followers of Jesus). Baptize them (identify the new followers as part of Jesus' body, the church). Teach them (instruct new followers to practice Jesus' teachings, day by day). This is the mission statement for Christians in every age, but there is more.

You see, Jesus is no distant taskmaster we must report to someday. He promised to *remain with* His humblest servant, always to encourage and strengthen. And Jesus always keeps His word. So pause often in a quiet corner of your heart. He is there for you.

*Thank You, **Jesus,** for being my constant companion. Teach me to follow You closely and openly share my heart with You. In Your name, amen.*

August 17, 18, 20–23. **Lloyd Mattson** is a retired minister and writer with 15 great-grandchildren. He lives in Duluth, Minnesota.

Priorities in Order

Your strength will be spent in vain, because your soil will not yield its crops, nor will the trees of the land yield their fruit (Leviticus 26:20).

Scripture: **Leviticus 26:14-26**
Song: **"God Will Take Care of You"**

A farmer named Anton Nelson attended the small, country church I served as a seminary student. He was not what you'd call religious, but he was kind, and he always took Sundays off. Hay down, grain ripe, corn ready to pick—it didn't matter. Come Sunday morning, Anton milked his cows then put on his white shirt. Sometimes his family included our young family in Sunday afternoon picnics on the nearby river. We fished with long cane poles.

Meanwhile, my more dedicated churchmen often rode their tractors on summer Sundays, from dawn to dusk. They worried about rain and hail. (Sudden storms can cost a farmer dearly, if grain is ripe and hay is down. The Lord understands, right?)

I talked with Anton about all of this one day. He spoke not a word against the Sunday workers, but smiled quietly. "Sure, I get rained on sometimes, but after farming a long time, I can't see that my neighbors are any better off than me." Anton raised good crops and a fine family. He seemed at peace with himself. He had his priorities right.

Heavenly Father, give me a long-range view. Let me not be tempted to compromise spiritual principles for immediate gain. In Jesus' name, amen.

Bending the Rules

[Samuel said,] "Why did you not obey the Lord?" . . . "But I did obey the Lord," Saul said (1 Samuel 15:19, 20).

Scripture: **1 Samuel 15:17-26**
Song: **"I Surrender All"**

King Saul was absolutely flabbergasted. He'd done what the Lord had asked him to do, and now Samuel was telling him the kingdom would be taken away from him because of his disobedience? Samuel had said to completely destroy the Amalekites and he had—except for their king, Agag. Saul knew that God had commanded him, "Totally destroy everything that belongs to them" (v. 3) and he'd done that—except for the very best sheep and cattle, which he intended to sacrifice to the Lord. Of course, his soldiers had also taken some sheep and cattle, but that was their right of plunder. In Saul's eyes the punishment was much too harsh for the crime of bending the rules a little bit. But God didn't see it that way.

Before we condemn Saul too harshly, we may want to look at our own tendencies to bend the rules to our own advantage. Whether it's speeding so we're not late for church, revealing some (but not all) of our income on a tax return, or lying to make ourselves look better than we are, we are all tempted to adapt the rules to suit ourselves. May God give us hearts to obey His commands to the best of our ability.

O Holy Father, how easy it is to make excuses for ourselves for failing to obey You. Help us to see our sin for what it truly is: an act of rebellion. Give us the strength and desire to do it Your way today. In Jesus' name, amen.

August 19. **Cheryl J. Frey** runs an editorial services out of her home in Rochester, New York. She spends her spare time with family—especially her grandchildren.

Harmony in the Trinity

The Father loves the Son and has placed everything in his hands (John 3:35).

Scripture: **John 3:31-36**
Song: **"The Family of God"**

A godly friend from a church other than mine worries about me. According to him, I neglect the Holy Spirit. He fears my grasp of biblical truth and style of worship fall short. My friend knows I love Jesus, but he says that's not enough.

I respect his faith and worship, but I am content with mine. I gently remind my friend that the Godhead knows no jealously. No one can honor the Father and Son yet grieve the Holy Spirit.

We can't fully grasp the mystery of the Trinity—Father, Son and Holy Spirit—three in one. Nor can we know the full meaning of the Incarnation—Jesus, true God and true man. Faith begins where human knowledge ends, so we thank the Father for sending His Son to redeem us, and we thank the blessed Holy Spirit for drawing us to the Son. When we worship one, we worship all.

Why should varying perceptions of the unfathomable truths divide us? As brothers and sisters in Christ, we serve together in the kingdom of God's infinite grace.

*Thank You, **Father Almighty**, for the rich variety of Christian thought that broadens the gospel outreach. Bless each church fellowship in my community that honors Your Son, my Savior. In the name of the Father, the Son, and the Holy Spirit, I pray. Amen.*

How's Your Appetite?

You would be fed with the finest of wheat; with honey from the rock I would satisfy you (Psalm 81:16).

Scripture: **Psalm 81:11-16**
Song: **"My Heart Is Yearning Ever"**

The finest banquet I ever ate was Spam baked with cloves and brown sugar, a generous serving of macaroni (lightly browned), and a tall glass of cold milk. I have often eaten more exotic fare, but that dinner was memorable . . . because I was *so hungry.*

I was on a walking kick. One hundred miles a month. And each week or so I would fast for 36 hours. I never felt better or enjoyed greater vigor. The weight loss was welcome, but I did it mainly for fun. I simply loved walking.

On that "banquet morning" I set out for Lakewood School, about three miles away, I figured. But I figured wrong. The distance was five miles. No problem. I'd phone Elsie. But the school was closed. Elsie's golf course was only three miles away. Likely she'd be there. But she wasn't. I phoned from the club house for a ride and heard my beloved say, "Hurry home. Lunch is about ready—baked Spam and macaroni." But I still had another mile to walk!

When you have a heart-deep appetite for God, the simplest gospel fare is honey from the Rock. What is your appetite for Him these days?

O God, help me listen closely to my heart this day. What will it tell me of my hunger for You? In Christ's name I pray. Amen.

No Quick Study!

The Lord **gives wisdom, and from his mouth come knowledge and understanding** (Proverbs 2:6).

Scripture: **Proverbs 2:1-11**
Song: **"Lord, Speak to Me"**

For several years my work called for writing books and articles on Christian camping. I was humbled one day to meet an adult Asian student who shook my hand warmly and said, "You are my guru." My philosophy and ideas on camping had resonated with him. He asked me to read his thesis. I did and heard familiar echoes.

My ideas, of course, came from others. Truly original thinkers are rare. I gleaned concepts from my own "gurus," which I digested, reshaped, and blended into my own writings. My Asian friend had shaped my second-hand ideas to fit his culture.

Another generation will probably find my borrowed wisdom obsolete, but God's wisdom remains timeless. And here is one place to find it: We turn too seldom to the early church fathers (Irenaeus, Polycarp, Augustine, and the others), who spent their lifetimes pouring over God's Word and defending the faith. They wrestled with many of the ideas that challenge Bible students today. We can learn from, and build on, their findings.

God's wisdom really doesn't lend itself to quick sound bites. Let us be ready to work hard at understanding.

Lord God in Heaven, speak to my heart of Your timeless wisdom. And let me be still long enough to hear! In Jesus' name I pray. Amen.

What's on Your Mind?

Talk about them when you sit at home and when you walk along the road, when you lie down and when you get up (Deuteronomy 6:7).

Scripture: **Deuteronomy 6:1-9, 20-24**
Song: **"Thy Word Have I Hid in My Heart"**

Where does your mind go when it's free? A member of a board I led could rarely get through a meeting without slipping away to check the stock market. He was a banker, and his subconscious continually scanned the ticker tape.

Ask a group of teens what is most on their minds. The boys will probably shout *Girls!* The girls will say *Boys.* Dating is big among adolescents.

In younger years I was given to trout fishing. The moment my mind was free, it wandered to a stream and calculated where to lay the fly.

Banking, dating, and fly fishing are worthy enough, but wouldn't it be great if a sense of God's presence became the background music of our soul? The blessed man of Psalm 1 knew about that: "On his law he meditates day and night."

Why not turn random thinking into conversation with God, rather than just a dialogue with yourself? Talk about ordinary things. Ask the Lord to help you plan your day, drive safely, and use your words wisely.

God, fill me with thoughts of You today. Let my every thought become prayer. And when things go wrong, help me to let You in on my problems, trusting Your wisdom for the way through. In Jesus' name, amen.

Joy at Lake Tahoe

He spread out a cloud as a covering, and a fire to give light at night (Psalm 105:39).

Scripture: **Psalm 105:37-45**
Song: **"God Is Working His Purpose Out"**

My wife, Juanita, and I were camping above Lake Tahoe in northern California. We'd just driven from Chicago, loaded down with everything we owned. We had no job, no place to stay. My anxiety was growing. What in the world were we going to do?

This must have been how the Israelites felt when they left Egypt and camped in the wilderness, loaded down with their silver and gold. What in the world were they going to do? They shouldn't have worried. As He had promised, God was with them—in the cloud, in the fire, in the bread and quail, and in water from the rock.

That night at Lake Tahoe, I remembered some Christian friends who lived near San Francisco. I hadn't seen them for 10 years. So what made me think of them? I have no doubt that God brought them to my mind. Through this miracle, He kept His promise to care for us. I called my friends the next morning from a pay phone. "Sure, you can stay with us," they responded. "Our home is your home."

Dear Father, *I praise Your faithfulness and constant presence. You always think about where I am and where I'm going. In Christ's name, amen.*

August 24–30. **Larry Brook** grew up in Cameroun, Africa, the son of missionaries. He is a tenor soloist with the Elgin Opera Company in Illinois.

Without a Doubt?

When they saw him, they worshiped him; but some doubted (Matthew 28:17).

Scripture: **Matthew 28:16-20**
Song: **"I Need Thee Every Hour"**

A few weeks after my wife and I moved to California, we rented a small apartment near Berkeley. Juanita found a part-time job in a fabric shop, but I was still looking for work. Then we faced a real crisis. I developed a blood clot in my leg and was consigned to complete bed rest. The days passed, and the bills kept coming. I sat in the room feeling bleak and hopeless. To be honest, I was filled with doubt.

There were people in Jesus' day who doubted. But how could they? I honestly don't know. (But then, look who's talking—how could *I* doubt?)

I've come to think that belief and doubt live side by side in all of our hearts. Jesus must have known this. I picture Him making bold eye contact with the doubters and saying, "I will be with *you* always."

A few days later, as I was trying to pray on my bed, I sensed Christ's presence in a special way. It was as if He were in my face, saying "I will be with *you*." In that moment, I was filled with gratitude. How little room for doubt there was then!

Dear Lord of my life, I believe in You. Please help my unbelief, as I thank You for the confidence You are building in my heart. Trusting in Your name, Christ Jesus, I pray. Amen.

God *Is* Great!

You are a forgiving God, gracious and compassionate, slow to anger and abounding in love (Nehemiah 9:17).

Scripture: **Nehemiah 9:16-20**
Song: **"How Great Thou Art"**

British writer Christopher Hitchens has come out with a new book titled, *God Is Not Great.* Right now it's in the top ten of the *New York Times* best-seller list. I heard Hitchens recently on the radio scolding a Baptist preacher who had called in to share his faith. The preacher said he and many others had been witness to the miraculous healing of his daughter—after much prayer.

Hitchens' reply? "How can you be so egotistical to believe that there is a God who cares about you and responds to your personal needs? You are deluding the public with false hopes, and you ought to be ashamed of yourself." What I wonder is why there are so many people who want to buy Hitchens' book and read about how indifferent—and *not* great—God is.

It makes me appreciate so much more Nehemiah's solid telling of the truth. Despite the refusal of the Israelites to "listen" and to "remember," despite their "rebellion," that God, in fact, was great. He was "forgiving" and "compassionate," "slow to anger," and "abounding in love."

He still is all these things, Christopher Hitchens, no matter what you say.

O God, I say this with complete joy and confidence—You are great! Thank You for Your love and care. In Jesus' name, amen.

Rebel Behind the Stove

Fear the LORD **and serve him with all faithfulness. Throw away the gods your forefathers worshiped beyond the River and in Egypt, and serve the** LORD (Joshua 24:14).

Scripture: **Joshua 24:14-24**
Song: **"And Can It Be That I Should Gain?"**

Dr. Walter Wilson, medical doctor and evangelist, once preached in a small country church that was heated by a wood stove at the back. During each service, a young man named Everett sat hidden behind the stove to listen to the sermon. Everett was "rough, ungodly, and given to wicked practices." But though he showed up for each sermon, he never stayed to talk. Instead, he bolted out the door.

Joshua, like Dr. Wilson, also knew the hearts of his listeners. He knew the people of Israel were disobedient. He challenged them to choose to serve the Lord and throw away the false gods of the Amorites. The people responded in faith: "We too will serve the Lord, because he is our God" (v. 18).

One evening, Dr. Wilson arrived at the little church to find Everett on the front step reading "the largest Bible I have ever seen." Everett explained that during the night he had chosen to serve Christ. "I have this big Bible," he said, "because I want everybody to know that Everett has been converted and loves the Bible."

Thank You, **God,** *for continuing to call people today to fear You and serve You in faithfulness. May I demonstrate Everett's commitment to openly share Your love. In Jesus' name I pray. Amen.*

Fish Faith

Who is it that overcomes the world? Only he who believes that Jesus is the Son of God (1 John 5:5).

Scripture: 1 John 5:1-5
Song: "Turn Your Eyes Upon Jesus"

When I was in Cambodia leading a Christian writers workshop, a young man told me his amazing story.

During the time of Pol Pot and "the killing fields" of the communist Khmer Rouge army, the young man's guards forced him to go down to the river and catch them a fish for dinner. They said that if he failed, they would cut his head off. The young man knew that his time had come, because the river was swift, and he had nothing with which to catch a fish.

Nevertheless, when he reached the river bank, he prayed, "Jesus, I know You are with me, and I release myself into Your hands." At that moment, he heard a thrashing sound beside the trail. He looked down and found the largest fish he had ever seen.

In a time of terror and massacre, my young Christian Cambodian friend had simply taken the apostle John's words to heart. He believed that only those who believe in Jesus and obey God's commands will "overcome the world." Could this be true for us, too, as we face the challenges of today?

Dear Lord, I probably won't find a fish thrashing in the back yard, but I pray for the faith to believe that with Christ, I can face any fear or conflict— or danger—that I encounter this day. Thanks be to God in Christ! Amen.

Identified with the Agony

The Lord is my rock, my fortress and my deliverer (Psalm 18:2).

Scripture: **Psalm 18:1-6**
Song: **"Rock of Ages"**

In the mining village of Aberfan, South Wales, a million tons of man-made coal slag turned into an avalanche. Heavy rains cause the slag to plow over cottages, homes, and Pantglas Junior High School. Over 160 bodies were recovered from the rubble, most of them children.

A survey taken in a nearby town asked the people if they believed God still cared for them. One person wrote, "No, not after the Welsh disaster."

Given such events, what are we to make of the psalmist's confidence that the Lord was a fortress and deliverer? Maybe the Lord was the psalmist's deliverer, we are tempted to say, but He sure wasn't for those 11-year-olds under the tons of coal slag!

Our only comfort is in believing, like the psalmist, that our confidence in God cannot be superficial. We are compelled to believe that, somehow, He hears our cries even amidst terrible suffering.

During the Aberfan disaster, one local minister, who had lost his son, declared, "We found Christ in our distress. Christ was identified with the agony . . . with those who wept."

Father, I love You. You are my strength, my rock in whom I take refuge, especially when destruction overwhelms me. Through Christ, amen.

Obey—and Live!

The LORD **will again delight in you . . . if you obey the** LORD **your God** (Deuteronomy 30:9, 10).

Scripture: **Deuteronomy 30:1-10**
Song: **"Here I Am, Lord"**

German philosopher Friedrich Nietzsche didn't think much of obedience. "If you are too weak to give yourselves your own law," he declared, "then a tyrant shall lay his yoke upon you and say: Obey! Clench your teeth and obey!"

Contrast this defiance to Mother Teresa's calming words: "If I belong to Christ, then He must be able to use me. That is obedience. Then we give wholehearted help to the poor. That is service. They complete each other. That is our life."

Why do we struggle with obedience? Especially when God promises to "delight" in us if we obey Him? (What greater reward for obedience could there be?) God further tells the people of Israel: "When you and your children return to the Lord your God and obey him with all your heart and with all your soul . . . then the Lord your God will . . . have compassion on you and gather you again from all the nations where he scattered you."

To obey God is to come home—to become fulfilled in ways we can only imagine. Mother Teresa understood this. Can we?

God, grant me the wisdom to see that obedience to You in no way stifles me, but rather brings terrific fulfillment and freedom. In Christ Jesus, amen.

Sweet Substitue

[Christ Jesus] who gave himself a ransom for all, to be testified in due time (1 Timothy 1:6).

Scripture: **1 Timothy 2:1-6**
Song: **"Nothing But the Blood"**

Years ago I attended a retreat for ministers. What an interesting group! The fellowship was awesome, and the discussions wide-ranging, to say the least. In fact, these ministers came from various denominations, spanning the spectrum of theological beliefs. That made things quite *interesting*. The sad part, which sticks so firmly in my mind, was a particiular sermon delivered one evening. The theme was "why we can't believe in substitutionary atonement."

Substitutionary atonement. I know those are big words, but they refer to Paul's words to Timothy in our Scripture today. It's the fact that Jesus, on the cross, acted as a *ransom* for sin. There's just no way around it. Christ, as the substitute ransom for sinners, dying in our place, is clearly proclaimed in myriad Bible passages. I remain amazed, to this day, that anyone could preach otherwise.

Hold tight to this glorious truth. If we had to pay the price of our sins, we could never erase the debt. But our ransom—our sweet substitute—paid the price for us.

Dear Lord, I am so thankful that salvation is a free gift of Your grace. Remind, me though, that it was not cheap. Jesus paid it's price in precious drops of His saving blood. In His name I pray. Amen.

Gary Allen lives with his wife, Carol, and Yorkshire terrier, Robbie Burns, in Moultrie, Georgia. He is acquisitions editor for *Devotions®*.

DEVOTIONS®

*L*ift up holy hands in prayer.

—1 Timothy 2:8

SEPTEMBER

Photo © iStock

Gary Allen, Editor

Come Up Higher

The LORD said to Moses, "Come up to Me on the mountain . . . that you may teach them" (Exodus 24:12, *New King James Version*).

Scripture: **Exodus 24:12-18**
Song: **"I Am Thine, O Lord"**

I agonized over some of my adult children's apparent indifference to spiritual things. They didn't attend church and rarely spoke with me of their faith. When I wrote letters and tried to begin a conversation along these lines, I received no response. "O, Lord," I prayed, "please bring my children into a deeper relationship with You!" I wanted them to have the joy and peace of salvation through Christ. I wanted it so much—and worried about it so much—that I lost my own joy and peace for a time.

Then one day, it was as if the Lord were saying to me, "You come closer to me. Intimacy with me is an individual thing. Each one must come alone."

Moses had to leave behind all the people for whom he was responsible. The 70 elders could go only part way with him up the mountain to God. In obedience, Moses went up to God in the fearful place of intimacy. Then God gave him the Commandments—and all the people saw the glory of God.

*Thank You, **Father,** for inviting me to know You. Please help my children to want this relationship as well. I pray in Jesus' name. Amen.*

September 1–6. **Judith Vander Wege** is a nurse and songwriter with 18 grandchildren. She and her husband, Paul, also have a music ministry in Oskaloosa, Iowa.

Any Envy Here?

Moses replied, "Are you jealous for my sake? I only wish . . . that the Lord would put his Spirit upon them all!" (Numbers 11:29, *The Living Bible*).

Scripture: **Numbers 11:24-29**
Song: **"Spirit of God, Descend upon My Heart"**

Do you ever feel jealous when others seem "more full of the Holy Spirit" than you? When I experienced a certain dryness of spirit due to grief and disappointment, I sometimes resented the bubbly joy of some other Christians. Was my own relationship with Christ lacking—and therefore I envied those who seemed to have this intimacy?

Moses reacted differently. He'd been having a hard time, overwhelmed with caring for so many complaining people, so he talked to the Lord about it. The Lord put His Spirit upon the 70 who had been chosen as elders. And Moses was close enough with God to know that envy was inappropriate. God had given these leaders His Spirit for Moses' benefit.

Moses wanted everyone to have the gift of the Holy Spirit. This wouldn't diminish his own ministry but enhance it. Similarly, love, when spread amidst a family or congregation, enhances each individual's love. Can we view God's gifts that way? What He gives to one member in the church will surely benefit the whole body of Christ.

Lord, thank You for Your indwelling Spirit within every believer. Help me to encourage His work in each and every one of us. In Jesus' name, amen.

Trust His Love

The Lord's anger was hot against them . . . for they had refused to do what he wanted them to (Numbers 32:10, 11, *The Living Bible*).

Scripture: **Numbers 32:6-13**
Song: **"Think About His Love"**

How is it for God when His beloved children fear to follow Him? Imagine a father who wants to surprise his child with a trip to an ice cream parlor, or take him to work to see what he does, or show him a train museum or a baseball game. What would you think if the child was afraid to go with Dad? The child must not trust the father, right?

It's true that some human fathers aren't worthy of trust. But God is love, and He is always trustworthy.

Moses thought the tribes who wanted to settle on the east of the Jordan River were afraid to go into Canaan, just as their fathers were. He discovered he'd misunderstood them. They were willing to go in and fight, but they wanted to go back and settle on the other side.

I sometimes wonder about my own willingness to "fight" for my spiritual inheritance—and help others pursue theirs. Salvation comes to us by God's grace alone. But then, following the Lord in discipleship often includes fighting some serious internal battles for obedience.

Father, forgive me for the times I've been afraid to go forward in faith. Give me strength to forge ahead, in Your strength, past every obstacle. And may the "sword of the Spirit" be my best weapon! In Christ I pray. Amen.

After Moses, Who?

May the LORD . . . appoint a man . . . who will lead them out and bring them in, so the LORD's people will not be like sheep without a shepherd (Numbers 27:16, 17).

Scripture: **Numbers 27:15-23**
Song: **"At Calvary"**

I once received bad news—and instantly knew that it was a consequence of my own sin. Thankfully, this incident actually strengthened my faith in God. You see, I began to realize that if God disciplines when we do wrong, then He also keeps His promise to bless us as we obey Him. I became more and more grateful for God's constant mercy.

Moses couldn't enter the promised land because he hadn't obeyed God. But Moses' final prayers weren't filled with arguments and excuses. He asked that God appoint a good leader to take his place. He wanted the people to succeed, even if he himself couldn't reap the rewards. So Joshua, son of Nun, lead the people. And, in His mercy, God showed Moses the land before he died.

May we, like Moses, enjoy such an intimate relationship with God. Then we'll go beyond merely trusting His decisions. We'll also take up a heartfelt desire that God's work be completed—whether by us or someone else.

Lord, thank You for forgiveness and mercy. I don't want to rebel against You ever again. Thank You for being my shepherd—and for the privilege of participating in Your work. Please continue to complete the good work You've begun in me. In the name of Jesus, my Savior, I pray. Amen.

Here's My Plan

Then Moses climbed . . . to Pisgah Peak . . . And the Lord pointed out to him the Promised Land (Deuteronomy 34:1, *The Living Bible*).

Scripture: **Deuteronomy 34:1-9**
Song: **"Sweet Hour of Prayer"**

An ancient philosopher, Mencius, once said: "Friendship is one mind in two bodies." I like that. And, by this definition, it seems to me that Moses was a "close friend" with God. God even showed Moses how the divine plans would unfold for the people of God. Yes, God was eager for Moses to see what He planned to give Israel, so He showed it to him from the mountain. What a tender scene amidst a profound friendship! And how disappointing that God's friend couldn't go into the promised land after all.

According to Bible scholar F. B. Meyers, Moses represents God's law, which "cannot lead the soul into the rest of God, nor give victory over our spiritual foes." Joshua, who completed Moses' job, represents Jesus, who completed the work of salvation for the world. When we accept what Jesus did for us, we come into a personal friendship with Almighty God.

The closer we grow to the Lord, the more the Scriptures come alive to us. Then we, too, begin to know the promises and plans He has for our lives.

Father, I love You and enjoy my relationship with You. Lead me, day by day, into Your plans—and empower me to follow. Through Christ, amen.

Lead My People

Be strong and of good courage; for you shall cause this people to inherit the land which I swore to their fathers to give them (Joshua 1:6, *Revised Standard Version*).

Scripture: **Joshua 1:1-11, 16, 17**
Song: **"He Giveth More Grace"**

For many years now I've had a plaque on my wall that says, "The will of God will never lead you where the grace of God cannot keep you." Do you believe it?

It was certainly true in Joshua's case. God told this valiant military man that he'd lead the Israelites into their inheritance if he would simply step forward with obedience and courage.

That is how I want to live each day. And I'm also claiming this verse for my loved ones. As I seek to obey God, I believe He will use me as His instrument to bring my loved ones into their own "inheritance," which is a close relationship with Him.

The great Christian apologist G. K. Chesterton once said: "Courage is almost a contradiction in terms: it means a strong desire to live taking the form of readiness to die." Though not every courageous decision is a matter of life and death, our commitment to God may well lead us to such a decision some day. Let us prepare ourselves for that possibility by saying "yes" to God's will within each moment of our daily routines.

Heavenly Father, lead me wherever You wish and use me as Your instrument to bring blessing to others' lives. In Jesus name I pray, amen.

We Are All Pencils

Brothers, think of what you were when you were called. Not many of you were wise by human standards; not many were influential; not many were of noble birth (1 Corinthians 1:26).

Scripture: **1 Corinthians 1:26-31**
Song: **"Make Me a Channel of Blessing"**

Mother Teresa said, "I am a little pencil in the hand of a writing God who is sending love letters to the world." During her life, she allowed God to sharpen her and write His love letter through her.

She was one of many ordinary young women when she went to India. She saw suffering people there and chose to help. She cared for street children and lived among the poor and sick. Her surprising willingness to give herself to those who were shunned impressed and stirred others, who began following her example. Soon she had many volunteers, along with financial support.

Mother Teresa died in September 1997, but her legacy continues. She taught us that one does not need to be a ruler or have access to riches and great talent to do great things for God.

The Lord is sending His love letters to the world, using His people to write them—whether they go somewhere far away or just next door.

O God, thank You for using ordinary people to "write" Your message of love. Remind me that I am a pencil in Your hands. In Jesus' name, amen.

September 7–13. **Mary Rediger** lives with her husband near the beautiful Rocky Mountains in Colorado Springs. She enjoys music, calligraphy, and literature.

Crying Out

Midian so impoverished the Israelites that they cried out to the LORD for help (Judges 6:6).

Scripture: **Judges 6:4-10**
Song: **"I've Got Peace Like a River"**

On September 8, 1900, Galveston, Texas, made history when it was hit by a massive hurricane. The terrible storm killed at least 6,000 people on Galveston Island, more than any other hurricane to hit American shores. The day after was a Sunday, and early that morning church bells rang, calling people to worship. Many turned to the Lord, crying out to Him for help.

Government officials immediately met to plan relief efforts, and the local newspaper, *The Galveston Daily News*, never missed an issue. Prayers were answered when Clara Barton and the Red Cross went to work in the devastated town. They built an orphanage, provided lumber to help rebuild houses, and raised much money.

The townspeople decided to rebuild their city, and soon water, telephone, and public transportation systems were up and running. The town was indeed rebuilt, but on higher ground, with an added seawall for protection.

In times of trial and tribulation, many of us cry out to the Lord. As well we should! For whatever situation we may face, He hears and is our ultimate source of help.

Father God, please help me turn to You in every trying circumstance. I know that You love me, listen to me, and long to remind me that You are with me always. I pray through my deliverer, Jesus. Amen.

The God Who Speaks

The angel of God said to him, "Take the meat and the unleavened bread, place them on this rock, and pour out the broth." And Gideon did so (Judges 6:20).

Scripture: **Judges 6:14-24**
Song: **"How Great Thou Art"**

I am unceasingly amazed at the ways God speaks to His people. I've always loved palm trees and enjoy watching their fronds wave in the wind. One brilliant day, I sat watching palms sway to and fro and recalled how people used palm branches to welcome and praise Jesus as He rode through town on a donkey. Since that day, seeing a palm tree stirs within me a desire to praise my creator.

The Lord used an ordinary tree to prompt me to worship. And He continues to use His creation to speak to His people. Throughout history, God has spoken, sometimes with an audible voice, or through angels, dreams, and—finally—through His incarnate Son, Jesus.

Like many patriarchs of old, Gideon received direct revelation from the Lord. You see, our spiritual ancestors of those days didn't have the Bible at hand as we do. Nor did they have the constant indwelling of the Holy Spirit who came at Pentecost. Since we Christians do have these aspects of revelation, the Lord usually speaks simply to us—quietly, in our intuition—to remind us He is Lord.

Creator God, please open my ears to hear what You are saying and open my eyes to see what You are doing. And I ask that Your will be done in my life each day, as I seek You. In Christ's holy name I pray. Amen.

Me Too!

Gideon took ten of his servants and did as the LORD told him. But because he was afraid of his family and the men of the town, he did it at night rather than in the daytime (Judges 6:27).

Scripture: **Judges 6:25-27**
Song: **"Be Strong and Take Courage"**

I vividly remember waiting for my high school art class to begin, when some other students nearby began speculating about what happens when someone dies. I was surprised at how easily I was able to enter into the conversation, explaining what Christians believe. Two of the students were listening intently and asking questions.

I saw the teacher walk into the room and was well aware of the controversial nature of our conversation in a public school. Knowing that class would begin and other students were listening, I hurriedly said that I would be happy to explain how one becomes a Christian. Then I whispered: "Would either of you like to know more?" Both said "Yes," and we decided to meet after school.

Even though my obedience was fearful and hurried, the Lord used an hour in art class for something more wonderful than I could have imagined. Yes, God uses fearful, imperfect people to carry out His will. He used Gideon that way—and me too!

Loving God, *thank You for using me for Your glory, even when I am afraid. Each day, give me the strength and courage to do what You have called me to do. In the name of Jesus, Lord and Savior of all, I pray. Amen.*

Mighty God

The LORD said to Gideon, "With the three hundred men that lapped I will save you and give the Midianites into your hands. Let all the other men go, each to his own place" (Judges 7:7).

Scripture: **Judges 7:2-8**
Song: **"What a Mighty God We Serve"**

In the movie *Chariots of Fire*, Scottish missionary and Olympic runner Eric Liddell said, "If you commit yourself to the love of Christ, then that is how you run a straight race." He committed himself and his ways to the Lord, desiring to please God above all else. One way he did this was to strictly observe each Sunday as a day of rest; he would not run on the first day of the week.

Many people thought this was foolish, that he would never be a winning runner because he didn't train enough. Against the odds, Eric ran and won the 400-meter race in the 1924 Olympics. Ultimately, the Lord received the honor for this win.

Eric understood that God would be glorified through his running. For him, the most important thing was to love God and obey Him. God is more than able to work marvelously through our circumstances, even when it seems there isn't much hope. But let us rely on His strength rather than our own. When our goal is to glorify Him, it's amazing what can be accomplished.

Mighty Lord of All, *You are worthy of all glory, honor, and praise. Thank You for being my strength in all situations. In Jesus' name, amen.*

What's in Your Hands?

Get up! The LORD has given the Midianite camp into your hands (Judges 7:15).

Scripture: **Judges 7:9-15**
Song: **"Take My Life and Let It Be"**

Growing up, I often visited an elderly widow named Marian Paakala. She lived a few miles from me and always welcomed company. She kept busy sewing but was never too busy to sit and talk, especially about the Lord.

One day she heard about some orphanages in Eastern Europe. These places had little money. They didn't even have enough blankets to keep the children warm during winter. So Marian decided to put her sewing skills to use for a good cause.

She joined with other ladies to collect scraps of fabric and stuffing. Working long hours together, they sewed 700 quilts per year! They packed the blankets in containers and sent them with clothing, medical supplies, and other necessities to the struggling orphanages.

Marian received many letters with photos of children holding the blankets she'd made. She proudly showed the pictures and letters to me when I would visit with her.

What an encouragement to me! I can't sew very well. But I know the Lord has placed other gifts and talents in my hands that I can use to encourage, bless, and inspire.

Gracious God, thank You for all the opportunities to be a blessing to others. Help me see how to use the abilities You have placed in my hands. I ask that You will use my life to inspire others. In Jesus' name, amen.

The Main Thing

When the angel of the LORD appeared to Gideon, he said, "The LORD is with you, mighty warrior" (Judges 6:12).

Scripture: **Judges 6:1-3, 7-16**
Song: **"Lord, Be Glorified"**

Stephen Covey said, "The main thing is to keep the main thing the main thing." (But sometimes just remembering what the main thing is can be challenging, right?)

At home, I begin to cook. I notice the counters are messy, so I stop to clean them. While putting the cleaning rag into the hamper, I realize there are clothes to wash, so I begin doing the laundry. Around this time I begin to smell slightly burned food—so I quickly refocus on cooking!

At work, I write down the details of a project. Then I receive a phone call and begin faxing information to the person on the line. More requests come, and I fulfill them. I stop to talk with a person and then . . . finally . . . stare at the notes I just wrote. *Now, what was I working on?*

Gideon needed to remember this main thing: God was with him, making him a valiant warrior. Have you too found how easy it is to be distracted? Yet I am thankful: During almost every day, God reminds me again and again of His loving presence. How I want that to be the main thing—above everything else that calls for attention!

O God, You are the most important one in my life. Help me keep my focus on Your goodness and grace. I pray that You will give me the right perspective and keep my mind from wandering. I also pray for the courage to tell others just how wonderful You are. Through Christ, my Lord. Amen.

The Weight of Shame

Blessed is he whose transgressions are forgiven, whose sins are covered (Psalm 32:1).

Scripture: **Psalm 32:1-5**
Song: **"From East to West, from Shore to Shore"**

"Child, what's troubling you?" my mother asked. I hung my head in shame, but I said nothing. At dinner, I ate poorly, stricken with guilt over my childish transgression. As we finished our meal, Mother said, "Tonight we're going to have 'Confession Time.' I'll go first." She proceeded to confess her rudeness to an inept cashier that day. My brother followed with his own admissions.

Their confessions freed me to confess my own sin. I felt a great weight lifted as I received the loving forgiveness of my family. As with David, acknowledging my sin removed the burden I was feeling.

Whether our sins are public or private, our consciences prompt us to confession. Perhaps we must confess to the person we offended—as well as to God—in order for our spirits to be lifted. If it's a private sin, confessing to our heavenly Father brings welcome relief. But when we confess our sins, we too must release them, remembering only enough to keep us from repeating them!

Heavenly Father, prompt me to recognize my guilt. Then help me to confess to You and to those I have wronged. May my confessions lift the load of guilt through the blessedness of forgiveness. In Jesus' name, amen.

September 14–20. **Lanita Bradley Boyd** is a freelance writer in Fort Thomas, Kentucky. Her writing springs from years of teaching, traveling, ministering.

A Lineage of Faithfulness

This Ezra came up from Babylon. He was a teacher well versed in the Law of Moses, which the LORD, the God of Israel, had given. The king had granted him everything he asked, for the hand of the LORD his God was on him (Ezra 7:6).

Scripture: **Ezra 7:1-6**
Song: **"Faith of Our Fathers"**

As a little girl, I loved to perform. One toddler accomplishment that my doting grandparents loved was when I stood on a stool and recited: "I stood upon the stage. My heart went a-pitty-pat. I thought I heard somebody say, 'Whose pretty little girl is that?'"

They loved to claim me as their girl, and I enjoyed identifying myself as "Lawrence Bradley's daughter" or "Luther Ralph's granddaughter." And by connecting myself to my parents or grandparents, I was also affirming my spiritual heritage; they were known for their faithful Christian lives.

Ezra's lineage was that of chosen priests of God, all the way back to Aaron. No doubt the Law was a common source of discussion and learning in his priestly family. Similarly, let us guide our families so that our descendants can acknowledge their heritage in the Lord. When we are well versed in the Scriptures and live them daily, others will see that the hand of the Lord is upon us.

Father in Heaven, help me to be a parent who guides my children in Your paths. Thank You for the faithful family members who have preceded me and taught me Your ways. In the name of Your Son I pray. Amen.

Live What You Learn

Ezra had devoted himself to the study and observance of the Law of the LORD, and to teaching its decrees and laws in Israel (Ezra 7:10).

Scripture: **Ezra 7:7-10**
Song: **"How Shall the Young Secure Their Hearts?"**

I know a boy who loved the game of baseball and hoped some day to play professionally. He studied great baseball players and absorbed the rules and nuances of the game. But he found that practicing and studying the game does not necessarily produce an exceptional player. He was adequate in Little League play, but his diligence could not make up for lack of natural talent.

He also accepted Christ at an early age and devoted himself to studying the Scriptures, applying them to his life. Since his early teen years, he has kept notebooks of "spiritual thoughts" based on his daily Bible study. And as an adult, he continues to add to his scriptural knowledge, always attempting to live what he learns.

Thankfully, success in knowing Scripture and serving Christ doesn't depend on *natural* talent. Daily communication with God through prayer and Bible study can put us in the company of Ezra, for it is the Holy Spirit who leads us to greatness in these things. As we devote ourselves to the Christ, we *supernaturally* grow to be more and more like Him.

Father, thank You for Your grace that allows me to grow in love and holiness. May all I do and say bring glory to You. In Jesus' name, amen.

The Heart of Authority

Praise be to the LORD, the God of our fathers, who has put it into the king's heart to bring honor to the house of the LORD in Jerusalem in this way (Ezra 7:27).

Scripture: **Ezra 7:25-28**
Song: **"A Safe Stronghold Our God Is Still"**

In the 1960s, Romanian citizen John Stanescu was arrested for daring to preach the gospel. Russian Colonel Albon, furious at Stanescu's declarations of faith, began to beat him. At that point, from elsewhere, a high-ranking Communist general summoned Albon.

Not only did that save Stanescu's life, but—typical in Russia at that time—Albon was thrown into prison with those he'd arrested. Stanescu, truly Christlike, defended Albon against the prisoners who attacked him.

God can use anyone to achieve His will. Just as Artaxerxes granted to Ezra everything that he requested for the house of the Lord in Jerusalem, so can people in authority today be used by God for His purposes.

It is our responsibility as followers of Christ to pray for those in authority and to recognize that God can work through them. Whether our leaders are active believers or not, we can be sure that God is in control. He can work through our political leaders, just as he did for Stanescu and for Ezra.

Almighty God, guide our country's leaders, whatever their beliefs. Help me to uphold them in prayer, since it is only by Your permission that they have any power at all. In the holy name of Jesus I pray. Amen.

A Safe Journey

There, by the Ahava Canal, I proclaimed a fast, so that we might humble ourselves before our God and ask him for a safe journey for us and our children (Ezra 8:21).

Scripture: **Ezra 8:21-23**
Song: **"Did You Think to Pray?"**

Our daughter's fiancé said he had to leave soon for his airline flight, but he lingered as we prepared dinner. As we urged him to stay and eat, he kept saying he had to be on his way. And yet he lingered.

Finally I understood. He'd been with our family enough that he knew we always prayed together before anyone left on a trip. "Let's pray together so Stephen can be on his way," I said. And the moment the prayer was over, off he went.

Our children and their companions may be more aware of our family habits than we are. With some families, arguing may be expected; with others, praying is the norm. One of the most "complimentary complaints" I ever heard about a man was that he was "so slow to decide anything because he has to pray about it first."

What are some of your family's habits? Do you lead your children to pray in every circumstance? That is a habit that will come back to you in many blessings.

Great and powerful God, please protect me on my journeys, both physical and spiritual. Help me to turn to You in prayer at every opportunity, encouraging my family members to do the same. I pray this prayer in the name of Jesus, my merciful Savior and Lord. Amen.

Emotion? OK!

"This day is sacred to the LORD your God. Do not mourn or weep." For all the people had been weeping as they listened to the words of the Law (Nehemiah 8:9).

Scripture: **Nehemiah 8:1-12**
Song: **"My Eyes Are Dry"**

Our friends assembled in the living room to hear Kate Campbell play and sing songs she'd written. Some were fun; many were spiritual. As she sang "Ten Thousand Lures," about how the devil lures us into doing wrong, I happened to notice Pete, a sturdy, middle-aged outdoorsman. I was touched to see tears streaming down his face just as Kate ended with "Three rusty nails, that's the cure, for ten thousand lures."

God's people wept upon hearing the words of the Law. And it was the appropriate response.

Why should we repress our feelings in similar situations? I may well weep as I read, "It is finished" (John 19:30). And my heart will surely ache when I read David's deep pleading: "Create in me a pure heart, O God, and renew a steadfast spirit within me" (Psalm 51:10).

Are your eyes moist when you say "The Lord has done great things for [me], and [I am] filled with joy" (see Psalm 126:3)? Our God is a *person*; that is, He has intellect, emotions, and will. We are persons too.

Dear Father, I know You love me deeply. Help me to absorb Your Word in my life so that it will naturally come out in my words and actions, affecting not only my mind but my will and emotions too. In Jesus' name, amen.

A Little Relief

But now, for a brief moment, the LORD our God has been gracious in leaving us a remnant and giving us a firm place in his sanctuary, and so our God gives light to our eyes and a little relief in our bondage (Ezra 9:8).

Scripture: **Ezra 9:5-11, 15**
Song: **"Burdens Are Lifted at Calvary"**

My Aunt Juanita has always loved the outdoors; she could still hike several miles a day when she was 80. Now, however, she stays indoors to care for her ailing husband. So when her daughter offered to take her on a little road trip to Georgia's beautiful Callaway Gardens in Georgia, she was delighted. The lovely landscape and flowering plants offered peaceful respite from her caregiver duties. She enjoyed "a little relief from her bondage."

Just as God saw the plight of the Israelites and gave them some relief, so we can help others in like manner. The "bondage" of a caregiver is different from slavery, but the feeling of relief when help comes is similar. Sometimes a person's bondage can be a time-consuming job, or overwhelming household duties, or the constant demands of several small children. Whatever the situation, we can look around us and uncover opportunities to offer welcome relief to a burdened soul.

Almighty Father, *thank You for the blessings You send into each of my days. I know that You see every burden I bear, and You will help me through each one. Help me also to see ways in which I can lift the burdens of others. In the name of Jesus, Lord and Savior of all, I pray. Amen.*

September 21

The Bridegroom Comes!

As a bridegroom rejoices over his bride, so will your God rejoice over you (Isaiah 62:5).

Scripture: **Isaiah 62:1-7**
Song: **"We Will Dance"**

Music from the massive pipe organ filled Wheaton Bible Church with intense, dramatic crescendos. Tears of joy glistened in the groom's eyes as his glorious bride appeared. She smiled radiantly, focusing on her beloved. At 46 years of age, she had long imagined this moment. Well-wishers stood and applauded in celebration of a long-desired union.

At the reception, the groom told his bride, "Many a prince has desired your hand, princess, but I am the one you chose to be your king—and you are my queen. Let the celebration begin!"

As this bridegroom rejoiced over his bride, so Jesus rejoices over His own. One day the New Jerusalem, Holy Zion, will ring with celebration as God's righteous bride, the holy church, is revealed. Her salvation will shine like a blazing torch, a crown of splendor, a royal diadem in the hand of God.

My King, thank You for loving me with the tenderness of a bridegroom. I praise You for preparing Your church to be a righteous bride through Your sacrifice on the cross. How I long for the day when I will see You, face to face, to celebrate for all eternity! In Your holy name I pray. Amen.

September 21-27. **Julie Kloster** is a teacher, speaker, and freelance writer. She lives with her husband and three teenage daughters in Sycamore, Illinois.

God of Comfort and Hope

When I heard these things, I sat down and wept. For some days I mourned and fasted and prayed before the God of heaven (Nehemiah 1:4).

Scripture: **Nehemiah 1:1-4**
Song: **"Sometimes He Calms the Storm"**

Just before dawn, the fiery, brilliant stars seemed unusually large and close. As I prayed and pondered the stars that morning, I had no idea of the enormity of the grief and disaster that would soon come from the sky. It was September 11, 2001—the day our nation reeled under the attack of hijacked commercial jets.

I wept at the devastation of my land, the grief of my people, and the helpless, hopeless feeling that deep suffering brings. I didn't understand what was happening, but I knew the one who did. I poured out my heart before God, asking Him for wisdom, comfort, peace, and hope for our nation.

Nehemiah had heard similar devastating news about his beloved Jerusalem. The people were in great trouble and disgrace, the city walls were broken down, and the gates burned with fire. Nehemiah wept and prayed.

We don't know what the future holds, but we know the one who holds the future. In sorrow and pain, may we turn to the God of comfort and hope.

O God, *You are my refuge and strength, an ever-present help in trouble. I cling to Your promise that You will never leave me nor forsake me. Thank You for Your gifts of hope, peace, and comfort. In Jesus' name, amen.*

Fervent Prayer

I confess the sins we Israelites, including myself and my father's house, have committed against you (Nehemiah 1:6).

Scripture: **Nehemiah 1:5-11**
Song: **"Pass Me Not, O Gentle Savior"**

"Our own beloved country, once, by the blessing of God, united, prosperous and happy, is now afflicted with faction and civil war," said President Abraham Lincoln on August 12, 1861. The purpose of Lincoln's proclamation was to call the American people to pray fervently for their country, which was ravaged by the devastation of civil war.

Lincoln implored the American people to "confess and deplore their sins and transgressions in the full conviction that the fear of the Lord is the beginning of wisdom; and to pray, with all fervency and contrition." He appointed the last Thursday in September as a national day of prayer and fasting.

Similarly, Nehemiah prayed fervently, day and night, for the nation of Israel. He opened his prayers with heart-felt praise, spent time in humble confession, claimed God's promises. And with patient perseverance he requested favor.

As we intercede for the good of our nation, let us model Nehemiah's prayer. God delights in the prayers of those who revere His name.

Awesome God, You redeem Your people by Your great strength and Your mighty hand. Please redeem the people of this land. In Jesus' name, amen.

Face-lift

The king asked me, "Why does your face look so sad when you are not ill? This can be nothing but sadness of heart" (Nehemiah 2:2).

Scripture: **Nehemiah 2:1-4**
Song: **"Blessed Be Your Name"**

"Uh-oh. Sarah must have had a bad day. She's upset," I told my friend Terry. From the picture window, we were watching my daughter, Sarah, get off the school bus.

"How do you know that?" Terry asked curiously.

Sarah's chin was on her chest; her shoulders were stooped. "I can tell by the way she's walking," I said.

Sarah opened the door and burst into tears. She told us her sorrows, and we prayed together.

The condition of our spirit often comes through in our facial expressions and body language. Nehemiah's grief was evident in his face. The king recognized it as sadness of heart. Though Nehemiah feared the king's reaction, he spoke truthfully to him about his grief. In his sorrow, Nehemiah sought God for wisdom.

We all have times of grief and frustration, but sometimes I wonder: What does my typical body language reveal about the condition of my spirit? Am I truthful with others about my feelings? When I am sad or angry, do I continue to talk to God and ask Him to help me?

Father, my highest joys and deepest concerns do not change Your love for me. Let my face radiate Your joy and peace as I trust You. Even in the troubling moments of life, help me overflow with hope. In Jesus' name, amen.

Request Granted

Because the gracious hand of God was upon me, the king granted my requests (Nehemiah 2:8).

Scripture: **Nehemiah 2:6-10**
Song: **"He Leadeth Me"**

"Our special education program is following state guidelines, and no changes need to be made," the superintendent told the school board.

"Julie, as the special education teacher, do you agree with this assessment?" the board president asked me.

I hesitated while I silently asked the Lord to help me. "The program *isn't* following state guidelines," I said. "We have too many students, and the age range of the students is too broad. The classroom has no windows, no heat, and no ventilation."

The board was silent. "What do you want?" the board president finally asked.

"I recommend that you build two new classrooms for this program and hire another part-time teacher," I said. And with little debate, the board granted my requests.

Here's what I learned: When we are following the Lord's leading, we can be bold in our requests. Nehemiah boldly presented his plan to the king. Because God's gracious hand was upon him, the king said: "Yes!"

Almighty and Sovereign God, for Your great wisdom and leading, I give You praise. Help me to be a bold defender of Your people. And thank You for allowing me to be part of Your work on earth. In the name of the Father, the Son, and the Holy Spirit, I pray. Amen.

Trumpet Tunes

Wherever you hear the sound of the trumpet, join us there. Our God will fight for us! (Nehemiah 4:20).

Scripture: **Nehemiah 4:15-23**
Song: **"In Christ Alone (My Hope Is Found)"**

Throughout the centuries, trumpets have been used strategically in war. They convey commands, remind soldiers of the valor of past heroes, identify troops, and advance psychological warfare.

It is dangerous for an order to go unheard or misunderstood. Thus trumpet signals are piercing, clear, unambiguous, and can be heard above the explosions of gunfire. Machiavelli, writing on military matters, said the trumpet was vital to the command and control of an army.

Nehemiah also recognized the value of trumpets during war, but he certainly didn't rely solely on human devices to win his battles. Yes, his soldiers were equipped with spears, shields, bows, and arrows. But it was prayer, diligent obedience, and complete trust in God that comprised Nehemiah's most important weapons.

We may be tempted to rely on our own strength and knowledge to fight the battles of life. After all, most of us desire to "be in control" of our own futures. But if we are wise, we will put our complete trust in God alone.

Eternal Ruler, You alone are mighty. Please forgive me for my tendency to rely on my own strength and power. I know that when I am walking in Your will, You will fight for me. I give You all the glory and praise, in the name of Your Son, my Savior, Jesus Christ. Amen.

September 27

Contagious Faith

I also told them about the gracious hand of my God upon me and what the king had said to me. They replied, "Let us start rebuilding." So they began this good work (Nehemiah 2:18).

Scripture: **Nehemiah 2:5, 11-20**
Song: **"Blessed Assurance"**

My daughter, Sarah, came home from Urbana 2006 (a college missions conference sponsored by Intervarsity) with a new radiance. What gave her such joy? The Lord had laid it on her heart to spend part of her summer in China. She'd be working at a youth camp teaching English as a Second Language.

When Sarah began to share her story of how God was leading her to China, other people wanted to be part of God's work in China too. Support money came in from the most unexpected places.

When Nehemiah shared his vision about rebuilding Jerusalem, the people wanted to be part of God's good work for Israel. Nehemiah's faith was contagious. He helped the people believe that they could accomplish this daunting task because God was behind it.

What vision has God laid on your heart to accomplish His work? And is your faith so contagious that it inspires others to glorify God too?

Heavenly Father, thank You for the blessed assurance that Jesus is mine. Praising You is the story of my life. Ignite the flame of passion in my soul so that my faith is contagious, and help me boldly proclaim Your love to others. In the precious name of Jesus I pray. Amen.

The Good Shepherd

As a shepherd looks after his scattered flock when he is with them, so will I look after my sheep (Ezekiel 34:12).

Scripture: **Ezekiel 34:11-16**
Song: **"Savior, Like a Shepherd Lead Us"**

One of my granddaughter's favorite nap-time companions is a white Beanie Baby lamb. She loves to finger his soft, white plush and cuddle him. "Fleece" allows her to shower affection onto him, to stroke him, and eventually pat him to sleep with her. This is how most of us picture lambs—soft, cuddly, and eager for our love and care.

Similarly, I have an image of Christ the Good Shepherd. I visualize Him leading a stray lamb out of a thicket or comforting a young one in His arms if it has wandered from its mother's side. Alone in the evening shadows, He stands guard as the flock sleeps, ready to fight an intruder if necessary. His life is devoted to guiding and caring for those in His keeping.

How comforting to know that I, His sheep, can rely on the Good Shepherd to lead me through the valleys and shadows. No evil can overcome me in His care. He has already laid down His life for me. Every day with this knowledge I rest in His keeping.

Jesus, tender shepherd, bless me, Your little lamb today. Thank You for Your comforting presence in my life as You walk with me through my hills and valleys. In Your precious name I pray. Amen.

September 28–30. **Cynda Strong**—minister's wife, mother of two, and grandmother of two—is a high school English teacher in Springfield, Illinois.

Thank God!

Give thanks to the LORD, call on his name; make known among the nations what he has done (1 Chronicles 16:8).

Scripture: **1 Chronicles 16:8-13**
Song: **"Praise God from Whom All Blessings Flow"**

Born and raised in the deep South, my children adopted the habits of our friends and politely responded at an early age with "Thank you, ma'am/sir." When we moved back to the Midwest, their good manners came as a surprise to many folks. Today it seems a simple "thank you" often goes unspoken. I know that I tend to take for granted what others do for me.

When I glance around at my blessings, a mere "thank you" to God seems insufficient, and yet this is what He asks of me—to thank Him in my heart and mind throughout the day. From the crops in the fields and the rain-filled streams, to the health of my family members, He asks that I acknowledge His goodness.

As I call upon His name in thankfulness, I also acknowledge the wonders of His name—the Counselor, the Mighty God, the Prince of Peace, the Savior. He is all this and much more. His goodness to me stretches beyond all time, even to eternity with Him. In love and thankfulness I share this wonder with others.

***Almighty God,** King of kings, I offer my thanks for all Your many blessings. I acknowledge Your majesty and power. In joyful praise, I ask that You help me to share Your greatness with everyone I meet, that they too may give You praise and thanks. In the name of Jesus, amen.*

Eternal Loyalty?

O LORD, God of our fathers Abraham, Isaac and Israel, keep this desire in the hearts of your people forever and keep their hearts loyal to you (1 Chronicles 29:18).

Scripture: **1 Chronicles 29:17-19**
Song: **"True-Hearted, Whole-Hearted"**

Maintaining customer loyalty is crucial to businesses today. Retailers want to be sure customers are pleased with a product so they'll buy it again. To ensure this, they may offer incentives like low financing, special guarantees, bonus gifts, or free repairs. Guaranteeing customer satisfaction can produce future sales and continued loyalty.

But businesses also know that the competition with bigger and better promotions is poised to lure customers away with even more enticing promises. Maintaining loyal clients and customers can be difficult. We always want the better deal, the better terms, and we are easily distracted.

God has blessed me richly in my life. Yet my loyalty to my Savior can waiver when I am lured by promises of things the world says are better than a commitment to God's kingdom. Today, will I rest in the knowledge that His guarantees are for much more than a lifetime?

Precious Savior, You offered the best bargain in the world, a lifetime guarantee of Heaven with You. You sealed the deal with Your death on the cross for me. Help me to remain committed to Your will for my life. In the name of the Father, the Son, and the Holy Spirit, I pray. Amen.

My Prayer Notes

DEVOTIONS®

*V*ery early . . . Jesus . . . went off to a solitary place, where he prayed.

—Mark 1:35

OCTOBER

Gary Allen, Editor

DEVOTIONS® is published quarterly by Standard Publishing, Cincinnati, Ohio, www.standardpub.com. © 2008 by Standard Publishing. All rights reserved. Topics based on the Home Daily Bible Readings, International Sunday School Lessons. © 2006 by the Committee on the Uniform Series. Printed in the U.S.A. All Scripture quotations, unless otherwise indicated, are taken from the HOLY BIBLE, NEW INTERNATIONAL VERSION®. NIV®. Copyright © 1973, 1978, 1984 by International Bible Society. Used by permission of Zondervan. All rights reserved. Where noted, Scripture quotations are from the following, used with permission of the copyright holders, all rights reserved: *The New King James Version.* Copyright © 1982 by Thomas Nelson, Inc. *Holy Bible, New Living Translation (NLT),* © 1996. Tyndale House Publishers.

Bargain Hunter

The LORD searches every heart and understands every motive behind the thoughts. If you seek him, he will be found by you; but if you forsake him, he will reject you forever (1 Chronicles 28:9).

Scripture: **1 Chronicles 28:6-10**
Song: **"The Way of the Cross Leads Home"**

I'm a garage sale hound. I love finding hidden treasures tucked in a box from someone's attic. I've often found things I couldn't afford if they were new—and things I didn't need at the time but found a use for later.

But it has taken time and energy. Searching for bargains, I never know what I might find just around the corner. Seeking the Lord, however, requires only that I listen to His Word and open my heart to His will. When I read His word, pray, or worship with His people, He comes to me with comfort and guidance amidst life's troubles.

Yes, God's treasures lie within my reach, already prepared for me. He waits to bless me daily as I grow in His grace. These wonderful "finds" bring more than momentary pleasure. They bring comfort, security, and eternal salvation.

Dearest Lord, sometimes I'm so caught up in all my activities that I forget Your constant presence. Forgive me, and help me to seek Your wisdom in my most difficult times and also within my ordinary, daily routines. In Christ's holy name I pray. Amen.

October 1–4. **Cynda Strong**—minister's wife, mother of two, and grandmother of two—is a high school English teacher in Springfield, Illinois. October 1–4.

Can You Hear Me Now?

If my people, who are called by my name, will humble themselves and pray and seek my face and turn from their wicked ways, then will I hear from heaven and will forgive their sin and will heal their land (2 Chronicles 7:14).

Scripture: **2 Chronicles 7:12-18**
Song: **"Prayer Is the Key"**

"Can you hear me now?" speaks the man into the cell phone as he moves from location to location. The obvious point of the TV commercial is that this company offers superior reception to its clients. They will experience no difficulty communicating on *this* phone.

As a child I wondered how God could hear the thousands of prayers flowing heavenward every minute. How would mine compete with all those others? But God's omniscience enables Him to know all things in the "eternal present," apart from time and space. My prayers encounter no interference as I seek His will and thank Him for His blessings.

Modern technology can't compete with our direct prayer-line to the creator. A simple whisper, a fleeting thought—such prayer is the response of my grateful heart. Through prayer I am able to confess, praise, and ask, just as any child would approach a loving parent. Best of all, God absolutely promises: I hear, and I will answer.

Father, thanks for the great privilege of praying—and for the assurance that You hear and answer. As I go through my daily life, may I speak to You frequently . . . and listen closely for Your responses. In Jesus' name, amen.

No Place Like Home

"The land is still ours, because we have sought the Lord our God; we sought him and he has given us rest on every side." So they built and prospered (2 Chronicles 14:7).

Scripture: **2 Chronicles 14:1-7**
Song: **"I'm But a Stranger Here"**

When we go on vacation, I love to stay at bed-and-breakfast establishments. Colorful linens, a room with a view, congenial hosts, and homemade breakfasts make me feel like a warmly welcomed guest. But no matter how comfortable I am or how delicious the meals, it's still not "home." I miss my own pillow and my brand of cereal. I love the familiarity that home offers, the feeling of safety and security.

My home and my country have been blessed by God. He daily provides all that I need—house, food, clothing, job, and health. As I remain faithful to Him and seek His will, He calms my doubts and fears, sustaining me through difficult times.

Though circumstances change, my future is never in doubt, because Christ has secured that for me. His death has sealed His promise never to forsake those who love and follow after Him. I rest in the comfort that my home now can't compare to the home He has prepared for me in Heaven.

Lord, as I seek Your will for my life, strengthen me to grow and follow You. I am so thankful that my home with You for eternity will be a joy I can't even imagine now. I pray this prayer in the name of Jesus. Amen.

Good News Travels Fast

Instead he went out and began to talk freely, spreading the news. As a result, Jesus could no longer enter a town openly but stayed outside in lonely places. Yet the people still came to him from everywhere (Mark 1:45).

Scripture: **Mark 1:32-45**
Song: **"Saved Through Jesus' Blood"**

The line at the local gas station stretched for several blocks. Every pump was running. For over three hours customers lined up to purchase gas selling for several cents below the norm. Word spread from friend to friend, and even local radio stations carried the news. Soon folks from neighboring towns were making the drive to fill their tanks. Good news traveled fast.

As Jesus went about healing the sick, word spread rapidly. People came from miles around to be touched and cured. I can only imagine the joy as dark futures suddenly gleamed bright with new hope because of Jesus' power to heal, and to heal immediately. And the news quickly spread . . . even though Jesus had requested silence.

Spreading good news brings others into our joy. In Christ, I know the miracle of salvation. I know His love, security, and comfort. These are things I can eagerly share with others.

Father, You've worked the miracle of salvation in my life. Thank You for the healing You've brought to my heart, and I pray that You will help me share this wonderful news with others who so need it. In Jesus' name, amen.

What Do My Actions Say?

John the Baptist sent us to you to ask, "Are you the one who was to come, or should we expect someone else?" (Luke 7:20).

Scripture: **Luke 7:18-23**
Song: **"Be the Center"**

The 10-year high school class reunion comes in two weeks. All across the country, former classmates prepare to see each other again. Each wonders: *Will people still recognize me?* Several stand for long minutes in front of mirrors. Mothers with a bit more post–baby weight than planned turn from side-to-side to see their figures. Men who haven't really worked out since the last football game adjust their belt loops a notch tighter.

But physical appearance isn't the only thing on their minds. Some have achieved their goals and advanced their careers. Others have taken detours that may or may not have taken them to highly desired destinations.

John's disciples had questions about Christ's identity. They wanted to be sure they'd recognize Him when He arrived. But when they asked Jesus directly, He simply pointed to his actions.

What we do is surely more important than how we look. Our actions tell others so much about us—and so much about our professed commitment to the Lord.

***Father**, if I am to be remembered by people, let it be because of the things I do for You. In the holy name of Jesus, my Lord and Savior, I pray. Amen.*

October 5–11. **Kate Schmelzer** recently graduated from Taylor University, Fort Wayne, Indiana. She has been a regular contributor to *Campus Life* magazine.

Poor Leadership

They made their lives bitter with hard labor in brick and mortar and with all kinds of work in the fields; in all their hard labor the Egyptians used them ruthlessly (Exodus 1:14).

Scripture: **Exodus 1:8-14**
Song: **"Give Me Jesus"**

No one liked the factory's head boss. He apparently wanted to serve himself and his name more than his employees and their customers. The shift workers felt unappreciated as they watched their benefits slowly being cut. And they must work as quickly as possible (though accuracy wasn't necessarily encouraged). Over time, of course, product quality suffered.

The company's executives soon learned how the workers were treated and how their once quality products were being degraded. The boss was fired, new leadership welcomed.

Many people today can relate to the ancient Israelites' struggles under Egyptian rule. Unfair treatment ripped apart their lives, yet these workers refused to let go of their identity as God's people.

When hard days come, we can remember who the true boss is. Under His wise and caring hand, deliverance will eventually come. Until then, we continue to pray in the words of the apostle John: "Come, Lord Jesus" (Revelation 22:20).

Lord, You are my Lord and Master, the one I will serve today. Help me to go about my work with joy in my heart. In Jesus' name, amen.

Welcome to the Forever Family!

I will take you as my own people, and I will be your God. Then you will know that I am the LORD your God, who brought you out from under the yoke of the Egyptians (Exodus 6:7).

Scripture: **Exodus 6:2-7**
Song: **"The Family of God"**

The adoption process can be grueling. First the mountain of paperwork. Then the interviews. And then some couples wait months—even years—before they're finally blessed with a child. Others never experience the joys that come with raising children.

Some children endure neglect and abuse before being removed from their circumstances. But thankfully, orphanages across the world, along with foster-care services, usually provide caring environments until a permanent home can be found.

Before people come to Christ, they are like neglected orphans, with no support system, no way to care for themselves, and little hope for a better future apart from a family. But God the Father "makes us his people," adopts us (see Ephesians 1:5), bringing us into the church through baptism, and making us brothers and sisters in Christ. Yes, that is why Christ left Heaven's glory for us, sacrificing His life on our behalf. Because of Him we are welcomed into an everlasting family.

Dear Father, I praise You for making me Your child. Thank You for all the blessings of Your family—including the presence of Your Holy Spirit, who is a down payment on my inheritance in Heaven. In Jesus' name, amen.

Are We There Yet?

If we hope for what we do not yet have, we wait for it patiently (Romans 8:25).

Scripture: **Romans 8:18-25**
Song: **"Eternal Source of Joys Divine"**

Small children rarely have an accurate concept of time. For most parents, car rides offer the best proof. No matter how long the trip may be, within five minutes from home, the kids feel they've been journeying for days. "Are we there yet?" rings out, along with the classic: "I have to go the bathroom."

It's in the nature of a child to want to "arrive" quickly. It's called instant gratification, and we adults are hardly immune to its temptations. Part of us seem to focus more on arriving in a future we try to "engineer" and less on arriving at a patient contentment with the present.

God does ask us to prepare and plan for the future, but not that we miss the immediate opportunities for worship and service in His name. According to the apostle Paul, patience is the key. Like the wise parent who doesn't let a young child participate in certain activities until he grows older, our heavenly Father waits for spiritual maturity before giving us the OK to move forward.

Father, keep growing me into the likeness of Your Son, day by day. Help me to relax in Your arms and take the long view of this process. Give me patience and hope, that through prayer, Scripture reading, and learning from the circumstances of life, I may come to a fuller and deeper faith in Your goodness and grace. I pray in Jesus' holy name. Amen.

Been There!

Because he himself suffered when he was tempted, he is able to help those who are being tempted (Hebrews 2:18).

Scripture: **Hebrews 2:14-18**
Song: **"Lead Us On"**

Ever confuse the difference between temptation and sin? It can be subtle. For example, we know that Christ lived a sinless life; nevertheless, He was certainly tempted, just as anyone with a human nature suffers temptation. (Remember that Jesus is one person with two natures—fully human, fully God.) Because He was tempted, we know that temptation, in itself, is not a sin.

There is a blessing here, as the writer of Hebrews tells us. The Lord of our lives fully understands each struggle and trial we face; He's been there. And by His power, He can deliver us as we rely upon Him.

Furthermore, not only does Christ understand temptations, He also experienced what it is like to be despised and rejected. Our temptations and struggles are real, but comfort comes in knowing that we are not alone in them.

Yet a practical matter remains: We must exercise caution and discipline in order to build our resistance. As Mark Twain once said about temptation: "It is easier to *stay* out than to *get* out." Or, to put it a little more vividly, in the words of John Dryden: "Better shun the bait, than struggle in the snare."

Lord, *thank You for taking on human nature to understand my temptations and offer the perfect sacrifice for my sins. In Jesus' name, amen.*

I Cry to You, Father!

You did not receive a spirit that makes you a slave again to fear, but you received the Spirit of sonship. And by him we cry, "Abba, Father" (Romans 8:15).

Scripture: **Romans 8:9-17**
Song: **"My Life Is in You"**

Statistically, "Da-da" is the most popular first word uttered by infants. Apparently, the "d" sound in the English language is easier to say first; then comes the "m" in "Ma-ma."

As an infant grows, he or she soon learns that cries, sounds, and words have specific meanings. And these meanings quickly attach to emotions, one of which is fear.

Children often fear the dark or become quite frightened when they're left alone. For adults, fearful emotions arise as any number of pressures build, whether related to finances, relationships, or just "making it through another day."

Children voice their concerns through cries. We can voice our concerns through prayer, a kind of crying out to our heavenly Father. Yes, God invites us, every day, to recollect that we are His sons and daughters by blessed adoption. No matter how horrible the situation we face, He knows our fears and will answer our cries.

O Lord, how little control I have over the circumstances of my life! Help me to rest in Your will for me, each moment of every day. May Your indwelling Spirit bring peace to my heart. Through Christ, amen.

Just Come As You Are

"Go home to your family and tell them how much the Lord has done for you, and how he has had mercy on you." . . . **And all the people were amazed** (Mark 5:19, 20).

Scripture: **Mark 5:1-13, 18-20**
Song: **"Accepted in the Beloved"**

I've noticed something truly wonderful about my Savior. He loves to take the ugly hurts and mistakes from yesterday and transform them into something beautiful for tomorrow.

Jesus did just that with the demon-possessed man. Suddenly freed, the man wanted to travel with the Lord. But Jesus told him to go home to his family and talk to the people he knew. What a beautiful message they received!

And we can learn a valuable lesson from the decision that man had to make. Despite being isolated from his family and friends, he chose to go home and face his past, willingly proclaiming the transforming work of Christ in his life.

We all have issues, shabby pieces of "baggage" from our past. But God can redeem the worst parts of us and use them for His glory. This is a miraculous work that only He can do. Yet, I must be willing. I must simply offer Him my heart, come to Him, just as I am.

Almighty Father, take my past, transform my failures, and use my redeemed life for Your purposes in my world. I claim no special talent or ability except the resources You've graciously provided through Your Spirit in me. All praise to You, in Jesus' name. Amen.

Beyond Their Ability

I testify that they gave as much as they were able, and even beyond their ability. Entirely on their own . . . (2 Corinthians 8:3).

Scripture: **2 Corinthians 8:1-7**
Song: **"Give Me Thy Heart"**

"You'll have to borrow the money. It's the only way you can build the addition you need. Besides, no one can raise that kind of money, especially a little congregation like yours." As I drove home from my meeting with our district official, I pondered the facts: We had 90 regular attendees, half of them retired people on limited incomes. We didn't have a building fund or extra money in the bank. Maybe the presbyter was right, but as senior minister I felt awkward putting our church into major debt.

That night, I took up my Bible, looking for direction. Everything I read told me to trust God for a way through this. At the annual business meeting on Sunday, I gave my report and let the church members decide. The vote was unanimous: no borrowing!

Our faith grew as the building fund increased. And . . . two years later we finished our half-million-dollar addition, debt free.

Lord, I am still amazed at what faith and sacrificial giving can accomplish. Your work at Calvary is my inspiration, where You put everything on the line for me. How could I do less? In Christ's name, I pray. Amen.

October 12–18. **Charles E. Harrel** was a minister for more than 30 before pursuing a writing ministry. He enjoys digital photography and camping with his family.

Belts of the King

Righteousness shall be the belt of His loins, and faithfulness the belt of His waist (Isaiah 11:5, *New King James Version*).

Scripture: **Isaiah 11:1-10**
Song: **"Jesus Shall Reign"**

"You're just one of them city-slickers." That's how my uncles from Oklahoma pegged me, and they were right. At 12 years old, I'd lived my whole life near the crowded metropolis of Los Angeles, California.

My uncles didn't dress like city people either. They all wore manila-white cowboy hats, made of straw, as big as umbrellas. I'd never seen anything like those hats. If I wore something like that to school, I would be laughed out of class. Even so, when Uncle Lance offered me one, I grabbed it without hesitation.

What impressed me most were the belts my uncles wore. Hand-tooled, made of tanned leather, they sported silver buckles the size of dinner plates. The buckles had various markings. My father told me these were brands, identifying the type of ranch each uncle owned.

Likewise, the Lord has belts symbolizing His kingdom. One represents His righteousness, the other His faithfulness. And He owns the entire realm—every star, every planet, and everything else beyond the waving of His hand.

*Even the garments You wear, **Father**, reflect the attributes of Your kingdom. One day, I hope to visit this kingdom and greet You in person. Through Christ, my Lord, amen.*

You Are Free Now

To open eyes that are blind, to free captives from prison and to release from the dungeon those who sit in darkness (Isaiah 42:7).

Scripture: **Isaiah 42:5-9**
Song: **"He Touched Me and Made Me Whole"**

Ever dreamed a dream that you believed came from God? One night a few years ago, I had one. It concerned my childhood friend, Robin. He sat alone in a dark cell screaming, "Help me! Would someone please help me?" The cries rattled my sleep, and I woke up trembling.

The next morning I phoned his mother. I'd thought Robin had been living in Sweden because of his business dealings. Instead, I discovered that he was serving a 20-year prison sentence! His mom believed that jealous associates had framed him.

Heartbroken for my friend, I began praying and fasting, asking God to vindicate him. My family prayed as well. Six months later, they released Robin—all charges dropped.

Most of us have never been a prisoner of war, incarcerated in a state prison, or locked up in a county jail. Like dungeons of old, these are dark places that darken the soul. In the midst of this hopelessness, Jesus stands with us, offering encouragement. He can still open doors and set captives free, especially those held captive by sin.

Dear Lord and Savior, *at times I feel trapped by circumstances beyond my control. Please deliver me, in the name of Jesus. Amen.*

Who Will Light the Way?

The LORD says . . . "I will also make you a light for the Gentiles, that you may bring my salvation to the ends of the earth" (Isaiah 49:5, 6).

Scripture: **Isaiah 49:1-6**
Song: **"Light of Light, Enlighten Me"**

Jeremy's hand rose first when I asked the question. As youth leader for children's church, I usually took requests for songs. Jeremy always requested, "This Little Light of Mine." He never tired of that song. Reluctantly, I said yes—but, for me, the song had lost its meaning years ago. At times I even despised it, including the repetitive hand motions.

I suppose the Lord was listening in to my thoughts. Halfway into the chorus, He seemed to speak to my heart: *So, how are you going to do that—be my light to a lost world?*

The question challenged and convicted me. After the morning worship service, I stopped by the prayer room. I waited in silence for an hour, listening for the Lord, and then I prayed, "Do You have any openings for Christian writers?"

Isaiah prophesied about a Messiah who would one day be a light to all people, Jew and Gentile alike. He, Jesus Christ, is the divine source of light, and we are His lamps. Each of us is called to carry and spread His light to our friends and neighbors.

Lord, fill my lamp with oil, and trim its flame to burn brightly. And use me to bring Your light to those who live in darkness. In Jesus' name, amen.

Come to the Glory

I know their works and their thoughts. It shall be that I will gather all nations and tongues; and they shall come and see My glory (Isaiah 66:18, *New King James Version*).

Scripture: **Isaiah 66:18-20**
Song: **"To God Be the Glory"**

The church bulletin read: "Come to the service tonight, and experience the glory of God." It sounded interesting. Being a new Christian, I wasn't sure what the glory of God was, so I decided to attend and find out. I half expected to see a pillar of fire or someone turning water into wine. Instead, I saw people kneeling at the altar or lying prostrate on the floor, their faces buried in the carpet. Some were silent; others cried softly. Most of the people just sat in their pews, eyes closed, with smiles on their faces. It didn't take me long to drop my preconceived ideas and move toward the altar.

Sometimes the glory of God comes as an outward manifestation, expressing itself in a visible sign or wonder. Other times it is inward, like a still small voice whispering that God is worthy.

We can see God's glory in His judgments or in His great mercy. Either way, it beckons us to watch in awe and then draw closer. One day, all people will experience His glory . . . but there's no penalty for starting early.

O Lord, from the first day of creation to now, Your glory remains in plain view. Each day, Your glorious presence draws me closer, and I fall deeper in love with You. In the blessed name of Jesus, I give You thanks. Amen.

Useless Fires?

Oh, that one of you would shut the temple doors, so that you would not light useless fires on my altar! (Malachi 1:10).

Scripture: **Malachi 1:9-11**
Song: **"The Heart of Worship"**

It only took a few seconds for the fire to start, helped along by some charcoal lighter. Soon the flames leapt high into the air. Not wanting to be scorched, everyone took a few steps back and watched as hot embers drifted up, disappearing into the night air. It was quite a show—like fireworks.

My high school friends knew how to make a roaring fire. Somehow, though, it seemed like a waste of good firewood. Their fire wasn't like the ones my father used to build. His campfires had purpose. They cooked meals, radiated warmth, provided security, and gave out a guiding light in the darkness.

Malachi gives us a similar analogy: he equates half-hearted worship to a useless fire on God's altar. It was superficial, having no purpose or passion, so God rejected it. The creator of the universe doesn't need more firework displays. He favors honest, meaningful praise from a pure heart. It's the kind of altar fire He desires most.

In the church today, the fires of worship burn in our hearts. They glow brightest when fueled with sincerity and compassion.

Lord, *You see all things, including the fire that inflames my soul. May Your goodness shine through in all my words and deeds. In Jesus' name, amen.*

Now That's Amazing

People were overwhelmed with amazement. "He has done everything well," they said. "He even makes the deaf hear and the mute speak" (Mark 7:37).

Scripture: **Mark 7:24-37**
Song: **"I Stand in Awe"**

My high school assembly featured a special guest that week, a local magician. His performance entertained and astonished the crowd. He floated a basketball in midair, made his lovely assistant disappear from a closed box, and read a student's mind. He did every trick in the book, except pull a rabbit from a hat.

Actually, he was quite good, his act well-rehearsed. But as the audience cheered him on, my mind drifted elsewhere. I thought about the signs and wonders my uncle experienced overseas. He had served as a missionary to Ghana, West Africa. One day I asked him, "Uncle Mel, are your stories about miracles really true?"

"Charles," he said, "I personally witnessed the blind see, the crippled walk, and heard two deaf mutes speak for the first time after receiving prayer. They spoke in English, too, a language they'd never learned."

The genuine works of God have a purpose: They overpower doubt, increase faith, and draw us closer to Him. When we experience real miracles, firsthand, they leave us overwhelmed with amazement.

God, *You amaze me. Your works are unmatched, Your deeds mighty, Your love unsurpassed. Praise to Your name, through Christ my Lord! Amen.*

The Greater Return

One man gives freely, yet gains even more; another withholds unduly, but comes to poverty (Proverbs 11:24).

Scripture: **Proverbs 11:24-28**
Song: **"Gladly We Will Go"**

Many of us would be a lot happier if we could manage the art of living simply. It doesn't necessarily mean living in poverty. In fact, it's more about attitude than money. But one principle of simple living is to give freely.

It's been said that you get what you pay for. It could also be said that you get what you give. "Give, and it will be given to you. A good measure, pressed down, shaken together and running over, will be poured into your lap" (Luke 6:38). Those who give are likely to receive joy in return. And, generally speaking, the love they give is lavishly reciprocated. In contrast, those who "withhold unduly" experience poverty by selfishly refusing to use what they have to help others.

The practical application? Simply give generously of your time, your heart, your resources, your expertise, your faith. Giving freely provides a greater return than any CD or savings account ever could.

Lord, I know that giving comes from a grateful heart, a satisfied heart, and a trusting heart. Because You satisfy my needs, I am able to give back in return. Even when I am financially hurting, help me to give away the riches of a smile, a hug, or a listening ear. In Jesus' name, amen.

October 19–25. **Brian J. Waldrop,** a Bible college graduate, works as a histology technician in the lab at Mercy Franciscan Hospital in Cincinnati.

Power of a Positive Influence

So give your servant a discerning heart to govern your people and to distinguish between right and wrong. For who is able to govern this great people of yours? (1 Kings 3:9).

Scripture: 1 Kings 3:5-14
Song: "Make Me a Blessing"

King Solomon is to be commended for wanting to govern wisely. He understood his place of influence over the citizens of Israel and humbly asked God for help. But you don't have to be an official leader in order to have a positive influence.

I recently signed an online obituary guest book. The book contained 11 pages of memories and messages from caring people. Many told how the deceased had positively influenced them. Ironically, this young father's death came by suicide. He believed himself to be a failure, never realizing the positive ways his life had affected others.

The opposite can be true as well. How we live our lives can negatively influence others more than we realize. Bad attitudes and brash decisions send out a ripple effect. Therefore, a prayer for proper perspective and attitude is more than a request for our own well-being. It is, in a sense, a prayer for others, as well.

Heavenly Father, like King Solomon, give me a discerning heart to positively impact my family, friends, coworkers, neighbors, and the many others with whom I come in contact each day. I want to be a blessing, not a curse. And thank You for those who have positively influenced me through the years. In the name of Your Son, my Savior, I pray. Amen.

He Uses Your "Little"

It is better to be godly and have little than to be evil and possess much (Psalm 37:16, *New Living Translation*).

Scripture: **Psalm 37:12-19**
Song: **"I'd Rather Have Jesus"**

My grandparents owned a modest, two-bedroom house. Though it was neat and cozy, it had a few oddities. The bathroom floor sloped. The bedroom doors consisted of folding, accordion-type partitions. And outside, a piece of foam insulation covered an opening where one could access the pipes that froze during harsh winters.

Although the house wasn't as nice as the one I grew up in, as a child I thought nothing of it. It was Grandma and Grandpa's house. Yes, it was small. But all of my many aunts, uncles, and cousins would gather there for family get-togethers to enjoy delicious, home-cooked meals.

Through the years I've been to a few church gatherings in the homes of wealthy Christians. Most of the home Bible studies, ice cream socials, and picnics, however, have been hosted in more modest houses and apartments. No one seemed to have any less fun in these homes than in the others. I think it just goes to show that Jesus blesses our "little"—a lot—when we use it for Him.

Dear Father in Heaven, though so many folks today seek to use what they own to impress, I want to use my belongings to bless. Please keep me from missing out on the joy of hospitality simply because I am not as wealthy as others. Remind me that everything we humans "own" is on loan from You. I pray in the name of Jesus, my merciful Savior and Lord. Amen.

Immortality: Not For Sale

They trust in their wealth and boast of great riches. Yet they cannot redeem themselves from death by paying a ransom to God (Psalm 49:6, 7, *New Living Translation*).

Scripture: **Psalm 49:1-7**
Song: **"Only Trust Him"**

It seems that with enough money, a person can buy just about anything. Some even try to buy immortality by investing in a process called cryonics—the practice of freezing someone who has died of disease in hopes of restoring life when a future cure is found. However, the means of "resurrection" from such a planned deep-freeze has yet to be developed.

Because of a disease called sin, which entered the world with the first human beings, nothing short of the second coming can save us from physical death. No doctor is smart enough. No drug is powerful enough. No amount of money can permanently prevent the inevitable. Therefore, it's best to trust in Jesus instead of money. He's the only one who can successfully reverse the process. "For as in Adam all die, so in Christ all will be made alive" (1 Corinthians 15:22). At the Last Day, our physical bodies will come alive. If we have the spiritual life of Christ within us, we will live with Him forever.

Heavenly Father, remind me that money can never buy that which only comes from You. May my wealth never distract me from trusting You. And may my boasting only point to Your faithfulness. Thank You for the gift of eternal life, with all the riches of Heaven. In Jesus' name I pray. Amen.

Protection and Praise

Let the righteous rejoice in the Lord and take refuge in him; let all the upright in heart praise him! (Psalm 64:10).

Scripture: **Psalm 64:5-10**
Song: **"Rock of Ages"**

I don't know about you, but I despise car alarms. These devices are so sensitive that they often blare at the slightest vibration—day or night. And some owners seem to take great pleasure in the attention their cars receive from onlookers.

God, too, has measures in place to protect us, we who are His most precious of possessions. Peter reminds us that we are "shielded by God's power. . . . In this you greatly rejoice, though now for a little while you may have had to suffer grief in all kinds of trials" (1 Peter 1:5, 6). And James 1:2 says to "consider it pure joy . . . whenever you face trials of many kinds" because such trials help us to mature in our faith.

The temptations the evil one devises to drive us *from* God can actually drive us *to* God. And the trials he devises to get us to *curse* God can actually motivate us to *praise* God. So, when someone or something tries to steal your faith, sound the alarm in praise to Jesus, your protector and Savior.

Dear God, I take great comfort in Your protection. You are all knowing, all powerful, and always present. You are the creator, sustainer, and redeemer of life. All life's problems pale in comparison to You. I love You. I thank You. I worship You. Accept my humble praise, through Christ my Lord. Amen.

Heart Decor

Watch out! Be on your guard against all kinds of greed; a man's life does not consist in the abundance of his possessions (Luke 12:15).

Scripture: **Luke 12:13-21**
Song: **"Count Your Blessings"**

I enjoy many of the home design shows on cable TV. Interior decorating can be a rewarding way to use one's God-given creativity, to organize and make the most of one's God-given resources, and to make one's home a place of hospitality.

But sometimes the designers on these shows seem to go too far. Have you noticed? They can take a perfectly usable room and redo it in over-the-top, impractical ways. So turn off the TV for a moment and ponder with me some questions about your own tastes in interior design. Do you worry more about the paint color of your kitchen than you do about those who live without food and safe water? Are you more concerned about matching furniture than you are with matching your talents to ministry opportunities? Do you regularly stop and count your blessings, or are you constantly looking for more treasure? If you're like me, there's probably room for some "interior redesign." Let us make not only our houses—but also our hearts—places of God-designed beauty.

O Lord, Your creative designs are second to none, as seen in the unparalleled universe You so graciously share with me. Help me make the most of my home without becoming obsessive about it. Through Christ, amen.

What Are the Odds?

It is easier for a camel to go through the eye of a needle than for a rich man to enter the kingdom of God (Mark 10:25).

Scripture: **Mark 10:17-31**
Song: **"Victory Ahead"**

Suppose someone is totally devoted to his or her possessions. What are the chances of that person getting into Heaven? According to Jesus, the odds are slim. Impossible, in fact. Jesus says it's easier for a camel to squeeze through the eye of a needle than for a rich man to squeeze into Heaven. "Who then can be saved?" (v. 26).

On our own, none of us. We're all addicted to our "riches," to some degree or another. Of course, riches aren't just money. Riches include anything we give our devotion.

If we're honest with ourselves, we're all in the same predicament as the rich young man in this passage. But thankfully, all things are possible with God. Jesus left behind the riches of Heaven to become poor for us. Jesus became a human, lived a perfect life, took the guilt of humankind upon himself, and then died as punishment for the world's sins. This is His gift to us; we're eternally rich. And the odds of that happening were about the same as a camel getting through the eye of a needle.

Loving God, when the fate of humankind seemed hopeless, You brought us hope. With You, all things are possible. Therefore, nothing I face in life is truly a hopeless situation. Help me remember how big and awesome You really are. In the name of my Savior I pray. Amen.

God's Treasure: You!

You are a people holy to the LORD your God. The LORD your God has chosen you out of all the peoples on the face of the earth to be his people, his treasured possession (Deuteronomy 7:6).

Scripture: **Deuteronomy 7:6-11**
Song: **"Chosen Seed and Zion's Children"**

Inside Nazi prison camps during World War II, prisoners frequently stood in lines. They often had no idea why. Someone had taken a quick look at them and told them which line to stand in. Some lines led to death; others to work—grueling hard work, to be sure—but these lines led to life. The movie *Schindler's List* was the story of a man who made these kinds of choices frequently.

Like Schindler, God has chosen a people—all who trust in Him—to be saved from death. We will work and toil while on this earth, but the elect will be with God in Heaven for eternity. Yet God has done much more than just tell us which line we occupy. He has made us His own—we are His treasured possession; we mean everything to Him. To God, we are of inestimable value.

Think about it. The God of the entire universe has chosen you to be one of His people. Picture it: there you are, in Heaven, with God. He has made you His treasure.

Lord, *thank You. I thank You for the peace that comes from knowing that You have chosen me to live with You forever. In Jesus' name, amen.*

October 26–31. **Robert Thompson** calls Denver home but currently lives near Washington, D.C. He is married with four children.

Love Will Lift You Higher

You yourselves have seen what I did to Egypt, and how I carried you on eagles' wings and brought you to myself (Exodus 19:4).

Scripture: **Exodus 19:1-6**
Song: **"He Will Hold Me Fast"**

This brief passage is really a love story. First, we see God protecting His love, the people of Israel, by working on Pharaoh's heart. God brought a number of different plagues on Egypt because their leader would not let God's love go free.

Then God carried His love on eagles' wings.

Eagles' wings—it is an apt description. Love lifts us up. Love buoys our spirits. Love, real love, brings hope and joy and peace. Love can make your spirit soar just like the eagle rides the wind, spreads his wings, and surveys all below from the clouds high above.

Love brings a unique closeness. We are drawn close to those we love and to those who love us. The Father, who has brought us to himself, suggests that He has brought us near. If you love someone, you just naturally want them to be close at hand. When we love, we revel in the other's presence.

Almighty and ever-living God, I thank You for Your love. Your love has lifted me up, and Your great love sustains me, especially in the dark times. I am so grateful, Lord, for the hope Your love brings into my life. May I rely upon it always! In the name of the Father, the Son, and the Holy Spirit, I pray. Amen.

Remember God

You will have these tassels to look at and so you will remember all the commands of the LORD, that you may obey them and not prostitute yourselves by going after the lusts of your own hearts and eyes (Numbers 15:39).

Scripture: **Numbers 15:37-41**
Song: **"Remember Christ, Our Savior"**

Memory is such a powerful thing, isn't it? In the Vietnam war, American prisoners have said that their memory of home, their memory of their loved ones, was the one thing that sustained them through the long years of their captivity.

Some of these men had a favorite photograph. Others treasured a letter, reading and rereading it, savoring every line. A physical reminder helped them focus on what was important to them.

This passage shows us the importance of remembering and tells us of the help that a physical or visual reminder can be. For the ancient Israelites, it was as simple as a tassel sewn to the corners of a garment. What is it for you?

This is just one place in Scripture where God encourages us to remember Him. When you get right down to it, that is a major reason He gave us His word to read. He wants us never to forget Him and never to forget the marvelous message of His gracious salvation.

Lord, when I am old, give me memories that bring joy, not shame. And today, when I see a cross, may I recall the deep love of Christ for me, a love that shined forth in an eternal sacrifice. Praise to You, Lord Christ! Amen.

Be Ready

"Men of Galilee," they said, "why do you stand here looking into the sky? This same Jesus, who has been taken from you into heaven, will come back in the same way you have seen him go into heaven" (Acts 1:11).

Scripture: **Acts 1:1-11**
Song: **"Rejoice, Ye Saints, the Time Draws Near"**

What do you think of when you look up into the clouds? When I was a child, I used to see houses, cars, and animals—they were my favorites. When I was a bit older, my mom bought me a telescope for Christmas. I used it to stare at the moon and the stars. It was great to pull the face of the moon so close that I could see its peaks and valleys.

But here's something more awesome to me: to ponder Jesus coming back on a cloud someday. Think about His return as you go about your busy routines this week. He is returning one day for all who believe in Him. When we look up—it will be the king of glory!

God won't require any telescope to see back into history—He will see every act of our lives clearly. The question isn't whether Jesus will return on a cloud . . . or on the next bus. The real question is: Will I be ready to face my Lord, my Savior, my Judge?

Father, I thank You for sending Jesus Christ to die for me and save me. I pray You will help me stay focused on You and not on this world, for I wish to grow in love, joy, and faith. I want to be living for Him when He returns for me. In His precious name, I pray. Amen.

The Storms of Life

Suddenly a sound like the blowing of a violent wind came from heaven and filled the whole house where they were sitting (Acts 2:2).

Scripture: **Acts 2:1-4**
Song: **"Sail On!"**

Hurricanes bring some of the most violent winds we will ever witness. The Saffir-Simpson scale for measuring these storms uses five categories. Category 5 hurricanes, the most severe, unleash winds from 156 miles per hour and above. I know the devastation such tempests can cause, so any sound "like the blowing of a violent wind" is bound to get my attention.

What does it take to get the attention of your whole household? In our home, it seems to vary depending on the circumstances. In periods of excitement, like Christmas morning, I have to talk quite loudly, just to get a word in. Other times, maybe the one-on-one times, a quiet voice actually seems to get the most attention. (I think they call those times the "teachable moments.")

I want to encourage you today: Let God's Holy Spirit rush over you like a fresh, cool breeze. Let Him breathe some new air into your sails. Get your second wind, and rise up to meet the stormy challenges life may throw at you this day.

Father, teach me not to be a hurricane when I communicate. Show me how to be humble, a quiet listener. Help me to fill my house with peace, which comes from leaning on Your Holy Spirit. In Jesus' name, amen.

New Birth = Living Hope

Praise be to the God and Father of our Lord Jesus Christ! In his great mercy he has given us new birth into a living hope through the resurrection of Jesus Christ from the dead (1 Peter 1:3).

Scripture: **1 Peter 1:1-12**
Song: **"The Mercy of God Is an Ocean Divine"**

It's always exciting to anticipate a birth. There's an expectancy, a certain excitement in the air. Everyone in my family looks forward to the birth of the next grandchild, no matter whose it is. Of course we all hope for the best when it comes to the baby's health. When that bundle arrives with all its fingers and toes, we have had an answer to our prayers.

Christ gives us new birth into a living hope. Hope is absolutely essential. Without hope human beings don't function very well. And our hope, as Christians, is the prospect of eternal life in Heaven. Without that goal before us—the Holy Spirit being our down payment on that blessed home—we tend to start shriveling.

I've noticed that people living without much hope don't stand as tall as they once did. They have lost the vision of a future resting in God's hands. As the great writer Herman Melville once said: "Hope is the struggle of the soul, breaking loose from what is perishable, and attesting her eternity."

Father, You give the ultimate hope—the promise of an eternity with You in Heaven. Thank You, Lord, I pray in the name of Jesus. Amen.

DEVOTIONS®

*T*hough you have not seen him, . . . you believe in him.

—1 Peter 1:8

NOVEMBER

Photo © Dreamstime

Gary Allen, Editor

DEVOTIONS® is published quarterly by Standard Publishing, Cincinnati, Ohio, www.standardpub.com. © 2008 by Standard Publishing. All rights reserved. Topics based on the Home Daily Bible Readings, International Sunday School Lessons. © 2006 by the Committee on the Uniform Series. Printed in the U.S.A. All Scripture quotations, unless otherwise indicated, are taken from the HOLY BIBLE, NEW INTERNATIONAL VERSION®. NIV®. Copyright © 1973, 1978, 1984 by International Bible Society. Used by permission of Zondervan. All rights reserved. Where noted, Scripture quotations are from the following, used with permission of the copyright holders, all rights reserved: *New American Standard Bible (NASB),* © The Lockman Foundation, 1960, 1962, 1963, 1968, 1971, 1972, 1973, 1975, 1977, 1995. *Holy Bible, New Living Translation (NLT),* © 1996. Tyndale House Publishers. *King James Version (KJV),* public domain.

A Focus on the Beloved?

Now that you have purified yourselves by obeying the truth so that you have sincere love for your brothers, love one another deeply, from the heart (1 Peter 1:22).

Scripture: **1 Peter 1:13-25**
Song: **"Love Surpassing Human Love"**

If you have lived beyond your teenage years, then you have probably experienced the pain of a love that turned out *not* to be what it first appeared to be. Perhaps you only had to endure a brief episode of "puppy love."

As we grow older and wiser, we begin to recognize the signs of mere momentary infatuation. While it may be deeply felt at the time, it's actually an insincere form of love—it has no real substance or staying power. It is focused on the lover's feelings rather than what's best for the one loved. In other words, what's lacking in insincere love relationships is this: commitment.

Without commitment, any so-called love relationship is doomed. With commitment, a relationship has a chance to grow and flourish. Between the sexes, it is in a committed love relationship, within the bounds of marriage, that we are free to love one another at the deepest levels. There we become free to love from the heart. Otherwise, we run for cover; it is just too great a risk.

Lord God, *thank You for my spouse. Help this relationship—and all my relationships—continue to grow in sincere love. In Jesus' name, amen.*

November 1. **Robert Thompson** calls Denver home but currently lives near Washington, D.C. He is married with four children.

His Requirements

What does the LORD your God require from you, but to fear the LORD your God, to walk in all His ways and love Him, and to serve the LORD your God with all your heart and with all your soul (Deuteronomy 10:12, *New American Standard Bible*).

Scripture: **Deuteronomy 10:10-15**
Song: **"With All My Heart"**

Some friends in grad school recently bewailed all of the requirements for getting into their respective programs—and for getting *out* of them as well! One friend faces a number of prerequisite undergraduate classes before she can even enter her graduate program. Another has to jump through many hoops to get his dissertation approved. In the meantime, he continually tweaks his scholarly masterpiece under ongoing faculty critique.

Sadly, we sometimes think that God has a long, but narrow list of requirements for all who enter His family. Each requirement starts with *should* or *must*—or so we tell each other. "You should do it this way"; "you must do this"—with each *should* or *must* laced with legalism. Now take a look at our verse today. In these words spoken by Moses to the people of Israel, there's not a *should* or *must* in sight. Love God; serve Him. And the field is pretty wide open as to the how.

God, *the "shoulds" and "musts" of life weigh me down. Teach me to walk willingly in Your ways, with a joyful heart. Through Christ, amen.*

November 2–8. **Linda Washington** is a seasoned writer and editor for numerous Christian publications. She lives in Carol Stream, Illinois.

November 3

A Storehouse for Our Trust

He gathers the waters of the sea into jars; he puts the deep into storehouses (Psalm 33:7).

Scripture: **Psalm 33:4-12**
Song: **"Strong Son of God, Immortal Love"**

The largest storehouse of water in the world is Lake Volta in Ghana. We're talking 3,275 square miles and 153 billion cubic meters of water! The man-made lake took four years to form after the Akosombo Dam was built to hold back the Black Volta and White Volta Rivers.

Think of all that water. Think of all that hydroelectric power. But just think: A massive amount of water like that is easily manipulated by God. After all, He's the one who formed the seas in the first place, establishing their boundaries. How fitting that a psalm of praise, which includes references to water storehouses, would remind its readers and singers of the perfect storehouse of our trust—God himself. He's the one whose plans "stand firm" (v. 11), the one whose knowledge and power are limitless.

When we feel buffeted by change, isn't it great to know that He who holds back the seas has a reservoir of strength and peace for us? Have you tapped into that reservoir lately?

Heavenly Father, I often feel tossed about by the whims of others or the ebb and flow of my own desires. How great to know that, just as You establish boundaries for the waters of the earth, You also establish boundaries for my life. Thank You so much, in Your Son's name. Amen.

Don't Count on It

Don't count on your warhorse to give you victory—for all its strength, it cannot save you (Psalm 33:17, *New Living Translation*).

Scripture: **Psalm 33:13-22**
Song: **"My Hope Is in the Lord"**

The Friesian was prized as a fine strain of warhorse during the early middle ages. Although it wasn't the heaviest of draft horses, this silky, black breed had the height, strength, and skill necessary to carry a fully armored knight. A warhorse—a destrier—cost a fortune. It was probably worth up to 20 average horses. And no wonder; this horse was trained for combat.

But isn't it interesting to see what our Bible passage stresses? That even such a valuable animal, with its years of training, should *not* be counted on for victory. You see, ancient Israel had a history of depending on a well-trained army or powerful allies for victory against their enemies. But they must constantly remember: God is the only surety in a war situation. Or *any* situation.

Warhorses have fallen out of fashion these days. But if we substitute computers, or cars, or money, or . . . well, the same message applies. If we put our hope in anything but the Lord, we're in for a rude awakening.

Almighty and Holy God, I often trust my own devices and plans instead of relying on Your power. Forgive me for my times of pure self-reliance. You are my only true hope, for this life and for the next one. In the name of Jesus, Lord and Savior of all, I pray. Amen.

No Favorites

Of a truth I perceive that God is no respecter of persons: but in every nation he that feareth him, and worketh righteousness, is accepted with him (Acts 10:34, 35, *King James Version*).

Scripture: **Acts 10:34-43**
Song: **"Together, Lord, We Come to Thee"**

In fourth grade, my best friend, Donna, and I used to make up scathing songs about the kids in class who were teacher's pets. We thought we were fighting an unfair system. Still, we envied those who seemed to have our teacher's favor. Had we been chosen, doubtless "the system" would have been more to our liking.

For centuries the Israelites were God's favored people. But through the sacrifice of His Son, Jesus, people of other nations could join a new body—the church. This meant there were no "favorites," since all shared equal status.

Thus the apostle Peter had to undergo a radical change of heart about associating with Gentiles. He readily admitted the change to his new brother in Christ, the Roman centurion Cornelius. Never in his wildest dreams could Peter have imagined that "favored status" would be shared by a member of the apparent enemy.

Perhaps there's someone in your life you can't imagine ever greeting with: "Welcome to the family of God!" But God invites all. May we do the same.

***Lord,** I'm thankful that, because of You, all are included in the invitation to salvation. When I feel excluded here on earth, may I rest in the assurance that I belong to a family far bigger than I imagine. In Jesus' name, amen.*

Less Talk, More Action

Great grace was upon them all. Nor was there anyone among them who lacked . . . and they distributed to each as anyone had need (Acts 4:33-35, *New King James Version*).

Scripture: **Acts 4:31-37**
Song: **"We Are One in the Spirit"**

I always considered my DVD collection to be something all of my friends could share. "Why rent when you can borrow one of mine?" I would say to those looking for a cinematic eveing. Of course, one rule must be heeded: return the discs—*asap.*

My altruistic motives went out the window when a friend not only borrowed—and kept—10 DVDs but also loaned one to a family member . . . who promptly lost it. I complained, but I had to question my true intentions. *Did I really mean to share my DVDs, or was that just talk? Did I care more about my possessions than I did the people who borrowed them?* The answer, sadly, was yes.

Not so with the first-century Christians. They didn't just talk about love or generosity; they acted. They willingly shared everything, no strings attached. Land was sold and the money given away—not loaned, but given—to those in need.

Can you imagine having no people in need in your community? These believers didn't have to imagine. They worked to bring it about.

Holy Spirit, only by Your presence can I desire to live beyond my usual self-centeredness. Help me talk less and act more. In Jesus' name, amen.

Bear Up

For this finds favor, if for the sake of conscience toward God a person bears up under sorrows when suffering unjustly (1 Peter 2:19, *New American Standard Bible*).

Scripture: **1 Peter 2:11-17**
Song: **"Precious Lord, Take My Hand"**

When one of my family members lost his corporate job, and I heard why, I was furious. Suddenly accused of lacking the managerial skills for which he had been promoted, he was given the option of resigning or being demoted—even after winning company awards for job performance. Sadly, he wondered whether his being a committed and outspoken Christian was the underlying reason for his problems on the job. He asked for prayer that he'd avoid bitterness, even as some folks "bad-mouthed" him during his last month of employment.

The apostle Peter suggests that kind of attitude in our Scripture today: In the face of persecution, continue doing what is right. Continue submitting to those in authority. Continue respecting others. Such behavior comes with a price, though. We sacrifice our pride along with any temporary satisfaction we might get from taking revenge.

As the apostle well knew, living the Christian life may cause us to lose jobs, friends, and possibly even our lives. Thankfully, we don't suffer alone. God suffers with us.

Father God, many times I've felt depressed and blinded by tears. It's hard to bear up, Lord, when life crashes down around me. I need Your strength to go on. I pray through my deliverer, Jesus. Amen.

Living Stones

You also, like living stones, are being built into a spiritual house to be a holy priesthood, offering spiritual sacrifices acceptable to God through Jesus Christ (1 Peter 2:5).

Scripture: **1 Peter 2:1-10**
Song: **"Christ Is Our Cornerstone"**

I work for a company whose motto includes part of today's verse. But many people don't get the connection when I tell them the company's name. They think of explorers like Stanley Livingstone, rather than the "living stones" of this Scripture. (I usually think of stones skipped across water; at least there's some movement.)

The truth is, I haven't always felt like a living stone. Instead, I've felt as still and lifeless as the average stone, especially when trouble plagues me as it has recently—trouble in the form of severe financial loss. Just as I'm feeling small and weak, I'm comforted by this passage. It describes someone who could easily have been described as small and weak—the cornerstone, Jesus. Having endured the pain of rejection by His own people, which resulted in His death, He established a family—"a royal priesthood" (2:9) given life by the Holy Spirit.

Even when we feel torn down, we're being built up. Ironic, isn't it? But it's all part of being a living stone—something so hard and lifeless being made into something alive, useful, and everlasting.

Spirit of the Living God, thank You for being the mortar that connects me and other believers with the cornerstone. In His precious name, amen.

Feel Like a Pinky Toe?

On the contrary, those parts of the body that seem to be weaker are indispensable (1 Corinthians 12:22).

Scripture: **1 Corinthians 12:20-26**
Song: **"We All Can Do Something for Jesus"**

Awhile back I stubbed my pinky toe while trying to find my way through a dark house. Although it really hurt—and turned out to have a small fracture—I figured the little wound wouldn't affect me much. After all, how important is a pinky toe? Quite important, I soon discovered: I could no longer climb stairs, reach to high places by standing on my toes, or even walk comfortably with shoes on.

Just like the pinky toe, some of us may be seen by others—or even ourselves—as pretty weak and useless. Maybe we have deep hurts that have disabled us emotionally or spiritually. Or maybe God has called us to obscure or lowly places of service.

But to God we are indispensable. We all need each other, whether weak or strong, whether holding positions of honor and prominence or not. God has designed a special place in His body for everyone, and we are all equal in His sight. You may only be a pinky toe, but without you, the rest of the body would have problems walking.

Thank You, Lord, for giving every member of Your body a ministry. May we realize how much we all need each other. Through Christ, amen.

November 9–15. **Renee Gray-Wilburn**, wife and mother of three, writes and edits for various ministries from her home in Colorado Springs, Colorado.

Trust Me!

By faith [Moses] left Egypt, not fearing the king's anger; he persevered because he saw him who is invisible (Hebrews 11:27).

Scripture: **Hebrews 11:23-28**
Song: **"Jesus, These Eyes Have Never Seen"**

Amidst the horror stories of the Holocaust nightmare, a few tales of triumph have emerged. Those who survived typically shared one common characteristic: they persevered by envisioning a brighter future. Simply put, they had faith.

Moses also relied on faith to equip him with the necessary courage to leave the only life he ever knew. By faith he would follow God into unchartered territories. He too persevered against all odds by setting his sights on what he could not yet see. He didn't know where God was leading him, but he knew his leader.

What obstacles do you face at the moment? What challenges lie ahead, evoking fear within you? God calls you to lay down your fears and arm yourself with faith. "Faith is being sure of what we hope for and certain of what we do not see" (Hebrews 11:1). No matter how difficult your circumstances, God says: "Trust me." When we start seeing "Him who is invisible" as the faithful one, we too will persevere.

Father, help me to walk by faith and not by sight. Give me the strength to persevere through all of life's challenges, knowing that You will be with me every step of the way. In Christ's name I pray. Amen.

The Secret Is Out

I have learned the secret of being content in any and every situation (Philippians 4:12).

Scripture: **Philippians 4:10-14**
Song: **"Hidden Peace"**

Not long ago, I befriended a lady who was new to our church. I enjoyed being around her because of her upbeat disposition. She was always full of joy and encouragement. One day I shared with her some difficulties I was experiencing. I hesitated to tell her at first, thinking she couldn't relate to my struggles. (Her life always appeared to be a walk on Easy Street!)

Once I started sharing, she opened up about her own hardships and trials. I could hardly believe all she'd been through—and was still going through. I chose to stop complaining about my "problems" and prayed God would help me develp an attitude like my friend's. He led me to Philippians 4:12. I reflected on everything the apostle Paul endured and how he still maintained contentment amidst his darkest hours.

So, what is this "secret" that Paul and my friend had discovered? They learned that once Jesus truly becomes all we need, He will also become our source of all peace and joy. And nothing will ever be able to take it away.

Dear Jesus, enable me to see You as my all in all—to know that You are all I need for deep contentment in my life. Help me look beyond my circumstances and stay focused on You and the perfect peace You've promised. In the name of the Father, the Son, and the Holy Spirit, I pray. Amen.

Do What You Ought to Do

Peter and the other apostles replied: "We must obey God rather than men!" (Acts 5:29).

Scripture: **Acts 5:27-32**
Song: **"I'll Live for Him"**

I frequently volunteer with a group that feeds the homeless. For a while we served food weekly at a busy downtown park. But then one day we were informed we could no longer serve there. Nearby businesses were complaining about our clientele.

Believing we had a biblical mandate to care for the poor, we wouldn't let a few complaints stop us. We left that particular location but began serving at several other parks in the same area. It wasn't long before the homeless once again knew where to find us.

Like Peter, we knew we must first obey God, regardless of public opinion. So we continued preaching the gospel and sharing our lives with the needy in our community.

There will always be opposition to God's Word and work done in Jesus' name. But we can't afford to be intimidated. As Thomas Carlyle, a great Christian of the past, once put it: "We do less than we ought, unless we do all that we can." As we determine to obey God, He will always make a way for us to do what we ought to do.

Dear Heavenly Father, give me wisdom and guidance in discerning Your will along with other Christians. Help us know what You would have us to do. Then give us the courage to move forward, with a spirit of goodwill and kindness, even in the face of oppositon. In the name of Jesus, amen.

Don't Jump!

They think it strange that you do not plunge with them into the same flood of dissipation, and they heap abuse on you (1 Peter 4:4).

Scripture: **1 Peter 4:1-6**
Song: **"No Compromise"**

Returning home from his first summer camp, our son shared that he was made fun of one day. Why? Because he wouldn't jump into a river with the other kids. Everyone took turns swinging from ropes and then jumping. But he didn't want to do it, because he thought the river water was "disgusting." He stuck to his guns but, apparently, never heard the end of it.

Sometimes it's hard, especially for new Christians, to leave the old life and live the new life in Christ. Our non-Christian friends continually invite us to jump into fairly "disgusting" waters of sin with them. It seems they just can't understand the transformation in us, now that Jesus has entered our hearts. But we can't afford to jump—not even once.

I'm proud of my son for not jumping into the river that day. I'm even prouder of him when he chooses not to jump into sinful behavior, despite the catcalls he may receive for his integrity.

Dear Heavenly Father, I praise You for rescuing me from the kingdom of darkness. Help me continue to live in Your strength, refusing to jump back into the old waters. In everything, keep me humble and ever open to the seekers around me. In Jesus' name I pray. Amen.

Work It In!

Above all, love each other deeply, because love covers over a multitude of sins (1 Peter 4:8).

Scripture: **1 Peter 4:7-11**
Song: **"A Little Bit of Love"**

As my husband and I prepared to welcome several friends to our home for an evening of entertaining, I noticed an orange-colored stain on my living room carpet. It was just moments before our guests were to arrive. Looking closer, I realized there were actually *several* small stains by our coffee table.

My toddler had been walking around with a cup of orange juice earlier in the day, so it wasn't hard to figure what had happened. Since I was so short on time, I did what any good host would do—I covered the stains with the coffee table.

Wouldn't it be great if our souls' "stains"—our mistakes, bad attitudes, hurtful words, and sins—could be covered as easily? God's Word says they can. When we love others with God's love, we will work to hide their imperfections and wrongdoings, not expose them. By conveying God's unconditional love instead of judgment, we allow opportunity for God's grace to bring them to repentance. The next time you encounter stains on someone, saturate them with God's love. Work it in, deeply.

Father, thank You for Your love shed abroad in my heart. You've not only covered my "stains" but completely removed them through the cross. Now help me to extend Your matchless love to others. In Jesus' name, amen.

Rejoice in Persecution

If you are insulted because of the name of Christ, you are blessed (1 Peter 4:14).

Scripture: **1 Peter 4:12-19**
Song: **"Do Not Be Surprised"**

Persecution against Christians steadily rises. In many places across the globe, preaching about Jesus, handing out Christian literature, or even carrying a Bible can bring imprisonment or possibly death. And while Christians in America aren't martyred for their beliefs, they're persecuted in other ways. For example, they may be forced to go against their values in the name of "political correctness" at work. And they often have to silence their prayers in public places.

The apostles were no strangers to persecution—it had a way of finding them wherever they went. That's because Satan will never step aside and allow us to freely advance God's kingdom. It will always be a fight, and even more so as we approach the return of Christ.

But rejoice! If you've ever been insulted or persecuted for the sake of the gospel, the Bible calls you blessed. You may not feel blessed at the time, but God will honor you for your commitment to Him. And His rewards—whether in this life or in Heaven—will make it all worthwhile.

Father, help me hold firm to Your Word when others insult me because of Jesus. Remind me that You have called me blessed because I am persecuted for Your name's sake—and that my heavenly reward will be great. Keep me loving others for Your sake, no matter what. In Christ's name, amen.

God Gives Us Our Abilities

Because you have been trustworthy in a very small matter, take charge of ten cities (Luke 19:17).

Scripture: **Luke 19:12-26**
Song: **"Help Somebody Today"**

In 1953, my mom, Dessolee Smith, thought she might be "losing her mind." She believed the Lord was calling her, a high school dropout and daughter of an alcoholic, to be a minister's wife. My dad, Keith Smith, also a high school dropout, was an introvert with speech impediments. And Dad had no intentions of leaving his factory job or his hometown. It seemed unreasonable that God could use either of them in full-time church work.

Mom pondered the whole matter, but she didn't share any of her thoughts with Dad. Then one evening my father broke the news that he believed God was calling him into pastoral ministry.

Their "inability" wasn't a problem to God, of course. They finished high school by correspondence while attending Bible college a thousand miles away from their hometown. God touched my dad's speech (with a lot of coaching from my mother) and used them in their ministry to lead many to Christ. Our lack of ability is a showcase for God's ability.

Heavenly Father, *help me to know and develop the spiritual gifts You've given me. May they bring glory to Your name. Through Christ, amen.*

November 16–22. **Linda Dessolee Roth** is a preacher's kid, a freelance writer, a mother of five, and a grandmother who lives in Adrian, Michigan.

The Sacrifice of Praise

I will sing of mercy and judgment: unto thee, O LORD, will I sing (Psalm 101:1, *King James Version*).

Scripture: **Psalm 101:1-4**
Song: **"I Will Sing of the Mercies of the Lord"**

Our adopted son, Ron, has never met his birth dad. He wasn't sure his biological father even knew of his existence. And Ron allowed the pain of it to fester into open bitterness. We understood Ron's struggles, but he refused our counsel. It was hard to sing God's praise amidst this heartache in our family, but we tried.

The hardness on Ron's face, the lack of respect for God and for us, the vulgarity of Ron's language, and the acceptance of questionable friends and habits were obvious. Year after year we waited upon God and continued to praise Him for what He must be doing in Ron's heart, even though we could not see Him working.

Recently we received a letter from Ron expressing regret for his actions toward God, us, and others. He signed his letter, "The adopted son of God."

I've begun to see that it isn't necessary for me to see the ending of my hard times. I only need to praise the Lord, God of mercy and judgment, and leave the unfolding of my days in His hands.

My dear Heavenly Father, only You could answer my prayer. Thank You for teaching me the value of praying a hedge of thorns around my son to separate him from ungodly friends. Teach me daily to sing of Your mercy and wisdom in the midst of my troubles. In Jesus' name, amen.

The Lies of Discouragement

A faithful witness will not lie: but a false witness will utter lies (Proverbs 14:5, *King James Version*).

Scripture: **Proverbs 14:2-5**
Song: **"Jesus Saves"**

All of us will face lies intended to discourage us. After my parents, Keith and Dessolee Smith, moved from their home town, Adrian, Michigan, to Omaha, Nebraska, so Dad could prepare for the ministry, Mom learned that her father, who did not know God, was dying.

Mom faithfully wrote letters to her father and enclosed scriptural tracts. Someone in Adrian laughed at Mom and told her the tracts were a waste of time—because her father was throwing them away without reading them.

But this apparently discouraging news pushed Mom even deeper into prayer and reliance on God. When the inevitable call of his worsening condition came, Mom knew she had to see her father one more time.

Our family returned briefly to Michigan. As Mom and Dad entered the hospital room, Mom said, "Dad, I've come all this way to see about your soul."

Grandpa looked at her and said, "That's all taken care of. I read one of those tracts you sent, talked to a minister, and Jesus has been my Savior and Lord for several weeks. "

But suppose Mom had listened to the lie?

Heavenly Father, strengthen me when I face lies that cut into the depths of my soul. No matter the intended discouragement, may I rely on Your faithfulness in loving and forgiving me, no matter what. In Jesus' name, amen.

God Can Use Anything

[Daniel] kneeled upon his knees three times a day, and prayed, and gave thanks before his God, as he did aforetime (Daniel 6:10, *King James Version*).

Scripture: **Daniel 6:6-10**
Song: **"He Is Able to Deliver Thee"**

As a timid junior higher, I attended a public school where our science teacher openly scoffed at Scripture and boasted that he was waiting for the next committed Christian to enter his class. He vigorously sought to destroy his students' faith, aggressivly teaching evolutionary theory from an atheistic perspective. So, every afternoon I faced that teacher, a large man with a booming voice. Each night I read the Bible and had discussions with my dad, who encouraged me to trust God's Word.

At the time, I was sure those were the worst days of my life. I often felt sick just walking into that science classroom. I couldn't grasp the depths of what God was doing for me.

Years later, when I faced standing alone once again, I felt the courage that God had developed in me through that science class. I found, as surely the prophet Daniel knew, that God is a faithful deliverer, even amidst the booming, roaring voices of opposition.

Heavenly Father, forgive me for my lack of understanding; my focus is often narrow. I cannot grasp, in the middle of a battle, how You are increasing my spiritual muscles. I do want to learn more of Your ways, to thank You for being my patient teacher. In the name of Jesus I pray. Amen.

For Us: Two Hours Less

Ye know not what hour your Lord doth come. But know this, that if the goodman of the house had known in what watch the thief would come, he would have watched (Matthew 24:42, 43, *King James Version*).

Scripture: **Matthew 24:42-47**
Song: **"Christ Returneth!"**

Does the reality of Jesus' return sometimes lose its grip on our expectations? It's not true for Heather Widdis of Jenison, Michigan. Heather, wanting her wedding to be a picture of the church's wait for the return of Christ, chose not to know the day of her wedding! The event's planning was done for her by family.

Heather was only told the month of the year (to represent the season). And for practical purposes, she had to be told about what time each day to be ready. After the invitations were sent to the guests, and the secret could accidentally slip out, Heather and her bridesmaids began staying together in her new home. By the activity and the excitement, Heather knew the time was close.

Then one day while Heather and her bridesmaids were having their morning devotions, her bridegroom, Dan, left his father's house and arrived with the sound of a trumpet. Dan told Heather that he would return in two hours to take her to the wedding. She didn't have much warning—but more than we will have.

Heavenly Father, help me live today so that others will see the reality of Your Son's sudden return to the world. In His name I pray. Amen.

We Each Take This Journey

The angel of the Lord spake unto Philip, saying, Arise, and go toward the south, unto the way that goeth down from Jerusalem unto Gaza, which is desert (Acts 8:26, *King James Version*).

Scripture: **Acts 8:26-39**
Song: **"He's Able"**

What is your desert these days? A few years ago my husband developed a form of dementia, throwing us into an emotional-financial-spiritual desert.

It has been three years since the Lord allowed us to walk out of that dry period in our lives. My husband is well now, but we are no longer the same; our spiritual strength has increased. Our footing is more secure as we walk by faith, and our prayer life has been revitalized.

We stared hopelessness in the face and found God's reflection. We couldn't answer all the why's, but He was there, ready to encourage us. It was a boot camp of intense spiritual training, and we are better off for having been enrolled.

There is always a reason that God leads us into a desert. When the heat of the trial initially hits us, however, as we head into that barren land, the *reason* isn't so important. No, it's all about our willingness to accept what God has allowed in our lives—and to let it deepen our faith.

Dear heavenly Father, thank You for the desert You allowed me to enter. It was hot and dry and appeared endless. However, while there, You deepened my refreshment in Your Word and allowed me to grow. In the name of Your Son, my Savior, I pray. Amen.

Looking Ahead

I will endeavor that ye may be able after my decease to have these things always in remembrance (2 Peter 1:15, *King James Version*).

Scripture: **2 Peter 1:3-15**
Song: **"Hold the Fort"**

My father's cousin told me about my great-great grandmother. Grandma Ballard was a godly woman whose favorite hymn was "Hold the Fort."

But what trials did God allow her to endure? What answers to prayers did she have? What was her Christian testimony? I asked, but no one knew the answers to any of my questions. Although I am grateful that I know Grandma Esther Ballard's favorite hymn, it would enrich my life to know more.

My grandchildren are very young. However, even if I died today, the stories of God's working in our family will not fade. I've preserved those answers to prayer, along with family stories and photos, in monthly "family magazines" that I've written.

Personalized family magazines aren't a necessity, but preparing a written testimony for those looking to us for an example is important. We can follow the apostle Paul's example and leave an epistle in some form—perhaps in an open letter to future generations—detailing God's faithfulness to us over the years.

Father, open my mind to what my testimony will mean to those who perhaps haven't even started their lives on earth yet. In Jesus' name, amen.

Drink It In

My soul thirsts for God, for the living God. When can I go and meet with God? (Psalm 42:2).

Scripture: **Psalm 42:1-11**
Song: **"As the Deer"**

Every living thing needs water, whether it's the tiniest flower in a hillside meadow, a huge elephant lumbering through the jungle, or a human being going about his daily routine. Without water, each of these life forms would eventually perish.

Just as all life depends on water, our souls need the water of God's Word to give us life and to sustain that life. God's well is deep, the supply is endless, and the water He promises will "become . . . a spring of water welling up to eternal life" in us (John 4:14) and that will touch others too.

We long to be in God's presence to quench our spiritual thirst with the life-giving water He has for us in His Word. Sometimes we feel spiritually parched, much like the deer panting for water. That's when we need the same vision as the psalmist: "Put your hope in God, for I will yet praise him" (Psalm 42:5, 11). Drink deeply and often of God's love, as you drink in His Word.

Father, may I be as thirsty for You as when I am physically parched from going too long without a drink of water. In You I find not only salvation but also the refreshment of Your life-giving words. In Jesus' name, amen.

November 23–29. **Sue Miholer,** a recent retiree in Salem, Oregon, runs Picky, Picky Ink, her freelance writing and editing business.

Besieged City

He showed his wonderful love to me when I was in a besieged city (Psalm 31:21).

Scripture: **Psalm 31:21-24**
Song: **"Faith Brings the Victory"**

I was able to visit Sarajevo and other neighboring cities in 2000, about five years after the horrible war in that region. Some rebuilding had occurred, but there were still bombed-out buildings, houses without roofs, walls pockmarked by small-arms fire, and whole blocks of vacant crumbling buildings. The horror of war had been silenced, but the telltale remnants told the story of a besieged city.

I realized that everyone over 5 years of age had lived through that terrible time of war. The missionaries told us about what some had endured. Many had lost close family members. Parents had risked—and sometimes lost—their lives to secure what little food was available. Proper healthcare and employment had been scarce.

And yet, there was an unmistakable joy in the Christians we met. Their souls—like their cities—had been besieged, and they searched for peace on many levels. Now, five years later, with the psalmist they could declare, "You heard my cry for mercy." He's ready, too, to hear and act on my cry for mercy when I feel cut off from Him.

Dear God, although I've never been under siege physically, I know what it's like to be under attack by verbal assaults. Thank You that even in those times I can know Your peace. In the name of the Father, the Son, and the Holy Spirit, I pray. Amen.

Dependence

From birth I have relied on you (Psalm 71:6).

Scripture: **Psalm 71:1-6**
Song: **"Jesus Is All the World to Me"**

Many of the physically disabled students I worked with over the years had to rely on parents and others for their basic needs—for bathing, clothing, feeding, nurturing, and protecting. Without such a support system, most would have died or been unable to live up to their potential.

Like a physical disability, my sin nature is a spiritual disability to me. I need someone besides myself to supply my deepest needs. I can't do it on my own—even when I think I can be independent.

For bathing, I need His cleansing from sin and for daily holiness—"the washing of rebirth and renewal" (Titus 3:5).

For clothing, I need His righteousness—"clothe yourselves with the Lord Jesus Christ" (Romans 13:14).

For food, I need His Word—"crave pure spiritual milk" (1 Peter 2:2).

For growth and nurturing, I need His grace—"grow in the grace and knowledge of our Lord and Savior Jesus Christ" (2 Peter 3:18).

For protection, I need the safety of abiding in His presence—"he will keep me safe" (Psalm 27:5).

Father, I am so dependent on You for everything. In You, I "live and move and have [my] being" (Acts 17:28). Thank You! In Jesus' name, amen.

Linked in the Darkness

I have put my hope in your word (Psalm 119:81).

Scripture: **Psalm 119:81-88**
Song: **"The Bible Is a Brilliant Lamp"**

Astronauts venturing outside an orbiting spacecraft must remain connected to the mother ship at all times. The tenuous, umbilical-like connection is their source of life-sustaining necessities. Outer space would be lethal without this linkage.

Have you ever been in a dark and scary place—a place where you felt cut off from God? In today's reading, that's where the psalmist is. He's fainting, his eyes are failing, he's being persecuted, and he feels as if he's been put "on hold" during a phone conversation.

But do you see his lifeline—what keeps him connected to God? It is those life-sustaining nuggets of truth interspersed in his complaints. He has put his hope in God's Word, he doesn't forget God's decrees, he remembers that he can trust in God's commands, and he has not forsaken God's precepts.

The same truths from God's Word that sustained the psalmist during his dark days are the very ones we can hang onto during our days of discouragement. Even when God feels so far away.

Dear Lord in Heaven, when I'm in a dark and scary place, remind me of the truths in Your Word that tell me You will always be with me. Thank You that You are as near as my next breath. I pray this prayer in the name of Jesus, my merciful Savior and Lord. Amen.

Against All Hope

[He is] the God who gives life to the dead and calls things that are not as though they were. Against all hope, Abraham in hope believed and so became the father of many nations, just as it had been said to him, "So shall your offspring be" (Romans 4:17, 18).

Scripture: **Romans 4:16-24**
Song: **"The Solid Rock"**

An elderly woman was lost in a remote area. After almost two weeks, the authorities called off the search, and her family began making plans for a memorial service. But an off-duty officer, against all hope, went out for "one last look" and found her.

Abraham and his wife, Sarah, were too old to have a child. God had promised one to them, and "against all hope" (Romans 4:18), Abraham chose to believe God. He couldn't explain how it would happen, but God had said it would, and he knew God could be trusted to keep a promise.

Against all hope, Jesus rose from the dead—a physical deadness as real as Abraham's "deadness" in his natural inability to become a father.

Against all hope, we can be made alive in Jesus Christ. The key is to be "fully persuaded that God [has] power to do what he [has] promised" (Romans 4:21).

Father, You have made so many promises to me—some that defy natural laws and others that simply seem outside the realm of the possible. You promise life instead of death, and I am so thankful. In Jesus' name, amen.

Blueprint for Missionary Work

Strengthening the disciples and encouraging them to remain true to the faith (Acts 14:22).

Scripture: **Acts 14:21-28**
Song: **"Tell Me the Story of Jesus"**

Everywhere Paul and his team went, they left behind a church—or at least a band of believers who met together on a regular basis. Paul spent his life planting the seeds of God's Word wherever he went, in lives and in entire cities.

I sometimes wonder what I leave behind in the lives of people. When I went with a team to Bosnia-Herzegovina, we left behind many of our personal clothing items for the missionaries to distribute. And we left behind the contents of eight huge suitcases (stuffed animals, craft supplies, camping equipment, teaching materials, etc.) for the missionaries to use. We helped the church by ministering to the children through Bible stories and an English-as-a-second-language program. We were guests in the homes of believers and encouraged them in their walk with Christ. I believe we, like Paul, "preached the good news" and strengthened the believers, encouraging them to remain faithful.

Paul's blueprint for missionary work is still the model being used effectively around the world today. It keeps planting the seed of God's Word in lives.

Lord, it's good to know that You can use us to bless others in much the same way You used Your early followers. In Jesus' name, amen.

Patience

The Lord is not slow in keeping his promise . . . He is patient with you (2 Peter 3:9).

Scripture: **2 Peter 3:1-13**
Song: **"Softly and Tenderly"**

When I worked with emotionally disturbed students, patience was the key to getting their compliance with the program's expectations. I never asked a student to do something because I had some scheme in mind. He needed to comply simply because it was in his best interest.

And I didn't care how long it took. I got paid whether I was actively teaching him how to read or waiting for him to decide to open the book. Sometimes it looked like I was ignoring a willful student. But that was usually a better tactic than getting in his face and demanding obedience. It often took longer than I liked, but it allowed the student to make his own decision.

Our patient God wants what is best for us. He's not interested in a specific time frame for our compliance—although "the sooner the better" is best. And sometimes it might feel like He's ignoring us. But the end goal of His incredible patience with us is that He wants us to choose Him so that not one of us will perish.

My Almighty God and Father, sometimes it seems like the unfolding of Your will takes too long. I want things to fall into place on my timetable. But show me how to step back and allow You to work in the way and time that suit Your sovereign purposes. In the name of the Father, the Son, and the Holy Spirit, I pray. Amen.

There All the Time

"I have been with you wherever you have gone, and . . . I will make your name great" (2 Samuel 7:9).

Scripture: **2 Samuel 7:8-11b**
Song: **"He Was There All the Time"**

I remember when my son Tim first saw the slide at our local park. It wasn't a big slide. But for him—being just a couple years old—it must have loomed as a Mount Everest to scale and conquer. Actually, I thought it might be a little too big for him, but he kept begging to try it. So I walked him over to it, and he grabbed the ladder to pull himself up. Sure enough, a few moments later, he stood at the bottom of that slide, beaming. "I *did* it, Dad!"

But let's go back and get the details. Yes, Tim took hold of the ladder, but I went up with him, my hand around his waist, giving him a little lift with each step. When he got to the top, I steadied him, helped him sit down on my lap, and held his hand as we enjoyed a controlled descent down that shiny metal. So, he did it!

Surely that's how King David became great. God was with him the whole way. Fighting battles on his behalf. Making David's name shine among the nations. The great king could never say he did anything purely by his own strength. Thankfully, we need never say it either.

Lord, I'm so thankful that my life rests in Your protecting hands. May I give You the credit for every accomplishment. In Jesus' name, amen.

November 30. **Gary Allen** lives in southwest Georgia with his wife, Carol. He has adult twin sons who love Christ and work as industrial engineers.

My Prayer Notes

DEVOTIONS®

You renew
the face of the
earth.

—Psalm 104:30

DECEMBER

Photo © by Liquid Library

Gary Allen, Editor

DEVOTIONS® is published quarterly by Standard Publishing, Cincinnati, Ohio, www.standardpub.com. © 2008 by Standard Publishing. All rights reserved. Topics based on the Home Daily Bible Readings, International Sunday School Lessons. © 2006 by the Committee on the Uniform Series. Printed in the U.S.A. All Scripture quotations, unless otherwise indicated, are taken from the HOLY BIBLE, NEW INTERNATIONAL VERSION®. NIV®. Copyright © 1973, 1978, 1984 by International Bible Society. Used by permission of Zondervan. All rights reserved. Where noted, Scripture quotations are from the following, used with permission of the copyright holders, all rights reserved: *Holy Bible, New Living Translation* (NLT), © 1996. Tyndale House Publishers. *New American Standard Bible* (NASB), © The Lockman Foundation, 1960, 1962, 1963, 1968, 1971, 1972, 1973, 1975, 1977, 1995. *The Revised Standard Version of the Bible* (RSV), copyrighted 1946, 1952, © 1971, 1973. *The New King James Version* (NKJV), Copyright © 1982 by Thomas Nelson, Inc.

December 1

Are You a Mentoring Influence?

I will raise up your offspring to succeed you . . . My love will never be taken away from him (2 Samuel 7:12, 15).

Scripture: **2 Samuel 7:11-17**
Song: **"Help Us to Labor On"**

Gunther and his wife served as missionaries to Indonesia, and then Russia, for over 30 years. Gunther's father had been a missionary to China, and when Gunther's son completed his education, he went on to serve in Cambodia. By word and example, Gunther followed—and then passed on—his commitment to worldwide outreach.

In today's reading God makes powerful promises to David regarding the son who will succeed him to the throne. David's heart must have swelled with gratitude upon hearing all that God declared for his successor.

Whether we have children or not, we want the next generation to honor and know God. We may not have a son like Gunther or David to whom we can pass along a godly heritage. But each of us can pray for the next generation of Christians. We are connected beyond the bonds of blood as "heirs of God and co-heirs with Christ" (Romans 8:17). We can trust God to lovingly raise up and establish this new generation, but He will surely use us to serve as its mentoring influences.

Father, I pray for my generation and the next. Empower me to pass along the importance of honoring You every day. Through Christ, amen.

December 1–6. Author and avid in-line skater, **Katherine Douglas,** lives with her husband in northwest Ohio.

O Sovereign Lord!

Is this your usual way of dealing with man, O Sovereign LORD? (2 Samuel 7:19).

Scripture: **2 Samuel 7:18-22**
Song: **"To God Be the Glory"**

We read of miraculous stories often. Some of us have lived them. Web sites, blogs, magazines, and books recount amazing tales of God's special help, deliverance, or miracles in the lives of children and adults alike. Whether we've had a "near miss" in a skidding automobile or seen a wayward family member surrender to God after decades of our prayers, we too sometimes ask, "Is this your usual way of dealing with [me], O Sovereign Lord?"

In the five short verses we read today, humbled King David addresses God as "Sovereign Lord" five times. The king struggles to find words of praise and thanks. He repeatedly acknowledges the one who reigns over all, yet lovingly focuses on him—one man.

What kind of God is this? He created vast galaxies of stars and planets with a word, yet He chooses to communicate with us, one on one? Surely along with David we too can exclaim: "How great you are, O Sovereign Lord! There is no one like you, and there is no God but you" (v. 22).

*Praise to You, **Lord,** for Your mercy and grace. You are God over all, forever praised. You are worthy of all praise, adoration, worship, and honor. To You alone be the glory, O Sovereign Lord. In Jesus' name, amen.*

The God of Covenant

You have established your people Israel as your very own forever, and you, O LORD, have become their God (2 Samuel 7:24).

Scripture: **2 Samuel 7:23-26**
Song: **"O Zion, Haste"**

As the story goes, Frederick the Great once challenged his chaplain on the Bible's validity. The royal skeptic demanded proof of biblical inspiration in one word. The chaplain thought for a moment and then said, "Israel."

As King David praised God, he focused in wonder on Israel—"the one nation on earth that God went out to redeem as a people for himself" (v. 23). Yes, God chose to make a name for himself through Israel. Thus He did mighty things for their benefit. Recalling all of this, David fell back on the covenant name of God with His chosen people: Lord God (v. 25).

Centuries later, Israel still exists as a unique nation. In spite of the Holocaust and frequent wars, Israel remains. As Christians, we too have been brought into covenant with God. "Christ is the mediator of a new covenant" and we too are "a holy nation . . . belonging to God" (Hebrews 9:15 and 1 Peter 2:9). Like King David, we can reflect on the marvel of our special relationship with the covenant-making Lord.

Lord, You are the God of covenant, worthy of all my devotion. Thank You for staying true to all that You have ever promised, down through the history of Your people. Praise to You, in Christ's name. Amen.

No Fair!

He will judge the world with justice and rule the nations with fairness (Psalm 9:8, *New Living Translation*).

Scripture: **Psalm 9:7-11**
Song: **"Joy Comes in the Morning"**

When Jonathan's friend gets a new bicycle for Christmas and Jonathan doesn't, "It's not fair!" he complains. Kristin, who has dreamed of being a mother but year after year can't conceive, cries, "It's not fair!" When the back-stabbing, long-lunch-taking, smooth talker at work gets a promotion and I don't, I say, *"It's just not fair!"*

All of us tend to keep long accounts when it comes to what's unfair and unjust. If we're not whining, "It's not fair," we're just as likely to remind another whiner, "Life's not fair, you know." Our violated sense of fair play grates on our nerves, whether the apparent injustice has occurred on the playground, at the workplace, or in our homes.

God's Word promises that justice won't take a backseat to injustice forever. The day is coming when the whole world will operate under principles of fairness and justice, without exception.

Feeling that life just isn't fair today? You're right. It's not. But God, who is fair and just, will one day set all things to right. Then, life will be fair indeed.

O God, when I'm disgruntled because of life's unfairness, help me remember that You're in control. Give me patience as I await the day when Your rule becomes explicit and every knee bows to You. In Jesus' name, amen.

December 5

Crowning Day Ahead

You have made me the head of nations; people I did not know are subject to me (Psalm 18:43).

Scripture: **Psalm 18:43-50**
Song: **"A Child of the King"**

In C. S. Lewis's *The Voyage of the Dawn Treader*, Prince Caspian keeps his identity a secret in order to reestablish his rule and upend the slave trade on one of his kingdom's distant islands. When he reveals himself as the Prince of Narnia, those who had mistreated him find themselves out of jobs.

There's a similar twist in the life of biblical David. While his predecessor, King Saul, reigned, few people knew that David had been secretly anointed for kingship. But after years of being on the run and hiding in caves, David rightfully assumed the throne. Then his enemies came "trembling from their strongholds" (v. 45). Yet David gave credit to the God who brought it all about. "From violent men you rescued me" (v. 48) he says to God.

From such persons God will rescue us too. We may not know the horrible things from which God has delivered us in this life—or will ultimately deliver us in the next. But because of our relationship to the King of kings, we too are royalty. Our victorious, crowning day lies ahead.

*Thank You, **Gracious heavenly Father,** that You've brought me into Your eternal kingdom through the work of Jesus Christ. Help me to live my life every day as a redeemed child of the Prince of Peace. Through the precious name of Your Son, I pray. Amen.*

And So It Begins

Praise be to the Lord, who this day has not left you without a kinsman-redeemer (Ruth 4:14).

Scripture: **Ruth 4:13-17**
Song: **"My Redeemer"**

The story of King David actually begins in the book of Ruth. There we meet his great-grandparents. Shockingly, perhaps, God chooses a Moabite woman to be in the ancestral line of David—and in the human line of Jesus Christ.

When Boaz first stepped forward to be the kinsman-redeemer of Naomi and her widowed daughter-in-law, Ruth, he wasn't able to assume the role. A closer relative held that position. But the closer relative wasn't willing to act as the kinsman-redeemer. He forfeited the role to Boaz, who was now able and willing to assume the responsibility. He took Ruth to be his wife.

Just as for Naomi and Ruth, God provided us a kinsman-redeemer. As Christ took on human flesh, He became related to us. In living a sinless life, He was both able and willing to redeem us. He paid the price for our redemption in His death. And the proof that His atoning work was eternally sufficient shines through in His resurrection. With Ruth and Naomi, we can praise the Lord too.

*You, **Lord,** are my kinsman-redeemer. You've paid the price for my sin and redeemed me to live a life that brings You praise. Thank You for filling me with Your Spirit and helping me to tell others of this great gift of Your grace. In the name of Jesus, Lord and Savior of all, I pray. Amen.*

Intended Peace

He will stand and shepherd his flock . . . they will live securely, for then his greatness will reach to the ends of the earth. And he will be their peace. (Micah 5:4, 5).

Scripture: **Micah 5:1-5**
Song: **"Peace I Leave with You"**

"Why is it that we're disappointed, to the point of frustration, with every organization we're in?" my husband asked me. The truth in his question stunned me. He was responding to my angry words about some apparently thoughtless decisions by the local school board. But in this revelatory moment, we both realized that my complaint echoed a frequent pattern: regular rantings about how things "should be."

"Why do we do this?" I asked him. "We're upset so often about the groups we love—whether it's scouts, the church, or even the credit union."

After much discussion, we decided that our frustrations grew out of a desire for righteousness and a secret fear that good might *not* triumph—at least not the good we had in mind. Jesus came to earth that we might live in Him who is our peace. We quickly realized that we were working in our own strength, not abiding in His.

Dear God, what am I thinking? Forgive me my fear and useless worries. Calm my heart and build my faith to trust Your plans, to know You will redeem this earth in Your own time. Through Christ I pray. Amen.

December 7–13. **Shelley L. Houston** lives in Eugene, Oregon, with her husband, Mark, of 38 years. She enjoys children's ministries and freelance writing.

Speaking the Truth

How often I wanted to gather your children together, the way a hen gathers her chicks under her wings, and you were unwilling. "Behold, your house is being left to you desolate!" (Matthew 23:37, 38, *New American Standard Bible*).

Scripture: **Matthew 23:29-39**
Song: **"Stand Up, Stand Up for Jesus"**

The woman cowered as she entered the meeting hall. Tonight many families would vote on a new vision for their Christian school. When she had read the preliminary draft, she knew she would need to speak against an important proposal. She felt the plan to be contrary to Christian principles, but maybe someone else would speak up. She was "just a mom," she thought, but one to whom God may well have revealed His wisdom.

"Is there any discussion?" the president asked after reading the motion to adopt the new vision statement. Chills ran down her spine as she raised her hand. She focused only on the words she believed God wanted her to say. When she finished, silence filled the room.

The secretary spoke first. "And who are you?" he asked, as if for the records. But his words emphasized her lack of status. The vote continued, and the new vision statement was voted in—as drafted. No one heeded the simple woman's warning.

Lord, how often do we "kill the prophets" that You send our way? Then we wonder why our house is "desolate." Instead, let me be faithful to You and Your will this day. In Jesus' name, amen.

Cherished, as a Child

After me comes he who is mightier than I, the thong of whose sandals I am not worthy to stoop down and untie. I have baptized you with water; but he will baptize you with the Holy Spirit (Mark 1:7, 8, *Revised Standard Version*).

Scripture: **Mark 1:1-8**
Song: **"Blessed Be the Name"**

He was a precocious child, reading before kindergarten, developing a taste for lobster at five. His parents doted on him, their only child, born in their late 30s. I came for a visit when he was 5 and was surprised to see the power this child held in their home. More than a prince, he was the king to whom we all paid homage!

This child knew little of honoring his parents. And his bouts of disrespect were wrong, of course. But to my way of thinking, the worst part was this: being so seemingly independent kept him from the sense of being protected and cherished *as a child.*

John the Baptist was well-respected by those who came out to the desert to hear him speak. Yet, he preferred a submissive role: serving at the feet of Jesus, but feeling unworthy even there. And this was no false humility. John was not the Messiah, so he seated himself under God's protective umbrella, as His cherished child.

Almighty God, maker of Heaven and earth, I praise You as my all in all. Thank You for loving me as Your cherished child. May I learn what it truly means to serve You from a pure heart. In the holy name of Jesus, my Lord and Savior, I pray. Amen.

God's Favorites

"Hail, O favored one, the Lord is with you!" But she was greatly troubled at the saying, and considered in her mind what sort of greeting this might be (Luke 1:28, 29, *Revised Standard Version*).

Scripture: **Luke 1:26-29**
Song: **"I'm So Glad I'm a Part of the Family of God"**

"Well, look who's here,—it's Shelley. It's been so long!" I attended a family reunion where people had names that I recognized from my mother's stories of her youth. Had we run into each other on the streets of Ponca City, we would have no idea we were related. But because I was "family," I was warmly enfolded here. Most of these folks didn't know about me, what I had accomplished, or where I'd failed miserably. It didn't matter to them. So, what a nice surprise: unconditional love and acceptance.

No doubt Mary was aware that God did indeed know who she was—and the things she had done and not done. Yet He loved her dearly.

When Mary heard the angel call her "O favored one," perhaps she had this same sense of surprise and wonder. Imagine hearing: "God is especially fond of you."

God chose Mary for this honored position because He loved her, not because she measured up. And He also loves each of His children long before they can even begin trying to be worthy. What a comfort!

My heavenly Father, You are my home and my family. Hold me near to You today, especially through each difficulty I face. In Jesus' name, amen.

December 11

Revealing the Son

All things have been delivered to me by my Father; and no one knows who the Son is except the Father, or who the Father is except the Son and any one to whom the Son chooses to reveal him (Luke 10:22, *Revised Standard Version*).

Scripture: **Luke 10:21-24**
Song: **"What Child Is This?"**

My high school daughter had an assignment to write about "My Hero." When she received her paper back, she asked me to read it. Only then did I see the title, "My Mother." I was surprised at what she wrote. Obviously, she had seen things in me that I never knew anyone noticed or valued. She knew me well. I was honored, and a little embarrassed, to have my life unfolded on paper.

My husband and I drove this same daughter to move into her college dorm. At a parent/teacher social I met one of her professors for the semester. I introduced myself, and the teacher said, "Tell me about your daughter." I had no trouble describing the sparkling delights of my daughter's personality. "You know her well," the professor responded.

She was right. Because we love each other and cherish our time together, we know each other. For the same reason, no one knows Jesus the way His Father does . . . and vice versa. If you want to know about one, ask the other.

Father God, thank You for loving me so much that You shared Your Son with me. In this season of celebrating His birth, please reveal more of His stellar qualities to me. In His precious name I pray. Amen.

Facing Your Fears

Grant us that we, being delivered from the hand of our enemies, might serve him without fear, in holiness and righteousness before him all the days of our life (Luke 1:74, 75, *Revised Standard Version*).

Scripture: **Luke 1:68-75**
Song: **"Deliverance Will Come"**

My husband asked me to sit down by him. Taking my hand, he explained that he had been chosen for active duty in Desert Storm. He would leave in two weeks. My thoughts swirled, and I felt a little dizzy. "Don't be afraid," he said. "I know that God wants me to go."

But my first thought was that our three young children might lose their father, certainly for the time he was gone—a year? or two? I wondered how I would make ends meet, since his pay would be cut.

Mary also received a mind-bending message: She'd been chosen to bear God's Son. To complicate matters, being pregnant before marriage would be a source of deep shame in her community. Yet, the angel approached her as if she'd just won the lottery! What was Mary's response? She had some questions, but she ended with: "Let it be to me according to your word" (1:38, *RSV*).

God had a plan for Mary, and He had a plan for me and my family. God used my husband in important ways, and he returned home four months after he left.

O God, how foolish are my worries and fears! Help me just to say: "Let it be to me according to Your word." Through Christ, amen.

Expecting the Impossible

Mary said to the angel, "How shall this be . . . ?" And the angel said to her, ". . . with God nothing will be impossible" (Luke 1:34, 37, *Revised Standard Version*).

Scripture: **Luke 1:30-38**
Song: **"Mary's Boy Child"**

My friend and I pressed our foreheads to the windows of the empty house. The For Sale sign had lured us to stop and dream, even though the houses in the neighborhood were clearly out of my friend's price range. After all, she was a Christian school teacher.

"It's so cute, but it's out of my league," she said. She was right, of course. We were on the outskirts of an exclusive community. But hadn't God called her to teach in a little Christian school there?

"I have a feeling about this place," I said. "Why not call the owner and check?" That was the beginning of an "impossible" deal God arranged for my friend. But to say "nothing is impossible for God" stretches my mind beyond any personal experience of good deals. The word *nothing* opens before me infinite possibilities.

So, Lord, give me faith. This Christmas season let my wish list hold all the things that seem impossible to me—like relationships healed, hearts changed, and Your eternal plan more perfectly realized in me, through the life of Your Son, Jesus.

Lord, my faith is weak as I approach You. Fill me with Your Spirit; help me believe Your will is more than possible in my life. In Jesus' name, amen.

Proclaim Emancipation!

God sent his Son, born of a woman, born under law, to redeem those under law, that we might receive the full rights of sons (Galatians 4:4, 5).

Scripture: **Galatians 4:1-7**
Song: "Redeemed"

Sadly, slavery didn't end after the Civil War. Around the world today, an estimated 12.3 million people suffer forced labor, even though slavery is legal in just a few countries. A 2004 State Department report indicates that 600,000–800,000 people are transported across international borders each year, 80% of which are women, and up to 50% minors. At least half face sexual exploitation. A 2006 report shows growth of such trafficking within the borders of many nations.

What can we do? One teenage boy travels across the country speaking on the issue, carrying chains once worn by child slaves. Some organizations urge the boycotting of products produced with suspected slave labor. Others raise funds to buy slaves and restore their freedom.

We can do these things in the name of Jesus. After all, He is the one born to set the whole world free from sin's slavery. Let us work in His strength to release, as well, the grip of one human upon another.

Lord, *I pray for women, children, and men living in any form of bondage. Bring salvation of both body and soul! In Christ I pray. Amen.*

December 14–20. **Patty Duncan** feeds the birds and watches them through her kitchen window. In winter she hosts juncos, chickadees, and red-winged blackbirds.

With Us in Trouble

I will make an altar there to God, who answered me in the day of my distress and has been with me wherever I have gone (Genesis 35:3, *New American Standard Bible*).

Scripture: **Genesis 35:1-4**
Song: **"Leaning on the Everlasting Arms"**

Ben Newell had already suffered a couple of heart attacks and received a pacemaker when his heart began to fail at age 29. Hospitalized, his name went to the top tier of the transplant list. His family waited on God. Their church members and other folks around the world prayed for the young man. His wife, Meaghan, lived at his bedside.

Ben's mother cared for their young daughter—and also for their 2-year-old son, who would soon begin treatment for an inoperable brain tumor. Ben's father had a heart attack and died a few days later in the room across the hall in the hospital. His mother's intestine ruptured, requiring emergency surgery. Wave after wave of trouble rolled over this already struggling family.

After two months of waiting, Ben received his transplant. Three weeks later, Meaghan wrote about finally seeing an end to their distress: "It is scary to say to God you'll go wherever He'll take you. But having been there, I can attest to His ability to carry us mightily through it all. Don't be afraid to trust Him. He is good."

Lord, *thank You for the Newell family, and others, who courageously testify of Your goodness in the midst of intense suffering. In Jesus' name, amen.*

Relationship Motivates

May the LORD our God be with us, as He was with our fathers; may He not leave us or forsake us, that He may incline our hearts to Himself, to walk in all His ways (1 Kings 8:57, 58, *New American Standard Bible*).

Scripture: **1 Kings 8:54-61**
Song: **"Nearer, My God, to Thee"**

From my mailbox at school, I picked up my annual performance evaluation and read it with interest. My principal noted that I'd mentored a new fourth-grade teacher and a student teacher during the year. The student expressed that time spent in the classroom had convinced her that she had made the right decision about becoming a teacher. Hmm, I didn't know that.

I read on. "Mrs. Duncan is creative and gifted in thinking outside the box." How nice to have my "sideways thinking" actually valued!

I read on. "I have appreciated seeing her growth in classroom management with an especially challenging group this year." My class of rowdier-than-usual boys pushes my boundaries, but I appreciate her assessment that I'm handling them. I finished the summary. "I appreciate her dedication and support of Christian education." Bolstered with new confidence, I smiled as I walked to my classroom, determined to work even harder for a boss who believes in me.

Lord, I underestimate the power of an encouraging relationship with You, my master. Thanks for Your constant support. In Jesus' name, amen.

Brothers at War

God is with us; he is our leader. His priests with their trumpets will sound the battle cry against you. Men of Israel, do not fight against the LORD, the God of your fathers, for you will not succeed (2 Chronicles 13:12).

Scripture: **2 Chronicles 13:10-15**
Song: **"Battle Hymn of the Republic"**

A month after Lincoln won the presidential election of 1860, South Carolina seceded from the Union. By the time of Lincoln's inauguration in March, seven states had banded together to form the Confederacy, and canon fire fell on Fort Sumter in April. The Civil War had begun.

Men on both sides rushed to enlist, and boys as young as 10 lied about their ages to sign on as drummer boys and buglers. Both armies expected to whip the other side and be home before summer. Instead, over the next four years, Americans slaughtered each other in wheat fields and peach orchards, on hilltops and beside creeks. About 620,000 soldiers died, more fatalities than in all conflicts from the Revolutionary War through the Vietnam War.

In its civil war with Judah, Israel lost 500,000 skilled warriors in this one battle, close to the number killed on both sides in our entire Civil War. God rescued the army that worshiped Him and helped them defeat all those who refused to.

Father, grant unity to the people who worship You around the world. Give us strength to rise up and fight injustice and sin, not each other. I pray this prayer in the name of Jesus, my Savior and Lord. Amen.

A Courteous Case

Be strong and courageous, do not fear or be dismayed because of the king of Assyria nor because of all the horde that is with him; for the one with us is greater than the one with him (2 Chronicles 32:7, *New American Standard Bible*).

Scripture: **2 Chronicles 32:1-8**
Song: **"Sound the Battle Cry"**

Dinesh D'Souza didn't wring his hands about a recent deluge of books by atheists attacking Christianity. He simply wrote a book of his own titled *What's So Great about Christianity?* It became a New York Times best seller.

D'Souza takes the challenge in stride, enjoying his debates with atheists on college campuses around the country. He intelligently analyzes the flaws in their arguments with affable good humor.

Born and raised in India in a Christian home, D'Souza came to America as a foreign exchange student and then stayed on for college. When professors humiliated Christian students, he questioned whether the God of his childhood faith was real. He studied to get answers to those challenges and soon launched a campus newspaper that confronted bias against Christians and conservatives. Now he serves as a respected commentator, courteously presenting a powerful case for Christianity.

Lord, I pray for the students on our college campuses. Equip Christian students to keep their faith by understanding thoroughly why they believe. Then use them, with winsome witness, to win others to You. In the name of Your Son, my Savior, I pray. Amen.

Choose the Right . . . Again!

Because this people has rejected the gently flowing waters of Shiloah and rejoices over Rezin and the son of Remaliah, therefore the Lord is about to bring against them the mighty floodwaters of the River (Isaiah 8:6, 7).

Scripture: **Isaiah 8:5-10**
Song: **"I've Got Peace Like a River"**

I still remember the conversation from so many years ago; another time, another place . . .

"I need to go to court with my son, so I'm going to Cincinnati tomorrow," my neighbor said. "I'm hoping we'll get him off, and he'll be home and ready to take classes during spring term. Could you feed my kitties for me? I'll be back Saturday."

"Sure," I said. A few days later she called to let me know she was home. "How did it go?" I asked.

"Not good," she said, and I didn't ask for details. I knew she believed in God, but she'd been involved in drugs. Actually, she had quit for some months, then she slipped back, then quit again. When her boyfriend went to jail, she was so upset that she lost her job. I think they lived in a travel trailer, and it was surely a hard life.

Today I prayed for her, just as I prayed for myself: May I choose God's gently flowing waters. May I know the peace that comes from making my next decision according to His ways . . . and then the next, and the next.

Lord, have mercy on us when we're drowning in the consequences of our choices. Give us courage to pursue Your ways. In Jesus' name, amen.

Welcome, Baby Jesus

"The virgin will be with child and will give birth to a son, and they will call him Immanuel"—which means, "God with us" (Matthew 1:23).

Scripture: **Matthew 1:18-25**
Song: **"O Come, O Come, Immanuel"**

"He's here," my son, Amos, announced when I arrived at the birthing center.

"You're an uncle!" I said happily.

"When was he born? How big is he? What's his name?" "An hour ago," Amos answered, "Ten pounds, thirteen ounces. Christopher Daniel."

"Oh, my," I said, then hurried to greet Kim and her husband, Dan—and my first grandchild. Swaddled in a blanket and wearing a knit stocking cap, baby Christopher was tucked into bed next to his mama. She was beaming.

I know the feeling, the all-time high of a new mother. I cooed over the baby, kissed my daughter, and hugged her husband. Then I held Christopher, took pictures of him, watched him get his first bath, took pictures of his Sumo wrestler physique under the warming lamp, held him again, took pictures of him . . . (You get the idea).

The point is, a stream of visitors to the little room continued after I left: other grandparents, friends, cousins, on and on. We all had to welcome him—our gift from the Lord.

Father, *thanks for babies and their reminder that You came in the same humble way to live with us. Thanks for entering our world to make a way for us to live with You, now and forever. Through Jesus I pray. Amen.*

Witness . . . and Trust God

Do not rebuke a mocker or he will hate you; rebuke a wise man and he will love you (Proverbs 9:8).

Scripture: **Proverbs 9:7-12**
Song: **"Go, Tell It on the Mountain"**

They were both homeless and appeared at my house two years apart. The first one dashed through my open front door and immediately took command of the household. The second one had to be lured in with a saucer of tuna fish to be rescued from the first freeze of winter.

I showered both kittens with love and gentleness. I tended to their needs and occasionally a want or two. Daily, I invited them onto my lap. The first hardly waited for an invitation, but curled up and purred contentedly. The second would sit on the other side of the room, looking as though she would actually like to approach me—but it took her 16 years to actually do it!

They both got the same treatment, because the message I sent was always the same: *I love you.* But the responses were so different.

When we witness to others, we are responsible for presenting the message in love. But we are not responsible for the response we receive.

Father, when I fear a negative response to my attempts to share my faith, remind me that Jesus and Paul met much rejection. Just help me to go tell it! In the precious name of Jesus I pray. Amen.

December 21, 24–27. **Wanda M. Trawick** is a retired "jack of all trades," whose last job was Director of Christian Education. She lives in Newark, Delaware.

God's Unique Purpose

"Wisdom and knowledge are granted to you; and I will give you riches and wealth"(2 Chronicles 1:12, *NKJV*)

Scripture: **2 Chronicles 1:7-12**
Song: **"His Way With Thee"**

My husband and I had little in common when we met. Roy was a pastor. At 21 years of age I could have counted on one hand the Sundays I attended church.

Roy's first ministry after we married was three hours from home. During those rides I read and studied my Bible. I didn't fit the role as a minister's wife. I couldn't sing or play the piano. I prayed that God would bless me with those talents.

God never answered those prayers. He went one step further, however. He showed me His will for my life. I found that my purpose had nothing to do with music. My prayer changed, as a result.

Today, I teach and write. I look back and thank God for not answering those first prayers. I find great joy in being the person God created me to be. God gave me the wisdom to know my purpose and the knowledge to follow through.

I am convinced that greater riches will come my way when I begin my eternity with Him.

I am ever grateful that Your fingerprints are on my life. Help me to always seek Your guidance in everything that I do or say. In Jesus' name, I pray and give thanks. Amen.

December 22 and 23. **Nancy B. Gibbs** is a wife, mother, and grandmother. She is the author of seven books, a freelance writer, motivational speaker, and newspaper columnist.

Gaining Knowledge

So teach us to number our days, That we may gain a heart of wisdom (Psalm 90:12, *NKJV*).

Scripture: **Psalm 90:11-17**
Song: **"Open My Eyes, That I May See"**

When my granddaughter, Hannah started first-grade, I often asked her what she learned that day at school.

"Nothing," Hannah usually replied. I knew, however, she was grasping new words and new math concepts on a daily basis. She just didn't realize it.

Toward the end of the school year, I received an email. "Hannah is an accelerated reader." I called to Hannah to offer my congratulations. She was bubbling over with excitement, as I told her how proud I was of her.

I have heard people say that since they cannot understand the Bible they don't read it on a daily basis. By reading God's Word, even when we think we don't understand, we are opening the doors to greater wisdom and knowledge.

God speaks to us, as we seek to know Him better. On a daily basis we may not think we are learning spiritual truths. But weeks, months and years later, we can look back and see how far we have come and how much closer we are to God.

I wonder if one day, God will smile at all those who faithfully read His word and proclaim, "Congratulations. I am so proud of you."

*Thank You, **God**, for the insight, knowledge and wisdom You give me. Help me to continue to grow through the reading of Your Word each day. My heart's desire is to know You better. Amen.*

Good, Better, or Best?

My son, preserve sound judgment and discernment, do not let them out of your sight (Proverbs 3:21).

Scripture: **Proverbs 3:13-23**
Song: **"God Rest Ye Merry, Gentlemen"**

He was in his mid-80s and confined to his upstairs bedroom when I met him. He was in chronic heart failure, and I had come to give him an injection. He pointed to the small Christmas tree on his bedside table that his granddaughter had decorated for him. He wanted to know if the snow had reached the valley or if it was still limited to the mountains. And were the community Christmas lights up? He listened eagerly for my answers.

The day before Christmas, his granddaughter called me. "Would it be too harmful if we took him out for Christmas Eve? I know this will be his last Christmas."

Harmful? Probably. But good for him? Yes.

Her husband and two athletic teenaged sons got him into the car on that frosty evening. They toured the town and saw the lights reflected on the snow. At his granddaughter's house they sat in front of her tree and the fireplace, drank hot chocolate, and recounted tales of Christmases long past. He never stopped smiling.

He died a few days after Christmas. She had no regrets; nor should she have. She discerned between what was good for him and what was best.

Father, *life is full of choices between good and better and between bad or worse. Give me the discernment to choose wisely. In Jesus' name, amen.*

How Still Was Bethlehem?

But you, Bethlehem, in the land of Judah, are by no means least among the rulers of Judah; for out of you will come a ruler who will be the shepherd of my people Israel (Matthew 2:6).

Scripture: Matthew 2:1-6
Song: "O Little Town of Bethlehem"

The year 2008 in the USA resounded with political rhetoric, accusations, denials, and public relations ploys. It was not a quiet year.

Can you imagine the mood of the crowd in Bethlehem on what we now call Christmas Eve? Think of the inconvenience of trips back to the home of their ancestors—just to have their noses counted for burdensome taxes.

Nothing seems to stir folks up like politics and taxes. And angry people don't make for the quiet, peaceful nights depicted on so many of our Christmas cards.

Nevertheless, in the midst of the noisy turmoil, God quietly entered into the humanity He created and altered human destiny forever. Witnessed only by a few powerless folks in the countryside, His action would be celebrated for centuries to come.

The crowd came to Bethlehem boisterous, angry, and unable to change a thing. God came quietly, lovingly, and largely unheard. Thus He changed the whole world.

Father, I tire of the everyday turmoil around me. Please remind me that in the midst of all the anger, the fear, and the violence, You are quietly at work to change me into what You want me to be. Through Christ, amen.

Living Among Alien Gods

They saw the child with his mother Mary, and they bowed down and worshiped him (Matthew 2:11).

Scripture: **Matthew 2:10-15**
Song: **"O Come, All Ye Faithful"**

My favorite Christmas poem is "Journey of the Magi," written by T. S. Eliot after he became a Christian. In it the narrator, one of the wise men, tells of the incredible hardships they encountered on the long trip to Palestine. But he concludes that it was all worth it, and that he would do it again.

Then the poem takes an unexpected turn. The narrator has worshiped an infant king among the Jews and is now miserable among his own people "clutching their alien gods." After this worship experience, he can never be the same.

Can't you feel with this man? Encountering Jesus makes us dissatisfied with our own culture and the gods of our culture. We long for the time when we will be with Christ forever, with no false gods to tempt us.

The narrator questions whether they had gone all that way to witness a birth or a death—and even says he longs for his own death. For he is no longer at home in his world. And neither are we. We are "in" the world, but not "of" the world.

Father, I usually know a false god when I see one, but that doesn't mean I can't be tempted by it. I need Your power daily to overcome temptation and to stay in a worshipful frame of mind. In the name of Jesus I pray. Amen.

December 27

Jesus—Refugee, Immigrant

He got up, took the child and his mother during the night and left for Egypt (Matthew 2:14).

Scripture: **Matthew 2:7-9, 16-23**
Song: **"This World Is Not My Home"**

As we struggle with immigration issues, let's remember that Jesus began his life as a refugee and immigrant. Just as their ancestors had fled to Egypt to escape famine, Joseph and Mary took their Son to the same land to save his life. So, when I see pictures of families fleeing warfare, persecution, and natural disasters—and when I see desperate mothers carrying their babies to safety—I also can see Mary carrying her child to a safe haven.

Doesn't Jesus' concern for "the least of these" drive me to my knees in intercessory prayer? Does His concern open my pocketbook? Does it cause me to look around my own community to find ways to help the less fortunate?

Yes, the problems are complicated and confusing. Solutions can be problematic and dangerous. Let us plead with our Father to give us wisdom as we attempt to deal justly with those who must leave their homelands. Some leave to *save* their lives; some leave to find *better* lives.

May I never forget that God's children are all strangers in this world. This is not my home. My home is where my Father is.

Lord, I've never been a refugee or an immigrant. But Your Son and His earthly family have. Teach me what it is like so that I may respond to them and their needs as You would have me to. In Jesus' name, amen.

By What Authority?

I will also ask you one question. If you answer me, I will tell you by what authority I am doing these things (Matthew 21:24).

Scripture: **Matthew 21:23-27**
Song: **"Jesus, Name Above All Names"**

On a day that our church designated as Family Sunday, I told two young children to sit with me for the worship service. These children ride our church bus to attend Sunday school and the children's worship service. Rather than have them run freely around the building, I have the children join me as I prepare for my preschool class.

My daughter observed the children obeying me and asked, "What authority do you have? You're not even their teacher." Although the children could ask that same question, they obey without question. Their parents are not present, and as an adult I assume the responsibility without explanations.

Just as I haven't had to defend my right to tell the children what to do, Jesus didn't explain His authority to those who questioned Him. The chief priests and elders asked why He performed an official act when He had no official status. Jesus answered with a question that implied exactly where His authority came from: God.

Father, please give me the wisdom to know what authority I should assume and what authority I should leave to others. In Jesus' name, amen.

December 28–31. **LeAnn Campbell** is a mother, grandmother, and retired special education teacher. She has taught children in church for more than 40 years.

A Greater One to Come

I will send my messenger ahead of you, who will prepare your way before you (Luke 7:27).

Scripture: **Luke 7:24-30**
Song: **"Jesus Is Passing This Way"**

For several weeks the spot announcement appeared on television screens and billboards along the highway. All the announcements featured twins—they might be older women, sometimes young boys with dark eyes, or babies. But the intriguing message was always the same: Twice as Nice. We didn't know what was coming but heard repeatedly that it would be twice as nice.

Then the day of revelation arrived. A hospital in a nearby town planned to open its second urgent care center. The original center was nice, and the hospital promised that adding another would be *twice as nice.*

In some ways, John the Baptist was like the town's first care center. John was a prophet, and he brought a special message to the people. Long before John's birth, Malachi prophesied that a messenger would come to prepare the way for the Messiah, God's Son. John was that messenger. He didn't go through the wilderness shouting "Twice as nice," but he spread the word that someone greater than he was coming. His announcement heralded the arrival of Jesus, our Savior.

Heavenly Father, sometime I might need the urgent care that the hospital provides, but it can never compare to the urgent care You offered, for You sent Jesus to heal my sin disease. Thankfully, in His name I pray. Amen.

What's Your Job?

Some Pharisees who had been sent questioned him, "Why then do you baptize if you are not the Christ, nor Elijah, nor the Prophet?" (John 1:24, 25).

Scripture: **John 1:24-34**
Song: **"Look to the Lamb of God"**

As a special education teacher in a vocational-technical school, I helped high school students train for jobs. I introduced them to local businesses and taught them to fill out applications, practice job interviews, and learn skills necessary for holding a job.

I loved the students and my work, but there were many challenges. Some of the students had attitudes: "If they want me to apply for a job, they'll have to give me clothes to wear," they might say. Or: "I'm going to run my own business, so I can take off whenever I want to."

In the midst of one trying day, a 16-year-old boy asked, "Mrs. Campbell, do you have a job?" Now what did that kid think I was doing in the classroom every day?

In today's Scripture, John had already told the priests and Levites what his job was—he baptized, but he wasn't the Christ. John's answer was not enough for the Pharisees. They probed deeper and asked John what reason he had to be there. They just couldn't see that he had one of the most important jobs in human history.

Dear God, You have given me a job too. You have told me to live for You and to tell others how much You love us. May I do what You have asked of me, so others won't ask "Why are you here?" Through Christ, amen.

Who Will Come?

Everyone who calls on the name of the Lord will be saved (Romans 10:13).

Scripture: **Romans 10:8-17**
Song: **"Calling for You"**

Our shower wouldn't work—only a trickle of water came through. My husband was sick and unable to fix it, and my plumbing abilities were nil. We could have called a plumber, but my brother came and installed a new shower head. All was well, until . . .

The next day we walked on the carpet in our other bathroom—and got our feet wet. This time the problem was a leak in the lavatory connection. That evening our son-in-law showed up with his toolbox and, within a few minutes, he fixed the leak.

Problems continued that week, but each time we called for help, and someone came. One brought a heavy-duty fan to dry the carpet, and when the furnace quit, a repairman quickly responded.

We all need to call for help once in a while. My brother and son-in-law came willingly to fix our plumbing dilemmas. But Jesus promises help in the most important matter of all, for He wants to save us from our sins. (In fact, He promises to save everyone who calls on Him.)

Dear God, thank You for those who come when I need help. I appreciate what they do. But nothing compares to the help You sent for my greatest need. Really, there was nothing I could do. Praise to You for Your goodness and grace! I pray through my deliverer, Jesus. Amen.